KF
AbdSamad Benkrid

Software and Hardware Architectures for FPGA-based Image Processing

Khaled Benkrid
AbdSamad Benkrid

Software and Hardware Architectures for FPGA-based Image Processing

VDM Verlag Dr. Müller

Impressum/Imprint (nur für Deutschland/ only for Germany)
Bibliografische Information der Deutschen Nationalbibliothek: Die Deutsche Nationalbibliothek
verzeichnet diese Publikation in der Deutschen Nationalbibliografie; detaillierte bibliografische
Daten sind im Internet über http://dnb.d-nb.de abrufbar.
Alle in diesem Buch genannten Marken und Produktnamen unterliegen warenzeichen-, marken-
oder patentrechtlichem Schutz bzw. sind Warenzeichen oder eingetragene Warenzeichen der
jeweiligen Inhaber. Die Wiedergabe von Marken, Produktnamen, Gebrauchsnamen,
Handelsnamen, Warenbezeichnungen u.s.w. in diesem Werk berechtigt auch ohne besondere
Kennzeichnung nicht zu der Annahme, dass solche Namen im Sinne der Warenzeichen- und
Markenschutzgesetzgebung als frei zu betrachten wären und daher von jedermann benutzt
werden dürften.

Coverbild: www.purestockx.com

Verlag: VDM Verlag Dr. Müller Aktiengesellschaft & Co. KG
Dudweiler Landstr. 99, 66123 Saarbrücken, Deutschland
Telefon +49 681 9100-698, Telefax +49 681 9100-988, Email: info@vdm-verlag.de
Zugl.: Belfast, Queen's University, Diss., 2000

Herstellung in Deutschland:
Schaltungsdienst Lange o.H.G., Berlin
Books on Demand GmbH, Norderstedt
Reha GmbH, Saarbrücken
Amazon Distribution GmbH, Leipzig
ISBN: 978-3-639-23923-2

Imprint (only for USA, GB)
Bibliographic information published by the Deutsche Nationalbibliothek: The Deutsche
Nationalbibliothek lists this publication in the Deutsche Nationalbibliografie; detailed
bibliographic data are available in the Internet at http://dnb.d-nb.de .
Any brand names and product names mentioned in this book are subject to trademark, brand or
patent protection and are trademarks or registered trademarks of their respective holders. The use
of brand names, product names, common names, trade names, product descriptions etc. even
without a particular marking in this works is in no way to be construed to mean that such names
may be regarded as unrestricted in respect of trademark and brand protection legislation and
could thus be used by anyone.

Cover image: www.purestockx.com

Publisher:
VDM Verlag Dr. Müller Aktiengesellschaft & Co. KG
Dudweiler Landstr. 99, 66123 Saarbrücken, Germany
Phone +49 681 9100-698, Fax +49 681 9100-988, Email: info@vdm-publishing.com

Printed in the U.S.A.
Printed in the U.K. by (see last page)
ISBN: 978-3-639-23923-2

Software and Hardware Architectures for FPGA-based Image Processing

By

Khaled Benkrid, PhD, CEng, MBA

AbdSamad Benkrid, PhD, MEng

Preface

This book presents software and hardware architectures for efficient Image and Video processing on Field Programmable Gate Arrays (FPGA). Central to the software environment is a high level, Prolog-based, hardware description notation called HIDE, and its implementation on Xilinx FPGAs, as well as a high level generator which takes an image processing high level algorithm description, and translates it into a HIDE hardware description. The book presents the details of an application development approach which allows application developers to think at the algorithmic level, and obtain an efficient hardware solution automatically from application-oriented abstractions. This is achieved in two stages: (a) by providing a mechanism for building a library of generalised, parameterised hardware blocks, and (b) by proposing the new concept of *hardware skeletons,* which are defined as reusable architectural *frameworks*, which can take function blocks as parameters, and which encapsulate all the low level hardware dependent optimisations. This is demonstrated in this book through an extensive library of basic building components developed for a range of data representations as well as a high level FPGA-based image and video co-processor, based on the abstractions of Image Algebra. The book describes a working implementation of the co-processor on a real FPGA based video board. The resulting system allows an image processing application developer with little FPGA knowledge to program a range of image processing algorithms at an application oriented level. It also automatically generates efficient FPGA configurations for real time video processing.

Contents

3 | Bit Serial implementation of the FPGA based Image Processing Coprocessor

64

6 HIDE4k descriptions of Image Algebra neighbourhood operations   140

7 Compound operations: towards the use of hardware skeletons   165

8 | Novel Image Processing Architectures | 199

11 Conclusion 278

Prologue

Prologue

The work presented in this book has a historical context which has influenced a number of its aspects. It was part of a project in the school of Computer Science at The Queen's University of Belfast to bring the power of high performance hardware to Image Processing (IP) application developers. One of the earlier outcomes of this research programme was a high level image processing language, called TULIP, developed by Steele (1994) and was designed for implementation on a range of high performance parallel architectures including the Transputer. TULIP includes a range of image-level neighbourhood operations based on the operations of Image Algebra.

By the mid-1990's, programmable hardware in the form of FPGAs had matured and had hence been considered by Donachy (1996) as a cheaper alternative to parallel machines for high performance image processing. Donachy pursued the objective of developing an FPGA based hardware implementation of TULIP with the aim of producing an image coprocessor. He took the operations of TULIP and developed a range of *static* FPGA architectures for the Xilinx XC6000 series. This was the first step towards implementing TULIP on FPGAs and targeted Xilinx XC6000 series.

In order to make Donachy's architectures more *dynamic*, flexible and powerful, Alotaibi (1999) developed a high level hardware description notation called HIDE. The latter is a Prolog based new hardware description notation designed specifically for the dynamic generation of parameterised and scaleable FPGA configurations. HIDE has been used to generate FPGA configurations for the standard operations in TULIP but was not brought through the stage where the system runs on a commercially available FPGA board. Many hardware-relevant abstractions were not fully developed in Alotaibi's HIDE as a result.

Both Donachy and Alotaibi targeted Xilinx XC6000 series which was discontinued by Xilinx in 1998.

The work described in this book was conducted between 1998 and 2000, and inherited a legacy which constrained a number of its aspects. The following summarises these constraints:

- This work is targeted to Image Processing applications and particularly to low level image processing operations.
- The use of Prolog as a description and implementation language.
- The use of HIDE and its tools as a starting point.
- Both Donachy and Alotaibi focused on bit serial arithmetic. This provided a benchmark for the work presented in this book.

The main contributions of the research presented in this book are:

- An extended HIDE hardware description environment for the Xilinx XC4000 series (HIDE4k system).
- An efficient library of architectures specifically tailored to Xilinx 4000 FPGAs. This library is much more extensive than the XC6000 based one both in its extent and diversity (e.g. supports different arithmetic types).
- The development of a high level generator which takes an image processing high level algorithm description (Tulip-like), and translates it automatically into an efficient FPGA configuration.
- The new concept of *hardware skeletons* is put forward in this book as a way of satisfying the dual requirement of generating efficient FPGA architectures while retaining the convenience and rapid development cycle of an application-oriented, high level programming model.
- The real implementation of the developed environment on a commercial FPGA based video board.

The remaining of this book is organised as follows:

We will start by an introduction to FPGAs in chapter 1. At the end of this chapter, we will make a decision on the FPGA architecture that we will target. The general motivation and aims of the research presented in this book will then be given.

The next chapter reviews a number of FPGA based hardware systems and software environments designed to exploit the performance of FPGAs for IP applications. In particular, the previous work conducted in Queen's by Steele (1994), Donachy (1996) and Alotaibi (1999), will be presented in some detail. At the end of this chapter, we present the objectives of the research presented in this book.

Based on a number of hardware implementation objectives, chapter 3 presents one possible way of implementing our FPGA based IP coprocessor, namely based on bit serial arithmetic. The hardware implementation starts with the standard set of Image Algebra (IA) neighbourhood operations. After that, chapter 4 presents optimised solutions (for speed and area) for two special cases, namely binary image processing and convolution.

Having presented the detailed hardware design of a core set of IP operations, chapters 5 and 6 present the software environment (HIDE4k) which will allow for the automatic generation of the previous hardware designs. Chapter 5 first presents the hardware description environment along with its implementation. Then, chapter 6 shows how HIDE4k is used to generate the full range of IA operators.

In chapter 7, we propose a generic framework for developing optimised FPGA architectures for a wider range of image processing applications (compound operations). This framework is based on the new concept of *hardware skeletons*.

Chapter 8 presents three novel IP architectures. The first is for perimeter estimation. The second is for median filtering, whereas the third is for Connected Component Labelling. These algorithms do not fall into the set of Image Algebra operations presented in chapter 3. The FPGA implementation of these algorithms is presented. Note that this chapter is not directly related to subsequent chapters and hence could be skipped at a first reading.

Next, chapter 9 presents a bit *parallel* implementation of the FPGA based IP coprocessor, for both the basic IA operators and an extension for compound IP operations.

Chapter 10 then presents a real hardware implementation of the IP coprocessor working on a commercial FPGA based video processing board (the Visicom VigraVision video board). This addresses a number of tricky hardware implementation issues, as well as the high-level software environment that runs the system.

Finally, Chapter 11 summarises the main contributions of this research, draws some conclusions, and presents a number of possible follow-on areas for future investigation.

The overall result of the work presented in this book is a system which is organised into several levels of abstractions. The following diagram shows the "big picture" which the various chapters of this book will build up. The relevant chapters (or sections) are indicated in bold between square brackets.

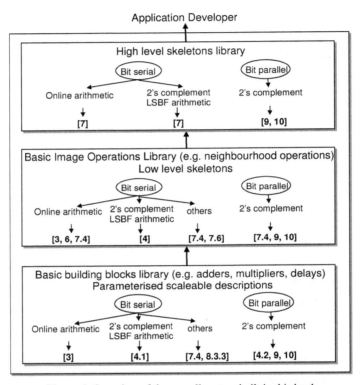

Figure 1. Overview of the overall system built in this book

As a result of the work presented in this book, the following papers have been published:

Benkrid K, Crookes D, Smith J, Benkrid A, 'High Level Programming for Real Time FPGA Based Video Programming', Proceedings of ICASSP'2000, IEEE International Conference on Acoustic, Speech and Signal Processing, Istanbul, June 2000, Vol. VI, pp. 3227-3231.

Benkrid K, Crookes D, Bouridane A, Corr P and Alotaibi K, 'A high level software environment for FPGA based image processing', Proceedings IPA'99, IEE Seventh International Conference on Image Processing and its Applications, Manchester, July 1999, pp. 112-116.

Benkrid K, Alotaibi K, Crookes D, Bouridane A and Benkrid A, 'An image processing coprocessor implementation for Xilinx 6000 Series FPGAs', Proceedings SPIE Configurable Computing: Technology and Applications, Boston, September 1999, pp. 104-111.

Crookes D and Benkrid K, 'An FPGA implementation of image component labelling', Proceedings SPIE Configurable Computing: Technology and Applications, Boston, September 1999, pp. 17-23.

Benkrid K and Crookes D, 'Design and FPGA implementation of a novel general purpose median filter', Proceedings IMVIP'99, Dublin, September 1999, pp. 280-287.

Crookes D, Benkrid K and Benkrid A, 'A General Framework for FPGA Based Image Processing using Hardware Skeletons', Proceedings IMVIP'2000, Belfast, September 2000, pp.117-124.

Benkrid K, Crookes D and Benkrid A, 'Design and FPGA Implementation of a Perimeter Estimator', Proceedings IMVIP'2000, Belfast, September 2000, pp.51-57.

Crookes D, Benkrid K, Bouridane A, Alotaibi A and Benkrid A, 'Design and Implementation of a High Level Programming Environment for FPGA Based Image Processing', *IEE Journal on Image and Signal Processing*, Vol. 147, No. 7, 2000, pp. 377-384.

Bouridane A, Crookes D, Donachy P, Alotaibi K, and Benkrid K, 'A high level FPGA-based abstract machine for image processing', *Journal of Systems Architecture* (JSA), Vol. (45) 10,1999.

Crookes D, Benkrid K, 'A Novel Algorithm for General Purpose Median Filtering on FPGAs', submitted and subsequently accepted to appear in *The SPIE Journal of Electronic Imaging*.

Chapter 1

Introduction to FPGAs

Chapter 1

Introduction to FPGAs

Image Processing application developers require high performance systems for computationally intensive Image Processing (IP) applications, often under real time requirements. In addition, an IP application development tends to be experimental and interactive. This means that the developer must be able to modify, tune or replace algorithms rapidly and conveniently.

Because of the local nature of low level IP operations (e.g. neighbourhood operations), one way of obtaining high performance in image processing has been to use parallel computing [CP90][KL96][LH95][YA94]. However, multiprocessor IP systems have generally speaking not yet fulfilled their promise [BBDS93]. This is partly a matter of cost, lack of stability and software support for parallel machines; it is also a matter of communications overheads particularly if images are being captured and distributed across the processors in real time.

A second way of obtaining high performance in IP applications is the use of Digital Signal Processing (DSP) processors [TI][RSR93][AAA94]. DSP processors provide a performance improvement over standard microprocessors while still maintaining the software programmability. This performance improvement is achieved by customising the architecture of a general purpose microprocessor to better suit DSP algorithm implementations. For example, DSP processors have multiple data buses to provide higher memory bandwidth. They, typically, are heavily pipelined to exploit data parallelism. Also, a Multiply-Accumulate operation, which is the most common DSP operation, can usually be done in a single clock cycle. However, because of the single flow of control, a DSP processor cannot fully exploit task parallelism.

At the opposite end of the spectrum from the above mentioned software based solutions, lie the dedicated hardware solutions. Application Specific Integrated Circuits (ASICs) offer a fully customised solution to a particular algorithm [DW81]

[MLM84]. Since it is a fully dedicated solution to the problem in hand, it allows the maximum performance in terms of speed and area. However, this solution suffers from the lack of flexibility provided by software solutions. Other disadvantages include the high manufacturing cost and the lengthy development cycle.

Reconfigurable hardware solutions in the form of FPGAs [BR93] [Con96][McLoe94] offer high performance, with the ability to be electrically reprogrammed to perform other algorithms. Though the first FPGAs were only capable of modest integration levels and were thus used mainly for glue logic and system control, the latest devices [Xil99a] have crossed the Million gate barrier hence making it possible to implement an entire System On a Chip. Moreover, the introduction of the latest IC fabrication techniques has increased the maximum speed at which FPGAs can run. Design's performance exceeding 150MHz are no longer outside the realms of possibility in the new FPGA parts, hence allowing FPGAs to address high bandwidth applications such as video processing. It is not uncommon for an FPGA to outperform a DSP processor by a 100:1 factor.

We will first start by an overview of the structure of an FPGA and its typical programming methodology. Then, section 1.3 will review some commercial FPGA architectures, after which a decision on the chosen target FPGA architecture will be made. Section 1.5 will then present the primary motivations and objectives of this project. Finally, the organisation of the book is given.

1.1 FPGAs overview

A Field Programmable Gate Array consists of an array of logic cells that can be interconnected via programmable routing switches. Logic cells are connected to the package pins via programmable Input/Outputs cells.

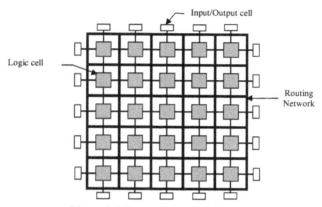

Figure 1.1 General structure of FPGA

FPGAs can be broadly discriminated according to:

- their *cell logic structure*, which ranges from simple cells (e.g. transistors, multiplexers and simple boolean functions) in which case they are called *fine grained*, to complex cells containing memories, Look-Up-Tables (LUTs), registers etc., in which case they are called *coarse grained*.

- their *routing architecture*, which can be either *hierarchical* offering both local interconnections for neighbour logic cells and non-local interconnections for distant cells, or *non-hierarchical* providing just local interconnections.

FPGAs are configured by setting each of their programmable elements (i.e. logic cells, routing network and I/O cells) to a desired state. These are programmed via *programmable switches*. Currently, the highest-density FPGAs are built using SRAM technology [MMS91][CSR99], similar to microprocessors. Other common process technologies are *antifuse* [GHB93][BCC92], *EEPROM* [Alt99] and *FLASH* [Xil99b].

SRAM-based FPGAs are inherently in-system reprogrammable. Some can even be *partially reconfigured* at run time, hence allowing *run time reconfigurability*. An external configuration memory source is usually used to load the FPGA with the configuration at power-up. The configuration time is typically less than 200 ms, depending on the device size and configuration method. We are particularly interested in this type of FPGA.

1.2 FPGA programming

A typical design flow for FPGA design is given in Figure 1.2.

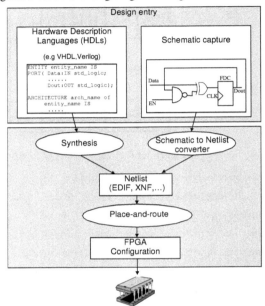

Figure 1.2 An overview of FPGA design cycle

We will describe these design steps in a top-down manner, starting from the design entry tools through to the FPGA bitstream generation.

1.2.1   Design entry

FPGA designs can be entered either schematically using a schematic editor or textually using a hardware description language.

1.2.1.1 Schematic design entry

In this case, a design is specified as a 2-D diagram by connecting together logic components (e.g. gates) with routing resources. These components are contained in a library supplied by the FPGA vendor. Because of the vendor specific nature of the components, schematic designs produced for a specific FPGA architecture are not easily portable to other architectures.

Once a design has been specified using schematic capture it can be converted into a netlist by a schematic-to-netlist converter tool.

1.2.1.2 Hardware Description Languages (HDLs)

There are many Hardware Description Languages (HDLs) available such as VHDL [IEEE87][Nav92] and Verilog [Moo92].

VHDL (Very-high-speed-integrated-circuit Hardware Description Language) is the most commonly used HDL. It uses the concept of a *design entity* to model hardware. Each design entity (see Figure 1.3) comprises an *entity declaration* and an *architecture body*.

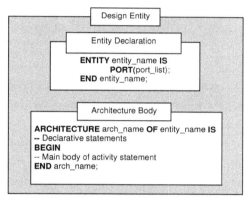

Figure 1.3 VHDL design entity

The *entity* declaration represents the external interface to the design entity i.e. the inputs and outputs to the circuit. The *architecture body* however, describes the function of the circuit by establishing the relationship between these inputs and outputs.

An *entity* can have different architectural descriptions associated with it. One way of describing the function of a design entity is to describe how it is composed of sub-modules. Each of the sub-modules is an instance of some entity, and the ports of the instances are connected using signals. Figure 1.4 shows an example of such architecture description, where an entity 'BLK_C' is composed of instances of entities 'BLK_A' and 'BLK_B'. This kind of description is called a *structural* description. Note that each of the entities 'BLK_A', 'BLK_B' might also have a structural description.

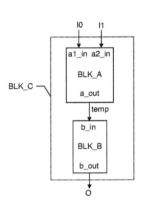

```
ENTITY BLK_C IS
    PORT( I0, I1 : IN STD_LOGIC;
                O : OUT STD_LOGIC);
END BLK_C;

ARCHITECTURE structural OF BLK_C IS
COMPONENT BLK_A
    PORT(a1_in, a2_in : IN STD_LOGIC;
                a_out : OUT STD_LOGIC);
END COMPONENT;
COMPONENT BLK_B
    PORT (b_in  : IN STD_LOGIC;
            b_out : OUT STD_LOGIC);
END COMPONENT;
SIGNAL temp: STD_LOGIC;
BEGIN
inst_A: BLK_A
PORT MAP(
            a1_in => I0,
            a2_in => I1,
            a_out => temp);
inst_B: BLK_B
PORT MAP(
            b_in  => temp,
            b_out => O);
END structural;
```

Figure 1.4 A VHDL structural description example

In many cases, it is not appropriate to describe a design entity structurally. For example, if a design is built from IC packages bought from an IC shop, there is no need to describe the internal structure of these ICs. In such cases, a description of the function performed by the module is required, without reference to its actual internal structure. Such a description is called a *functional* or *behavioural* description. The following is an example of such behavioural description for an exclusive-Or (XOR2) function. This particular type of behavioural description is also referred to as *dataflow* description.

```
ENTITY My_XOR2 IS
    PORT( I0, I1 : IN STD_LOGIC;
                O : OUT STD_LOGIC);
END My_XOR2;

ARCHITECTURE My_XOR2_arch OF My_XOR2 IS
BEGIN
        O <= (NOT(I0) AND I1) OR (NOT(I1) AND I0);
END My_XOR2_arch;
```

Figure 1.5 A VHDL dataflow description of a XOR2 port

More complex behaviours cannot be described purely as a function of inputs. In systems with feedback, the outputs are also a function of time. VHDL solves this problem by allowing description of behaviour in the form of an executable program. Extra programming facilities, similar in syntax and constructs to high-level programming languages such as ADA, have been added to VHDL for that purpose.

These include data types (e.g. integers, floating points, physical, enumeration, arrays etc.), data objects (constants, variable and signals), sequential statements (e.g. *if* and *case* statements), subprograms (procedures and functions), packages etc. The following is a simple example of a behavioural VHDL code implementing an edge triggered D flip-flop.

```
ENTITY My_DFF IS
        PORT(CLK, D : IN STD_LOGIC;
                    Q : OUT STD_LOGIC);
END My_DFF;

ARCHITECTURE My_DFF_arch OF My_DFF IS
BEGIN
reg: PROCESS(CLK)
        BEGIN
            -- detect the clock rising edge
        IF(CLK'event and CLK='1') THEN
            -- set the output 'Q' to the input value 'D'
            Q<=D;
        END IF;
        END PROCESS;
END My_DFF_arch;
```

Figure 1.6 A VHDL behavioural description of an edge triggered D flip-flop

Describing a digital design as registers (see Figure 1.6) and logic between the registers (see Figure 1.5) is referred to as RTL (Register Transfer Logic) level descriptions. Such descriptions are FPGA target independent and hence are portable (though it may not always lead to an efficient implementation). The VHDL code is then synthesised into a specific FPGA technology netlist using a *synthesiser* (compiler) tool.

Recently, synthesiser tools have been made so sophisticated that they are capable of understanding very high-level descriptions such us '+' for addition and '*' for multiplication and automatically infer the corresponding *optimised* FPGA implementations. The synthesiser tool would work out automatically the number of clock stages necessary to satisfy the user supplied constraints (e.g. throughput, latency etc.), with no subsequent user intervention [ZB99][SD99]. In FPGA jargon, it is this sort of coding which is referred to as *behavioural* HDL as opposed to the previously discussed RTL level coding. It is totally independent from the target FPGA technology. As the whole process is handled automatically by the synthesiser tool (mapping, retiming etc.), the design time is dramatically reduced. In addition, the user can make architectural trade-offs very conveniently since the same code is used to target different hardware structures.

1.2.2   Netlist representation

A netlist is a standard textual representation of a developer's design. It contains a more structured description of the functionality of the design and tends to contain an FPGA vendor specific information by using component names and cell attributes associated with a particular target architecture. Most vendors' netlist representations allow placement constraints that bind a particular component in the design to a particular location on the FPGA. The netlist format can be in the standard Electronic Data Format Interchange (EDIF) format [Cra84], or in another vendor specific format (e.g. Xilinx Netlist Format -XNF from Xilinx).

1.2.3   Place-and-Route tools

Place-And-Route (PAR) tools map the component and routing information defined in a netlist onto the FPGA architecture. Each FPGA vendor has its own PAR tools. The mechanism of placement and routing is usually based on flattening the hierarchy in the netlist, performing some optimisations (e.g. redundant gate removal) and then using simulated annealing (calculating the efficiency of a particular placement, moving cells slightly, then recalculating the efficiency) to try to find the best placement for the cells. Routing between the cells is then performed based on this placement and the routing resources available. Timing-driven routing is automatically invoked if PAR finds timing constraints associated with the design (e.g. in a user constraint file).

Once the PAR operation has been successfully performed, a bitstream file can be generated. The latter contains all the FPGA configuration information.

1.3 FPGA architectures

In this section, we will present some selected commercial and research SRAM based FPGA architectures.

1.3.1 Xilinx XC6200 series

The Xilinx XC6200 FPGA series [Xil96] is the successor of the CAL architecture from Algotronix [Alg91][Kea89]. It is an SRAM-based FPGA with an array of identical, fine-grained cells and a hierarchical routing network. The first implementation of the architecture, the XC6216 (see Figure 1.7) consists of an array of 64 by 64 cells. Each of these cells provides nearest neighbour connections as well as employing a hierarchical cellular array structure. Neighbour connected cells are grouped into blocks of 4x4 cells which themselves form a cellular array communicating with neighbouring 4x4 cell blocks. A 4x4 array of these 4x4 blocks form a 16x16 block. In an XC6216 device, a 4x4 array of these 16x16 blocks form the 64x64 cell array.

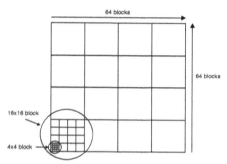

Figure 1.7 The XC6216 device architecture

Logic cells are interconnected to their nearest neighbour using local interconnect which runs North (N), South (S), East (E) and West (W). A hierarchy of longer connections (called FastLane™ connections) is also provided. Length-4 routing segments span each 4x4 block in the four directions: North (N4), South (S4), East (E4) and West (W4). Similarly, length-16 routing segments span each 16x16 block in the four directions. The final level of routing hierarchy spans the device at chip length (see Figure 1.8).

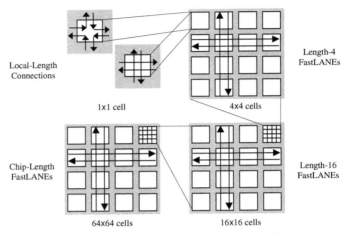

Figure 1.8 The XC6200 hierarchical routing architecture

The structure of an XC6200 basic cell is given in Figure 1.9. Each of these cells can be configured as any two-input gate function, any flavour of a 2:1 multiplexer, a constant 0 or 1, a single input function (buffer or inverter) or any of these in addition to a D-type register. The configuration of each cell is controlled by a configuration register associated with each function unit. These registers are memory mapped into the address space of the host processor and can be reconfigured dynamically at run-time. The host system can reconfigure all or part of the device in microseconds.

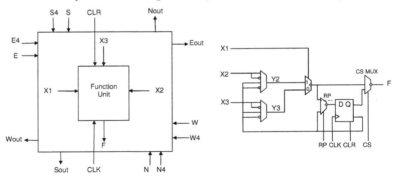

Figure 1.9 XC6200 basic cell structure

Another special feature of XC6200 is that the content of any register on the device can be written or read by simple memory Read/Write from the host processor

(FastMap™ processor interface). This effectively reduces routing problems in an FPGA design since inputs/outputs do not need to be routed to the package pins.

Despite the attractive dynamic reconfiguration feature and the FastMap™ processor interface, the XC6200 has mostly been used for research purposes. Xilinx does not support this FPGA family anymore. Instead it has added the dynamic reconfiguration feature, partially, to a new FPGA architecture called Virtex (see section 1.3.5 below).

1.3.2 Xilinx XC4000 series

The XC4000 architecture supersedes previous XC2000 and XC3000 devices and is the most successful FPGA architecture commercially [Xil99c]. It consists of an array of programmable function units called *Configurable Logic Block* (CLBs), linked by *programmable interconnect resources*. The internal signal lines interface to the package through programmable *Input/Output Blocks* (IOBs).

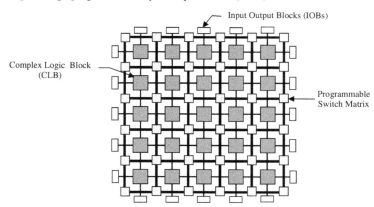

Figure 1.10 XC4000 architecture overview

In the following, we will present these parts in more detail. Unless otherwise stated, the information given below is valid for all XC4000 series. The information related to XC4000X series includes XC4000EX and XC4000XL families.

Configurable Logic Block (CLBs)

The CLB structure is given in Figure 1.11. It comprises two 4-input function generators (i.e. Look-Up-Tables) 'F' and 'G', plus a 3-input boolean function 'H'. Either zero, one, or two of the three inputs of the 'H' function generator can be outputs of 'F' and 'G'; the other input(s) are from outside the CLB. This configuration can implement certain functions of up to nine inputs. Each CLB contains two storage elements that can be used either to store the function generator outputs, or to store inputs from outside the CLB.

An important feature of XC4000 series is that the Look-Up-Tables (LUTs) 'F' and 'G' can be configured as an array of Read/Write memory cells. A single CLB can be configured as a 16x1, 16x2 or 32x1 RAM. These can be configured as edge triggered (synchronous RAMs) or level sensitive (asynchronous RAMs). Synchronous RAMs can be used to implement very fast shift registers (up to 32 bit shift on one CLB) when addressed by an external counter. The 16x1 mode in particular can be configured as a dual port RAM.

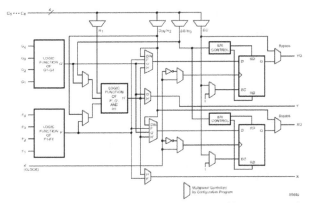

Figure 1.11 XC4000 Complex Logic Block (CLB) architecture overview

Another very important feature of XC4000 series is the fast carry logic. Each CLB 'F' and 'G' LUT contains dedicated arithmetic logic for fast generation of carry and borrow signals (<1ns). This extra output (C_{out}) is passed on to the function generator in the adjacent *vertical* CLB. The dedicated fast carry chain is independent of normal routing resources. The two 4-input LUTs can be configured as 2-bit adders, subtracters, incrementers or decrementers with built in hidden carry that can be expanded to any length. Note that the carry chain in XC4000E devices can run either up or down. In the XC4000X devices, however, the carry chain can travel upward only. At the top and bottom of the columns where there are no CLBs above and below, the carry is propagated to the right.

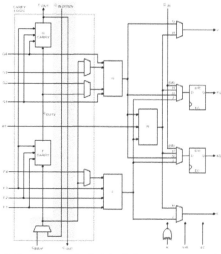

Figure 1.12 XC4000 dedicated carry logic (shaded area not present in XC4000X)

Programmable interconnect

CLB inputs and outputs are distributed on all four sides (North, South, East and West), providing maximum routing flexibility. These are then interconnected using Programmable Switch Matrices (PSMs) as shown in Figure 1.13.

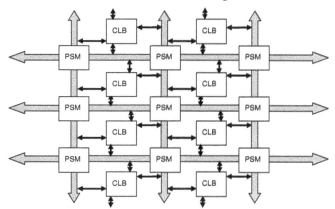

Figure 1.13 XC4000 routing architecture overview

Single-length lines offer fast routing between adjacent CLBs. *Double-length* lines are twice long as the single length lines. There are four vertical and four horizontal double length lines associated with each CLB. They are grouped in pairs with each line going through a PSM every other row or column of a CLB. Also provided are *longlines*- segments that run the entire length or width of the FPGA. These are intended for routing high fan-out, time critical signal nets and signals that are distributed over a long distance.

The XC4000X devices include twelve vertical and twelve horizontal *quad lines* per CLB. These are four times as long as single length lines. They are grouped in fours; with each line of them going through a buffered switch matrix every fourth CLB location in that row or column. The XC4000X series also offer two *direct*, fast connections between adjacent CLBs and between IOBs and CLBs. These do not compete with general routing resources and have less interconnect propagation. Note that a pair of 3-state buffers is associated with each CLB. These 3-state buffers can be used to drive signals onto the nearest horizontal longline (see Figure 1.14).

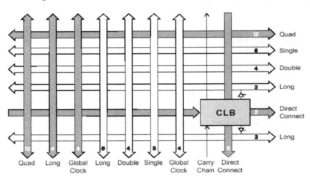

Figure 1.14 High-level routing diagram of a XC4000 series CLB
(Shaded arrows indicates XC4000X only)

XC4000 series have dedicated global networks, which distribute clocks and other high fanout control signals throughout the device with minimal skew. A certain number of vertical longlines (four in XC4000E and eight in XC4000X) in each CLB column are driven by special global buffers situated in the corners of the device. There are different types of global buffers. In general, placement of a library symbol called BUFG causes the Xilinx software tools to choose the appropriate global buffer (e.g. BUFGP, BUFGS etc.), based on the user supplied timing constraints.

Input/Output Blocks (IOBs)

The FPGA's internal logic interfaces to the external package pins by user-configurable Input/Output Blocks (IOBs). Each IOB controls one package pin and can be configured for input, output, or bi-directional signals. Two input paths (see I1, I2 in Figure 1.15) bring input signals from the package pin into the internal logic. Inputs can also connect to a register, which can be programmed as an edge-triggered flip-flop or a level-sensitive latch. Output signals can be optionally inverted within the IOB, and can pass directly to the pad or be stored in an edge-triggered flip-flop.

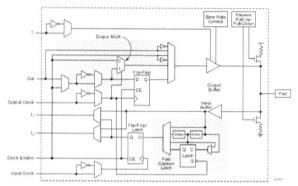

Figure 1.15 Simplified block diagram of XC4000X IOB
(The shaded area is not existent in XC4000E)

1.3.3 Altera Flex10K series

The Altera Flex10K FPGA is the most popular competitor to Xilinx 4000 [Alt00a]. It is composed of an array of Logic Array Blocks (LABs) and Embedded Array Blocks (EABs) joined by row and column interconnect buses (FastTrack™ interconnect) as shown in Figure 1.16.

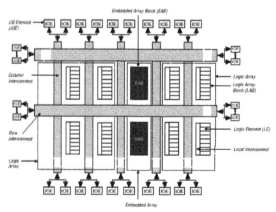

Figure 1.16 Altera Flex10K Block diagram

Each LAB contains 8 Logic Elements (LE's) and a local interconnect. The structure of a LE is given by Figure 1.17.

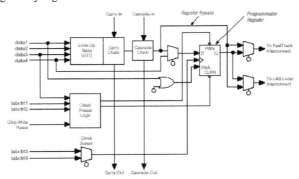

Figure 1.17 Altera Flex 10K Logic Element architecture

The Logic Element (LE) contains a 4-input LUT, a flip-flop and dedicated fast carry and cascade chain. As in XC4000, the dedicated carry logic is used for the construction of fast adders and adder based structures. The cascade chain is used to connect the output of one LE to the input of the next adjacent very quickly (~1ns).

Note that when the carry chain is used, the 4-input LUT is broken into a pair of 3-input LUTs, one for the carry to the next bit and one for the sum function. One input to each of these is the carry from the previous bit. That limits the number of inputs of any arithmetic function to two. Moreover, if the register clock enable is used, another LUT input is stolen too. That limits the number of arithmetic inputs to one if it is to be implemented in one level (one LE). As can be seen from Figure 1.11, the Xilinx 4000 architecture allows the function generators 'F' and 'G' to be configured to implement any 4-input arithmetic function independently of the carry mode. Another shortcoming of Altera's Flex10K architecture (compared to XC4000) is that the LUT cannot be configured as synchronous RAMs. Shift registers are then implemented using multiple LE 1-bit registers.

The Embedded Array Block (EAB) is comprised of an array of RAM surrounded by programmable logic. Typical functions implemented on an EAB are RAMs, multipliers and error correction functions. The RAM can be configured in a number of forms: 256x8, 512x4, 1024x2, or 2048x1 bits. It also may be configured as single or dual port RAM, ROM or FIFO. This feature does not exist in XC4000.

Recently, Altera has announced the new Apex family, which combines and enhances the strengths of the previous FLEX10K, FLEX6000, and MAX7000 architectures. Based on 0.22um, six-layer metal technology, some Apex devices exceed 2 million gates. Among the new features introduced in Apex, which were not existent in Flex10K, are Content Addressable Memories (CAMs), Phase Locked Loops (PLLs) and product term logic used for combinatorial intensive functions [Alt00b].

1.3.4 Atmel 40K series

The Atmel 40K series are SRAM based, dynamically reconfigurable FPGAs from Atmel [Atm99]. It comprises an array of up to 48x48 configurable cells grouped in 4x4 blocks separated by *Vertical Repeaters* (RV) and *Horizontal Repeaters* (RH). Each repeater provides interconnection into one length-4 local bus and two length-8 express buses. These three buses form a *bus plane*. There are five such bus planes in a device. At each repeater crosspoint, there is a block of 32x4 RAM, which can be configured as single or dual port-RAM, in both synchronous and asynchronous modes.

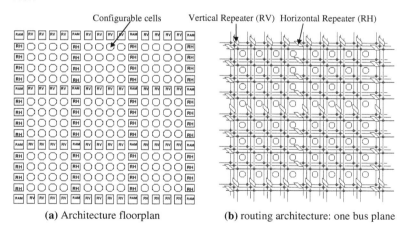

(a) Architecture floorplan   (b) routing architecture: one bus plane

Figure 1.18 Atmel 40K

There are direct connections between each cell and its eight neighbouring cells (see Figure 1.19a). The connections between the cell and the five bus planes are shown in Figure 1.19b.

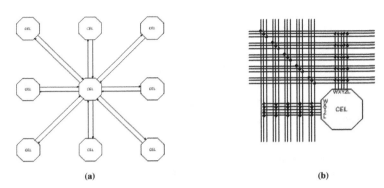

(a)   (b)

Figure 1.19 (a) Atmel 40K direct cell interconnection
(b) Cell interconnection with the five bus planes

Each cell consists of two 3-input LUTs and a register as shown in Figure 1.20. The LUTs may be used to implement any two 3-input functions or combined to implement any 4-input one. Note the presence of an AND gate, which allows the implementation of a gated full adder configuration useful for the production of a multiplication partial product and carry outputs. This feature, along with the octagonal routing structure at the local level, makes the Atmel40k very efficient in implementing array multipliers.

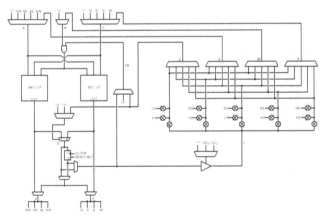

Figure 1.20 Atmel 40K configurable cell architecture

However, here again, unlike XC4000, the cell LUTs cannot be configured as synchronous RAMs. Shift registers are then implemented using the configurable 1-bit register. In addition, the routing resources are fewer compared to XC4000 FPGAs.

1.3.5 Xilinx Virtex series

The Virtex [Vir99] FPGA family, from Xilinx, was announced at a late stage of this project. The Virtex gives a significant increase in silicon efficiency by optimising the architecture for place-and-route efficiency and using a 5-layer-metal 0.22-μm CMOS process. It is based on the highly successful XC4000 cell architecture. An overview of Virtex architecture is given in Figure 1.21.

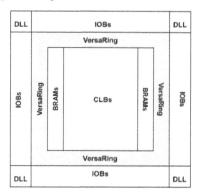

Figure 1.21 XC4000 architecture overview

Each Virtex CLB comprises two 'slices'. A Virtex slice is very similar to a XC4000 CLB and has all its features (see Figure 1.22).

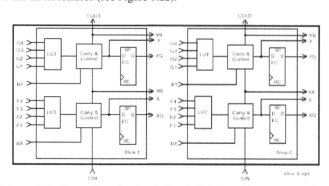

Figure 1.22 Virtex Complex Logic Block (CLB) architecture overview

The most important new features of Virtex are:

- Each of the four Look-Up Tables (LUTs) in a Virtex CLB can be configured as a 16-bit shift register with no extra logic (no external address counter). As in

XC4000 FPGAs, LUTs can also be configured as 16x1 or 32x1 synchronous RAMs.

- Virtex contains large Block SelectRAM™ memories. These complement the distributed LUT synchronous RAMs implemented in CLBs. Block SelectRAM memory blocks are organised in columns. All Virtex devices contain two such columns, one along each vertical edge. These columns extend the full height of the chip. Each Block SelectRAM memory block is four CLBs high. It is a fully synchronous dual-ported 4096-bit RAM with independent control signals for each port. The data widths of the two ports can be configured independently, providing built-in bus-width conversion.

- Four dedicated digital Delay-Locked Loops (DLL) are provided. A DLL can be used to eliminate skew between the clock input pad and internal clock input pins throughout the device. In addition to eliminating clock-distribution delay, the DLL provides advanced control of multiple clock domains. The DLL provides four quadrature phases of the source clock (0°, 90°, 180°, 270°). It also can double the clock, or divide the clock by 1.5, 2, 2.5, 3, 4, 5, 8, or 16.

- Virtex allows for partial reconfiguration. However, unlike the XC6200 family in which the whole chip could be partially reconfigured, Virtex has a column oriented partial reconfiguration facility.

The Virtex family members range from XCV50 (16x24 CLBs) to XCV1000 (64x96 CLBs). The latter has a density exceeding 1 Million gates. Recently Xilinx has announced the new Virtex-E family, which is built on the Virtex architecture. Virtex-E family provides more internal block memory, more I/O pins and higher performance. Leveraging the 0.18um, six-layer metal technology, Virtex-E devices push the traditional FPGA measurements to over three million gates, 804 I/Os and over 311 MHz performance. Virtex-E family is designed to support very high bandwidth requirements.

1.4 Deciding on an FPGA

The basic functions required for nearly any signal processing operation include addition/subtraction, shifts and delays. These blocks can then be used to construct more complicated structures such as multipliers. It is then crucial for an FPGA to have efficient support for addition and delay queues. An ideal FPGA architecture for DSP applications would then contain:

- Dedicated carry logic and routing necessary to implement fast adders, which in turn will allow for high throughput multipliers.
- An efficient implementation of shift registers and delays.
- Large amounts of on-chip RAM for storing intermediate data (buffers).

Moreover, many research projects [RFLC90][RGV93] have demonstrated that an FPGA architecture based on 4-input LUT coupled to a flip-flop provides optimal implementation density for DSP applications. It is then clear from the above arguments that Xilinx XC4000 and Altera's Flex10K architectures are superior to other architectures as far as DSP applications are concerned. Our choice was then restricted between Xilinx XC4000 and Altera's Flex10K. While Flex10K offer large amounts of on-chip memory, it falls seriously short for flexible dedicated carry logic and efficient delay queue implementation (see section 1.3.3). This has led us to choose Xilinx XC4000 as a target FPGA architecture. The availability of a XC4000 based prototype board (Xilinx Xchecker™) and the support software (XACT™) locally has also consolidated this choice.

Unfortunately, Virtex based systems were just becoming available at a late stage of this project. Had it not been the case, we would have targeted this FPGA family since it offers great facilities for DSP designs (e.g. large BlockRAMs).

1.5 Motivation and aims of the book

Though FPGAs seem to enjoy many of the advantages of both the dedicated hardware solution and the software based one, many people are still reluctant to move towards this new technology because of the low level programming scheme of FPGAs. Although behavioural synthesis tools have developed enormously, structural design techniques often still result in circuits that are substantially smaller and faster than those developed using only behavioural synthesis tools [HBH99]. This is particularly true in most demanding applications such as image and video processing. Moreover, even with optimised libraries of most common functions like adders and multipliers, the user still has to think at the logic level rather than at the algorithmic level. This can cause the FPGA design process to be slow, tedious and error-prone.

The general goal of this book is to show how we can eliminate these unfortunate consequences *in Image Processing applications specifically* by implementing an FPGA based Image Processing Coprocessor. In particular, this book shows how to:

- Provide a *high-level programming environment* for FPGA based Image Processing. This environment should ideally *hide FPGA hardware details completely* from the user's point of view. This would enable the IP application developer to exploit the performance of a direct hardware solution while programming in an application oriented environment.
- The *environment should produce an efficient FPGA configuration directly* from a very high-level algorithm description, which would ease and speed up the design cycle.

Chapter 2

FPGA based Image Processing

Chapter 2

FPGA based Image Processing

Since the emergence of dynamically reconfigurable hardware in the form of FPGAs in the mid-1980's, there has been a considerable and continuous growth of the programmable logic market [SIA]. Both hardware and software for FPGAs have developed very significantly since the dawn of this new technology. A considerable amount of research has been spent into the use of FPGAs in computationally intensive applications, such as data compression [RTR99][MMcC99], data encryption [PCC99][WWD98] and other Digital Signal Processing applications. Digital Image Processing is a computationally intensive and inherently parallel application, and thus has been able to take advantage of the parallelism offered by FPGAs [PA96][CNH93].

In this chapter, we will first present some commercial hardware systems along with some real world applications implemented on these systems. Section 2.2 will then present some software environments developed to exploit the performance of FPGAs. Section 2.3 takes a closer look at previous work, which forms the direct starting point for the work presented in this book. Finally, the objectives of the research presented in this book will be given in section 2.4.

2.1 FPGA based hardware systems

In this section, we will firstly present some commercial FPGA based computing machines. The various architectural features of these boards are then reviewed.

2.1.1   The HOTWorks XC6200 development system

The HOTWorks PCI board from Virtual Computing Company [Vcc99] comprises a Xilinx XC6200 device used as a Reconfigurable Processing Unit (RPU), along with a Xilinx XC4013 FPGA used for PCI interface. It also includes 4 banks of SRAM for a total of 2MB as well as a mezzanine connector for the addition of daughter cards.

The HOTWorks board has been used to implement a 2D DCT transform [WTH98] and an image correlator [KD97].

VCC has another package, called HOTII™ Development System which is based on Xilinx XC4062XLT device (XL version) or the Xilinx Spartan XCS40-4 FPGA (Standard version). More recently, VCC introduced the Virtex Workbench™, which is based on the latest Xilinx Virtex family.

2.1.2   SPLASH and SPLASH II

Splash, and its second generation Splash II were among the first FPGA computing machines, and were developed by Maryland SuperComputer Research Center [Mok90][ABD92]. The Splash II system is an attached special purpose parallel processor. It uses 16 Xilinx 4010 devices connected in a linear array augmented by a crossbar, each with its own SRAM. The Splash II system has been successfully used in a wide range of applications such us the genetic database search application [Hoa93] and an automatic target recognition system [RH97].

2.1.3   The G-800 system

The G-800 [Gig94] is a configurable video rate computing engine. It is a VESA local bus interface board capable of supporting up to 16 computing modules. The basic computing module (called VCMOD) can support up to 2 FPGAs and 4MB of RAM. The G-800 interface unit provides either 133 MB/sec through the VESA local bus or 100 MB/sec through the VESA media channel video bus. The high speed I/O and scaleable computing modules make the G-800 well suited to high performance SIMD (Single-Instruction-Multiple-Data) image processing applications [COPS99].

2.1.4   PCI Pamette

The PCI Pamette board from Digital's System Research Centre [PAM96], contains 5 Xilinx XC4000E devices. One Xilinx XC4010E FPGA implements a master and slave PCI interface supporting 32 and 64-bit transactions and contains a DMA engine capable of transferring data at full PCI-bus speed. The PCI Pamette board features a PCI mezzanine card connector (PMC) for daughter cards. Two independent SRAM banks are provided, each is 64k x 16-bits. Implementations based on this board include the PAM-Blox circuit libraries [MMF98] including Jacobian relaxation and matrix multiplication.

2.1.5   Mirotech's Aristotle

Aristotle™ from MiroTech [Mir99] is a PCI reconfigurable board designed for the academic sector. It is based on TI's TMS320C44 DSP processor combined with Xilinx XC4036EX FPGA. Mirotech claims that Aristotle™ is the first DSP-based PCI reconfigurable computer designed exclusively for the academic sector.

MiroTech offers Corespex™, a development toolkit specifically designed for MiroTech's High-Performance Reconfigurable Computing (HPRC) architecture.

2.1.6   Visicom's VigraVision

Visicom's VigraVision™ product family exploits FPGA technology to provide real-time image and video processing [Vig98]. The VigraVision PCI board is an accelerated Super VGA display board with an onboard colour frame grabber and an FPGA based video processor. The functional block diagram of the VigraVision PCI board is shown in Figure 2.1.

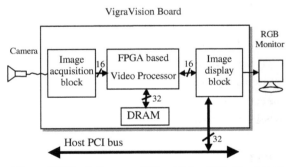

Figure 2.1 Block diagram of VigraVision PCI video board

Many image and video processing algorithms have been implemented on the VigraVision board giving real time processing of video data. These include laplacian edge enhancement, frame averaging with 3x3 convolution, median filtering and motion detection.

2.1.7   Review of hardware design features

The above FPGA based computing machines can be analysed and compared in terms of a number of design features:

- **Multiple FPGAs**: A board containing multiple FPGAs achieves higher performance. However, this involves a more *complex programming model* and more *complex control* (e.g. by processing different parts of an image at the same time). This also involves *higher cost*. Splash II, PCI-Pamette and G-800 have multiple onboard FPGAs.

- **On board processor**: It has been shown in some studies [SS98] that an onboard processor (e.g. a microprocessor) can lead to a considerable performance improvement. The processor can be used to off-load critical tasks from the host system processor such as DMA memory transfer between the host's memory and the on board RAM. It also can be used to off-load the FPGA(s) from certain complex and area consuming control tasks (e.g. On-board memory control). Among the aforementioned boards, only the Mirotech board contains an onboard processor in the form of the C44 DSP processor.

- **Video transfer facilities**: For video processing, it is essential that a board contains certain facilities for high bandwidth data transfer, such as a high rate video transfer bus to the FPGA. This is offered by the G-800™ board. The VigraVision™ goes as far as offering a direct video input to the FPGA with on board video capture.

Other factors include the level of software support offered by the vendor, the cost and the extensibility.

2.2 Software environments for FPGA platforms

Although behavioural synthesis tools have made significant progress in the last few years, structural design can still improve the performance of FPGA designs, both in smaller area and faster speed [HBH99].

Though it is possible to design structural circuits using VHDL and even include manual placement directives, structural VHDL is extremely verbose, making it difficult to read and maintain. Moreover, VHDL has not been designed to support physical placement. Thus, physical placement directives are not standard and differ from one synthesis tool to another.

As a result, several other HDLs have been designed to benefit from structural design and manual placement of at least some parts of the design. These include:

2.2.1 Lola

Lola is a small modula-2 like language for the specification of digital circuits [GLW94][Wir95]. This language is supported by an integrated software environment called *Trianus*. The Trianus software consists of a suite of tightly integrated tools for the efficient design and implementation of algorithms using a custom-computing machine. It comprises a compiler for the Lola hardware description language, a layout editor, a circuit checker, a technology mapper, a placer, a router and a bitstream generator and loader for the Xilinx XC6200 architecture [GL96a].

A design can be described textually by means of a program written in a HDL (i.e. Lola), or schematically using a schematic editor, or physically using a layout editor to give complete control over the circuit.

In a textual description, a circuit is described statically as a set of assignments of boolean expressions to variables. In order to describe sub-circuits, new *types* can be created which group together variable declarations and assignments. Variables of such types can be instantiated and connected together, for instance, to build bit-sliced designs. Instances of types can also be declared within other types, allowing for the hierarchical composition of circuits from sub-circuits. The static description can be augmented with placement information. The following code gives an example of Lola code for a 1-bit full adder:

```
MODULE Fulladder;
  TYPE fa;
    IN a,b,cin : BIT;
    OUT sum, cout : BIT;
    BEGIN
      sum := a – b – cin;
      cout := (a*b) + (a*cin) + (b*cin);
    END fa;
  VAR
  fa1 : fa;
  x, y : BIT;
  BEGIN
    fa1(x, y, '0);   (* initially cin=0 *)
  END Fulladder.
```

2.2.2 Pebble

Pebble [LMcW98] is an alias for *Parameterised Block Language*. The two primary objectives for Pebble are to facilitate the development of efficient and reusable designs, and to support the development of designs involving run-time reconfiguration.

Pebble can be regarded as a much simplified variant of structural VHDL. It provides a means of representing block diagrams hierarchically and parametrically. The basic features of Pebble [LMcW98] are:

- A Pebble program is a block defined by its name, parameters, interfaces, local definitions, and its body.

- The block interfaces are given by two lists, usually interpreted as the inputs and outputs. An input or an output can be of type *WIRE*, or it can be a multidimensional vector of wires.

- The GENERATE-IF statement enables conditional compilation, while the GENERATE-FOR statement allows the concise description of regular circuits.

The following code gives an example of Pebble code for a 1-bit full adder:

```
BLOCK Fulladder [a, b, cin] [sum, cout];
BLOCK Fulladder [a, b, cin] [sum, cout]
  VAR
    Temp1, Temp2, Temp3, Temp4, Temp5 : WIRE;
  BEGIN
    XOR2 [a,b] [temp1];
    XOR2 [cin, Temp1] [sum];
    AND2 [a, b] [Temp2];
    AND2 [a, cin] [Temp3];
    AND2 [b, cin] [Temp4];
    OR2 [Temp2, Temp3] [Temp5];
    OR2 [Temp5, Temp4] [cout]
  END;
```

2.2.3 Ruby

Ruby [JS90] is a declarative language which has been used in describing and developing various architectures, including image processing designs [AL96], butterfly networks [JS91] and systolic data structures [LGSZ96].

The general idea is that circuits and circuit components are represented by relations between the signals at their inputs and outputs. Larger circuits are assembled from components by a suite of functions, such as relational composition and various combining forms that represent regular arrays of components.   For instance, components might be composed horizontally (using *beside* and *row*), vertically (using *below* and *column*) or in a triangular way (using *tri* and *irt*). The algebraic properties of these functions, such as the associativity of composition, yield equations between circuits with different structure but the same behaviour.

With Ruby, a design by refinement process is advocated, where the initial specification of a circuit is a Ruby expression that describes its behaviour in gross terms which it would be unrealistic to implement directly. This specification is then rewritten using a succession of laws until it assumes a form in which all the relations are known, implementable components [JS94]. The sequence of transformations applied to the specification can be read as a proof that the implementation meets the specification.

Ruby does not have a standard version available because several research groups have adapted the language to their own needs [Sin95]. The complexity and rather mathematical nature of Ruby have meant it has not been as widely used as it might have been hoped.

2.2.4   JHDL

JHDL [HBH99] is a complete structural design environment, including debugging, netlisting and other design aids. In JHDL, circuits are described by a JAVA code that programmatically builds circuits using JHDL libraries. Each circuit element is represented by a unique JAVA object. These objects inherit from core classes that set up the netlist and simulation model. Circuits are created by calling the constructor for the corresponding JHDL object (by **new**) and passing 'Wire' objects as constructor arguments to be connected to the ports of the circuit. JHDL also provides a core structural design class (**Logic** class), which provides a quick-hardware API to build circuits efficiently. In this case, logic functions are instantiated by method calls instead of constructors. These in turn call the appropriate constructor. The circuit can add FPGA target specific placement directives. The following code gives an example of a JHDL code for a 1-bit full adder (targeted to XC4000 series):

```
Public class FullAdder extends Logic{
/* Define the ports for a 1-bit full adder */
  public static final String[]
    portnames  ={ "a", "b", "cin", "s", "cout"},
    portwidths ={ "1", "1", "1", "1", "1"},
    portios    ={ "in", "in", "in", "out", "out"},

  public FullAdder(Wire a, Wire b, Wire cin, Wire s, Wire cout){
  /* Connect wires to my parts */
  port("a", a); port("b", b); port("cin", cin);
  port("s", s); port("cout", cout);

  /* Instantiate the logic functions */
  or3(and(a,b), and(a, cin), and(b, cin), cout); /* cout is output */
  xor3(a, b, cin, s); /* s is output */

  /* Map the gates to LUTs and place */
  map(a, b, cin, s); place(s, "R0C0.F");
  map(a, b, cin, cout); place(cout, "R0C0.G");
}
```

Once the circuit is constructed, it can be debugged and verified with the design browser, a circuit verification and debugging tool. Then, an EDIF 2.0.0 file [Cra84] can be generated. The latter is then passed to vendor specific placement and routing tools to create an FPGA configuration file. At the time of writing, JHDL supports Xilinx XC6000 and XC4000 series, and HP chess devices.

2.2.5 Handel-C

Handel-C from ESL [ESL99] enables a software engineer to target directly an FPGA without recourse to hardware description languages. Handel-C is a programming language designed to enable the compilation of programs into synchronous hardware. Handel-C is not a hardware description language though; rather it is a programming language aimed at compiling high level algorithms directly into gate level hardware in the form of an EDIF netlist.

The Handel-C syntax is based on that of conventional C, so programmers familiar with conventional C will recognise almost all the constructs in the Handel-C language. However, although Handel-C is inherently sequential (as conventional C), it is possible (and indeed essential for efficient programs) to instruct the compiler to build hardware to execute statements in parallel (**par** statement). This exploits the fact that the target of the Handel-C compiler is low-level hardware rather than a conventional microprocessor.

Unfortunately, Handel-C has been made available at a late stage of this project and thus has not been considered.

2.2.6 JBits

The JBits API from Xilinx [JBits99] is a new JAVA based tool set, or application programming interface (API), that permits the FPGA bitstream of the Xilinx XC4000 and Virtex series to be modified quickly, allowing for fast reconfiguration of the FPGA. This interface operates on either bitstreams generated by Xilinx design tools, or on bitstreams read back from actual hardware. With Virtex FPGAs, the JBits API can partially or fully reconfigure the internal logic of the hardware device. The programming model used by JBits is a two dimensional array of Configurable Logic Blocks (CLBs). Each CLB is referenced by a row and column, and all configurable resources in the selected CLB may be set or probed. Additionally, control of all routing resources adjacent to the selected CLB is made available. Because the code is written in JAVA, compilation times are very fast, and because control is at the CLB level, bitstreams can be modified or generated very quickly. JBits has been used to construct complete circuits and to modify existing circuits. In addition, the object oriented support in the Java programming language allows for small libraries of parameterisable, object oriented macro circuits or *Cores* to be implemented. Finally, this API may be used as a base to construct other tools. This includes traditional design tools for performing tasks such as circuit placement and routing, as well as application specific tools to perform more narrowly defined tasks. Unfortunately, JBits has been available at a late stage of this project and thus has not been considered.

2.3 Towards an application oriented environment

Despite the great amount of research done on FPGAs, many FPGA-based applications have been algorithm-specific. An environment for developing *applications* needs more than just a library of static FPGA configurations, since it should allow the user to experiment with alternative algorithms and develop his/her own algorithms. There is a need for bridging the gap between high level application-oriented software and low level FPGA hardware.

In order to bridge this gap specifically for Image Processing (IP) applications, the school of Computer Science at The Queen's University of Belfast developed a research programme in High Performance Image Processing. One goal of this research was to exploit the performance of novel architectures while providing a convenient high level, application friendly programming model. The programme originally started using parallel computing. More recently, FPGAs have been considered as an alternative, for high performance and relatively low cost. We will firstly summarise the most relevant projects in this programme, and then consider those in more details.

As mentioned in the prologue, one of the earlier outcomes of this research programme was a high level image processing language, called TULIP [CS94][Ste94], which was designed for implementation on a range of high performance architectures. TULIP includes a range of image-level neighbourhood operations based on the operations of Image Algebra (IA) [RWD90]. After this, Donachy [Don96] pursued the objective of developing an FPGA based hardware implementation of TULIP with the aim of producing an image coprocessor. He took the operations of TULIP and developed a range of static FPGA architectures for the Xilinx XC6200 series. This was the first step towards implementing TULIP on FPGAs and targeted Xilinx XC6200 series.

As a way of developing Donachy's architectures to be more dynamic, flexible and powerful, Alotaibi [Alo99] developed HIDE: a Prolog based new hardware description notation, which has been used for dynamic generation of a range of scaleable FPGA configurations for all the standard operations in TULIP.

Each of these projects is now described in more details.

2.3.1 TULIP

TULIP is a high level algebraic programming language for parallel image processing applications [CS94][Ste94]. It was designed for portable implementation across a range of parallel machines. It is based mainly on providing a range of neighbourhood operations, on both 2-D and 1-D structures. Both non-recursive and the less common recursive operations are available. TULIP included the basic set of low level image processing operators of Image Algebra Language (IAL) [CMMc90], which was a precursor to TULIP.

An entire neighbourhood operation takes the form of a 2-D or 1-D array (a *window*, or *template*) of coefficients applied to all possible regions of an image in a defined manner. The manner in which the window of coefficients is applied to an image depends on the window mode and the neighbourhood operation taking place. A window may be applied in one of the following types:

- **Template**

Templates are applied to all possible neighbourhoods of the source image, conceptually simultaneously. These neighbourhoods will clearly overlap.

- **Tiles**

A tile is the same as a template, except it is moved over the image with a step size equal to its template's size. So, for instance, applying a 2x2 tile to a 256x256 image produces a 128x128 image result.

There are two more modes of templates, which are used for *recursive* neighbourhood operations. With recursive processing, each result pixel is stored back in the *original* image as the image is scanned. This means that the neighbourhood used in the calculation will consist of some of the original pixel values and some of the newly calculated values. In this type of neighbourhood, the old and new parts are "spliced" together. According to the direction of image scan, we distinguish:

- **Splices**

A Splice is a type of recursive neighbourhood operation in which the image is scanned from top left hand corner to lower right hand corner.

- **ISplices**

An ISplice is a type of recursive neighbourhood operations in which image data is scanned from lower right hand corner to upper left hand corner.

Templates in TULIP are static. Variant templates of Image Algebra are not implemented. A 2-D template can be declared and defined in TULIP as follows:

```
laplace : template[3,3] of integer;
value laplace = [ [ ~, -1, ~ ],
                  [ -1, [4], -1 ],
                  [ ~, -1, ~ ] ];
```

The '~' coefficient indicates that this pixel is not used in the calculation. The coefficient corresponding to the target pixel location (in the result image) is surrounded by the inner most []'s.

A template may be applied to an image using one of the following six built in neighbourhood operators:

- **Convolution** (@): The coefficient values are multiplied by the corresponding image pixel values and the result pixel is the summation of all of these partial results.

- **Absolute convolution** (|@|): This is similar to convolution, only the result pixel is the *absolute* value of the summation of all of the partial results.

- **Additive maximum** (+V): The coefficient values are added to the corresponding image pixel values and the result pixel is the maximum of all of these partial results.

- **Additive minimum** (+Λ): Similar to additive maximum, only the result pixel is the minimum of all of the partial results.

- **Multiplicative maximum** (*V): The coefficient values are multiplied by the image pixel values and the result pixel is the maximum of all of these partial results.

- **Multiplicative minimum** (*Λ): This is similar to multiplicative maximum, only the result pixel is the minimum of all of the partial results.

For instance, an *Absolute convolution* neighbourhood operation (using the previously defined *laplace* template) can be written in TULIP as follows:

> Imageout := Imagein |@| laplace;

New user-defined neighbourhood operators may be written in 'C' and imported as new machine instructions. The machine (or environment) then needs to be recompiled. Thereafter, these user-defined operators can be imported by a TULIP program.

Tulip has a Pascal-like syntax. The following is a complete TULIP program, which performs Sobel edge detection:

```
program EdgeDetect;
const   threshold = 150;
var     img1, res      : image[256, 256] of integer;
        sh,sv          : template[3,3] of integer;
value   sh =     [ [ 1,  2, 1 ],
                   [ ~, [~],~ ],
                   [-1, -2,-1 ] ];
        sv =     [ [1,  ~, -1 ],
                   [2, [~],-2 ],
                   [1,  ~, -1 ] ];
begin

{Add the result of two absolute convolutions (|@|) on the input image. The result
image is then thresholded (>). The resulting binary image is finally multiplied by 255}

  res := ((img1 |@| sh  + img1 |@| sv) > threshold)*255 ;

end.
```

The compiler generates code for the Tulip abstract machine, designed by Steele & Crookes [Ste94]. Prototype implementations of the machine have been developed for the Transputer and for the AMT DAP.

2.3.2 Donachy's FPGA Based Image Processing Coprocessor

This section outlines the architecture of an *ideal* FPGA based Image Processing Coprocessor (IPC) proposed by Donachy [Don96]. Donachy proposed an Image Processing oriented high level programming model implemented in C++. This provides automatic and efficient FPGA implementation of low level image processing operations. The IP operations implemented were mainly neighbourhood operations and were based on TULIP's operations.

2.3.2.1 The IPC instruction set

Most common neighbourhood operations can be split in two stages:

- A *local* operator applied between an image pixel and the corresponding window coefficient.

- A *global* operator applied to the set of local operation results to generate a result image pixel.

The set of local operators includes 'Add' ('+') and 'multiplication' ('*'), whereas the global operators include 'Accumulation' ('Σ'), 'Maximum' ('Max') and 'Minimum' ('Min') operators. With these local and global operators, the following neighbourhood operations can be built:

Neighbourhood Operation	Local Op.	GlobalOp.
Convolution	*	Σ
Additive maximum	+	Max
Additive minimum	+	Min
Multiplicative maximum	*	Max
Multiplicative minimum	*	Min

Table 2.1 Image Algebra core operation set

These two operators (Local and Global) along with a user-defined *window* (with specific size, and a set of weights) and a *template mode* (template, tile, Splice or ISplice) completely define a neighbourhood operation. A general neighbourhood operation (nop), for the generic PxQ window template shown in Figure 2.2, is defined by the following high level instruction operator object:

```
nop =new Instructionoperator(Neighbourhoodoperation(Local_op,Global_op),
                             Template_mode,
                             window(SizeP, SizeQ, targetP, targetQ,  C₁,₁, C₁,₂, ...C₁,Q,
                                                                      C₂,₁, C₂,₂, ...C₂,Q,
                                                                      ........................,
                                                                      CP,₁, CP,₂, ...CP,Q )
                  )
```

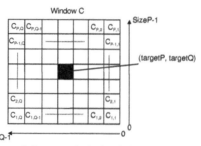

Figure 2.2 A generic PxQ window template

Given an instruction operation object (**nop**), an input image object (**input_im**) and an output image object (**output_im**), an image instruction object (**Im_ins**), which encapsulates all the details of IP operation to be performed, can be generated as follows [Don96]:

```
Im_ins = new Imageinstruction(output_im, input_im, nop)
```

Once this object is created, the corresponding IP operation can be executed on an FPGA by a call to a member function (*perform*) with two operands (the input and output image):

```
Im_ins.perform(output_im, input_im)
```

2.3.2.2 Implementation of the IPC Instruction Set

Before implementing the FPGA-based IPC instruction set, Donachy set the following implementation objectives:

- **Scaleability:** An efficient hardware implementation should be generated regardless of the window size and coefficients of the neighbourhood operation.

- **First Time Place and Route:** There should be no Non-Recurring-Engineering (NRE) design costs. A design generated from the high level instruction set should guarantee a first time place and route with no user intervention.

- **Reusability:** The instruction set should be implemented from reusable components. This may require extra hardware for the implementation of the basic components, but in the context of providing reusable hardware components, this can be tolerated.

Architectures were designed *by hand* for *3x3 windows* for the set of neighbourhood operations given in Table 2.1, for each template mode.

The following gives the design of a convolution operation in template mode, as used by Donachy. The design of other neighbourhood operators (e.g. Multiplicative Maximum and Additive Minimum) using other window modes (Tile, Splice and ISplice) was based on this convolution template operation [Don96].

A 2-D Convolver

As in any other neighbourhood image operation, a convolution involves passing a 2-D window over an image, and carrying out a calculation at each window position, which, in this particular case, is a Multiply-Accumulate operation.

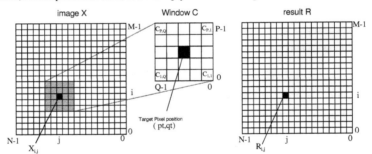

Figure 2.3 A 2D neighbourhood operation process

The result image is defined as follows:

$$R_{i+pt,j+qt} = \sum_{l=1}^{Q} \sum_{k=1}^{P} C_{k,l} * X_{i+k-1,j+l-1} \qquad \forall i,j \in 0, 0 \times M - P, N - Q$$

which can be rewritten as:

$$R_{i+pt,j+qt} = \sum_{l=1}^{Q} c(l)^T . x(i, j+l-1)$$

where *c(l)* are coefficient column vectors.

For instance, a 3 by 3 window may be reorganised as follows:

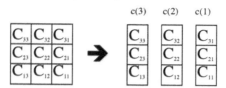

and x(i, j+l-1) are input image column vectors and where

$$c(l)^T.x(i,j+1-1) = \sum_{k=1}^{P} C_{k,l} *X_{i+k-1,j+l-1}$$

This has split the overall convolution into a sum of scalar-products. Each of these vectors of coefficients c(l) and column vectors x(i, j+l-1) produces a partial result. These can be calculated independently and finally added to produce the result value $R_{i,j}$.

To allow each pixel to be supplied only once to the FPGA, internal line delays are required. These internal line delays synchronise the supply of input values to the processing elements units ensuring that all the pixel values involved in a particular neighbourhood operation are processed at the same instance [Ple88][Sho94][KKSH90]. Figure 2.4 shows the architecture for a 2-D convolution operation with a 3 by 3 window kernel assuming a vertical scan direction of the input image.

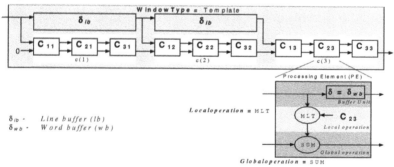

Figure 2.4 Architecture of a standard 2-D, 3 by 3 convolution operation.

Each image pixel within the 9 pixels involved in a particular neighbourhood is simultaneously multiplied by its corresponding window coefficient. Partial sums are then accumulated by a 9 adder chain, with one pixel delay 'δ_{wb}' between adjacent pixels in an image column, and a delay 'δ_{LB}', between image columns, equal to the image height (if the image is scanned vertically).

One principle feature of Donachy's approach was to have a standard framework, which accommodates the full range of neighbourhood operators. The appropriate two local and global operator sub-blocks were plugged into this standard framework.

Since a complete convolver (or similar operator) had to fit on a single XC6200 FPGA chip, parallel multipliers were not feasible. That's why bit serial arithmetic was used (rather than bit parallel). Note, secondly, that the need to pipeline bit serial Maximum and Minimum operations suggested processing data Most Significant Bit first (MSBF). Following on from this choice, because of problems in doing addition MSBF in 2's complement, it was better to use an alternative number representation to 2's complement in which addition can be performed in MSBF fashion independently of the pixel wordlength i.e. a number system with no carry propagation. Redundant carry free number representation in the form of radix-2 signed digit system was chosen. Therefore, the solution, which Donachy has implemented to meet the design constraints, is based on the following choices:

(i) Bit serial arithmetic

(ii) Signed Digit Number Representation (SDNR) rather than 2's complement

(iii) Most Significant Bit First processing

Because, in Donachy's model, image data may have to be occasionally processed on the host processor, the basic storage format for image data is, however, 2's complement. Therefore, processing elements first convert their incoming image data to SDNR. This also reduces the chip area required for the line buffers (in which data is held in 2's complement). A final unit to convert a SDNR result into 2's complement will be needed before any results can be returned to the host system. With these considerations, a more detailed design of a general Processing Element (in terms of a local and a global operation) is given in Figure 2.5.

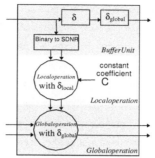

Figure 2.5 Architecture of a standard Processing Element

The constant coefficient bits are hardwired in the logic. The ability to dynamically reconfigure gates on the XC6200 means that the image template can be rapidly reconfigured an unlimited number of times.

The pixel wordlength was fixed and set to 16 digits regardless of the actual neighbourhood operation to be carried out. The basic building blocks were designed to fit each other conveniently with as little wastage area as possible (the so called *design to fit* approach). This opens the way for the possibility to generate the corresponding architectures dynamically from a very high level software tools with first time place and route.

2.3.2.3 Overview of the software interface

Donachy proposed an overall design for a complete software interface, which provides the high level programming model that hides all details of configurations from the user (see Figure 2.6).

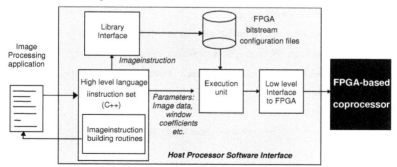

Figure 2.6 Overview of the software interface proposed by Donachy

To implement an IP operation on the FPGA, the software interface provides the user with a set of building routines to construct *imageinstruction* objects. A library of configuration files (bitstream) is provided for 3x3 neighbourhood operations in different template modes. These configuration files are available to the software interface at run-time. The library interface examines the high level *imageinstruction* object and selects the appropriate configuration file. The content of this configuration file in addition to a number of user supplied parameters (e.g. image data, reconfiguration information etc.), is used by the execution unit to perform the required IP operation on FPGA.

However, even with this software interface, Donachy's work had a number of limitations:

- The architectures were all generated by hand, and were static. This restricted the application programmer to a fixed set of operations and window configurations.
- Donachy's environment did not reach the full implementation stage. Bitstream configurations were produced, but a working hardware-based system was not produced.

2.3.3 Alotaibi's HIDE system

Given the fixed nature of Donachy's FPGA library, Alotaibi [Alo99] addressed the problem of extending the library dynamically without having to be an expert in FPGAs. In his work, he aimed to bridge the gap between the IP oriented application high level and the low level FPGA hardware configurations. He proposed a high level Hardware Description environment called HIDE (Hardware Intelligent Description Environment), which comprised:

- A high level hardware notation (called HIDE) particularly suited to describing architectures for IP neighbourhood operations.
- A Prolog-based translator which automatically and dynamically generates hardware architectures (in EDIF) from a HIDE description. This translator was specific to Xilinx XC6200.

The following will introduce the basics of HIDE notation.

2.3.3.1 Essentials of the HIDE Notation

Rather than invent a brand new notation, Prolog [CM94][Cro88] has been used as the base notation for describing and composing basic building blocks in order to build FPGA chip configurations. Prolog, after all, was designed for expressing logic, and it supports the representation of knowledge (e.g. of common sense routing heuristic) using rules. It also provides the concept of unbound variables for representing parameters of uncommitted details.

The HIDE notation has a simple and small set of constructors for putting sub-blocks together in order to build an FPGA chip configuration.

HIDE configuration description

The main component of a HIDE configuration description is a *block*. A *block* is either:
-   *A basic block*: an individual component or
-   *A compound block*: a hierarchical composition of sub-components.

A block also has a set of input/output *ports*. A complete FPGA chip configuration is a block with its input/output ports connected to chip pins. An initial suite (a library) of *basic blocks* is provided within the HIDE system. This library normally covers various primitive components, which are required to build up full operations (e.g. bit serial adders, multiplier sections, etc.). The basic building blocks can be generated by using popular synthesis tools (e.g. ViewLogic™) and stored later in the library in a format such as EDIF (netlist).

A *basic block* is a rectangular, non-overlapping block, which completely contains a predefined circuit. At the outer edges of this block, there are input and output *ports*. Basic block properties are expressed as a data object as follows:

> *block_properties(name, width, height, signals_list , ports_list)*

where:

name: a unique name for the basic block.

width and *height*: *width* is the number of cells occupied on the chip by the basic block on the **X** (horizontal) axis, while *height* is the number of cells on the **Y** (vertical) axis. Both width and height are computed from the basic block origin (0,0) which is assumed to be the bottom left hand corner of the basic block.

signals_list: a list of clock and clear signals used in the block. In an asynchronous basic block, the *signals_list* attribute is represented by an empty list [].

ports_list: a list of input/output ports to/from the block located at the perimeter cells of the block.

The decision to limit blocks to be rectangular and non-overlapping was taken to simplify subsequent block assembly. The above attributes are illustrated in Figure 2.7.

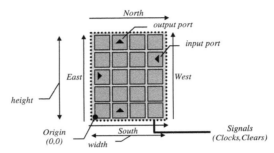

Figure 2.7 HIDE Basic block properties

A **block port** has a *name, position*, and *direction*. The *name* is a locally unique identifier for the port. The port *direction* is either **in** or **out**. The *position* is a point on the outer edge of the block (using X-Y cell co-ordinates relative to the block origin). All properties for a port are grouped in one object and expressed as follows:

port(name, direction, X, Y)

The set of ports is grouped into four sub-lists. These four sub-lists represent the ports along each of the four block sides: *north, south, east* and *west* (see Figure 2.7):

ports_list([North_sub-list, South_sub-list, East_sub-list, West_sub-list])

If there are no ports at any side, the sub-list is represented by an empty list []. Ports within a list are held in order of increasing co-ordinate as shown in Figure 2.7.

In the following, we will show how these basic blocks can be composed into more complex blocks in order to build up **compound blocks**.

Compound Blocks

A *compound block* is a set of sub-blocks, which are composed together. The composed compound block is also a rectangular, non-overlapping block with many of the same types of attribute as a basic block.

A compound block can be built from sub-blocks by the following *constructors*:

- **vertical([B₁, B₂, ...Bₙ])** used to compose the supplied sub-blocks together vertically.

- **horizontal([B₁, B₂, ...Bₙ])** used to compose the supplied sub-blocks together horizontally.

- **v_seq(N,B)** used to replicate the supplied block 'B', N times vertically.

- **h_seq(N,B)** used to replicate the supplied block 'B', N times horizontally.

- **offset(B, X, Y)** used to offset the supplied block 'B' by 'X' positions horizontally and 'Y' positions vertically.

These constructors are illustrated in Figure 2.8. Note that the composed sub-blocks are aligned on the left hand side (in the case of vertical composition) or along the bottom (in the case of horizontal composition).

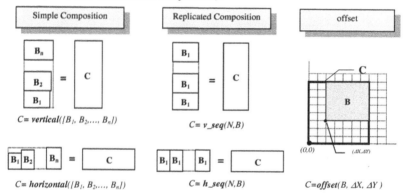

Figure 2.8 HIDE's five basic constructors

The resulting compound block's width and height are computed according to the following formulas:

- For horizontal constructors (*horizontal* and *h_seq*):

$$width\_of(C) = \sum_{i=1}^{n} width\_of(B_i)$$

$$height\_of(C) = \max_{i=1}^{n}(height\_of(B_i))$$

- For vertical constructors (*vertical* and *v_seq*):

$$width\_of(C) = \max_{i=1}^{n}(width\_of(B_i))$$

$$height\_of(C) = \sum_{i=1}^{n} height\_of(B_i)$$

Sub-Blocks interconnection

During sub-block composition, the ports on the corresponding sides of adjacent sub-blocks are connected together. These corresponding sides are: *north_of(B$_1$)* and *south_of(B$_2$)* in case of vertical composition, and *east_of(B$_1$)* and *west_of(B$_2$)* in case of horizontal composition. If the ports (input-output or output-input ports) along two adjacent sides can be connected '*exactly*', then these connections will be made immediately by HIDE (see Figure 2.9a). Two ports can be connected *exactly*, if their directions are complementary (i.e. input-output or output-input) and their X-position attributes (in case of vertical composition) or Y-position attributes (in case of horizontal composition) are equal. If the ports cannot be matched exactly, HIDE system will automatically generate a **network block** as shown in Figure 2.9b. Alternatively, the user can connect the ports explicitly by giving a network block (**nb**), which specifies all logical port connections:

$$\text{nb}([\ (i, j), \ ... \ ]) \qquad\qquad i > 0, \ j > 0$$

where:

i : is a port sequence number on the first side.

j: is a port sequence number on the second side.

This is illustrated in Figure 2.9c. Note that the network block is a special type of block, which is used exclusively for routing. An important feature of this block is that its ports are *floating*. In other words, the position of the I/O ports is not finalised until it is included in an actual circuit.

Note that, when the enclosed rectangle for a compound block leaves internal gaps, any unconnected 'exposed' internal ports are extended to the perimeter of the resulting compound block. As a result, position attributes (X, Y co-ordinates) of the ports, are updated (see Figure 2.9d).

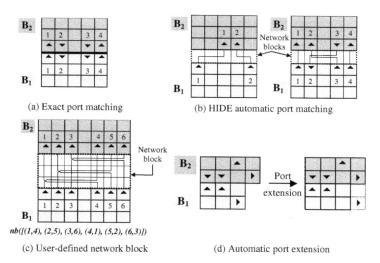

(a) Exact port matching   (b) HIDE automatic port matching

nb([(1,4), (2,5), (3,6), (4,1), (5,2), (6,3)])

(c) User-defined network block   (d) Automatic port extension

Figure 2.9 Examples of port connectivity in HIDE

To assist in automatic port matching, HIDE made the positioning and direction of ports more flexible by introducing two high-level types of ports: ***hinged ports*** and ***floating ports***.

Hinged Ports

Sometimes, when joining a sequence of instances of blocks, ports at the corner of a block may have to connect in different directions depending on whether the block is in the middle or at the end of the sequence. In other words, some corner ports can be considered as part of two different sides (e.g. either north or east). These corner ports can be stated as *hinged ports*. These hinged ports are defined to have one of two possible directions, by defining a new 'pseudo' direction for corner ports (e.g. North-East: NE). This solution is better than creating different versions of the component for each specific direction. Figure 2.10 illustrates this problem with its proposed solution for *north-east* case.

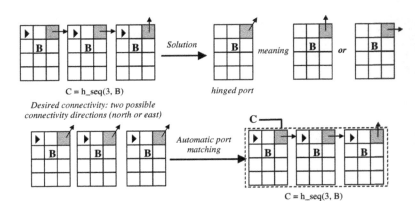

Figure 2.10 Hinged ports problem illustration (north east case)

In general, 4 new pseudo-directions have been added: NE (either *north* or *east*), NW (either *north* or *west*), SE (either *south* or *east*) and SW (either *south* or *west*) as shown in Figure 2.11.

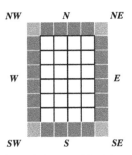

Figure 2.11 Block layout with eight port groups

These new groups are now added to the natural groups (N, S, E and W) in the port list which will have the following form:

ports_list([N, S, E, W, NE, NW, SE, SW])

When sub-blocks are to be connected, the ambiguity for corner ports directions has to be resolved. HIDE's resolving algorithm is based on the following reasoning:

■ For *horizontal* composition of *N* blocks with hinged ports :

  • Hinged ports between blocks in a sequence must be horizontal.

  • Hinged ports at the *ends* of a block sequence must be vertical since otherwise they could all have been defined using East and West.

■ For *vertical* composition of *N* blocks with hinged ports :

- Hinged ports *between* blocks in a sequence must be vertical.
- Hinged ports at the *ends* of a block sequence must be horizontal since otherwise they could all have been defined using North and South.

Figure 2.12 below shows the application of the algorithm for these two cases.

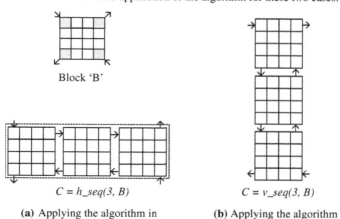

Block 'B'

$C = h\_seq(3, B)$ $C = v\_seq(3, B)$

(a) Applying the algorithm in   **(b)** Applying the algorithm
horizontal composition.   in vertical composition.

Figure 2.12 Hinged ports processing.

When the above algorithm does not give what is desired, HIDE offers the possibility of overriding the automatic resolution, by altering the solution explicitly. This is carried out by a port alteration constructor as follows:

alter_ports(Old-direction, New-direction, Selected_ports, Block)

where **Selected_ports** is a list of the ports to be altered.

Figure 2.13 illustrates an example of altering the direction of a port (number 1) of a block B, from *east* to *north*.

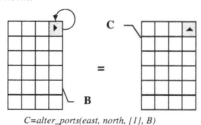

C=alter_ports(east, north, [1], B)

Figure 2.13 A port alteration from east to north.

Floating Ports

The concept of floating ports has been already introduced in the network block description. This is an instance in which the position of a block's ports cannot be determined in advance.

When seeking to make descriptions more flexible, it is common to use floating ports in conjunction with parameterised block descriptions (in which even the shape of a block may depend on user-supplied parameters). The final properties of these *dynamic* blocks can only be finalised when they are included in an actual circuit.

A common example of the use of both these features is the line buffer used to hold an image column (see section 2.3.2). A line buffer is a memory block with three parameters: overall size (in bits of memory), height and width. It is necessary to specify only the overall size and one of the two dimensions (height or width). The other dimension (width or height) is determined automatically by HIDE. Because the input and output positions of a line buffer depend on the adjacent blocks, the input and output ports of a line buffer are *floating* ports and are positioned automatically to align exactly to the corresponding ports of the adjacent blocks. The HIDE constructor for a line buffer has the following format (see Figure 2.14):

lb(Type, Size, Width, Height)

where:

Type: the line buffers position relative to the adjacent blocks- either *top*, *bottom*, *right*, or *left*.

Size: Line buffer size in bits.

Width, Height : width and height of the rectangular area enclosing the line buffer. One of *Width* or *Height* can be unbound, but not both.

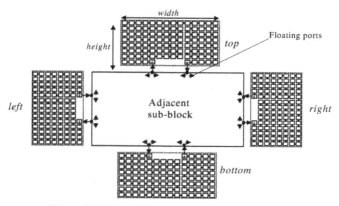

Figure 2.14 Four different positions of line buffers.

Note that the basic memory element is a 1-bit register. This is due to the structure of the XC6200 FPGAs, in which each logical cell contains one flip-flop.

2.3.3.2 Overall structure of the HIDE System

An outline of the overall structure of the HIDE system is given in Figure 2.15. At the top level, the IP *application developer* describes his/her image processing architecture in the HIDE notation. The latter offers a simple way of combining basic building blocks to describe IP application architectures. The basic building blocks are designed by the *architecture builder* and stored in EDIF [Cra84] format in a *Basic Component Library* (BCL). Different tools can be used for this process such as schematic design entry and VHDL, or even using HIDE itself. A short description of these blocks' properties should be provided (see section 2.3.3.1) and stored in an *Object Description Library* (ODL). The latter also holds higher level blocks, whose descriptions are stored in the HIDE notation, and for which an EDIF description will be generated later.

The HIDE engine takes the high level HIDE notation and produces two output files: an *EDIF* file and a *report* file. The EDIF file contains the actual configuration for the described design whereas the report file contains some characteristics such as size, and location of tailorable bits for partial reconfigurability. The generated EDIF contains full placement and routing[1] information of the circuit. It is then loaded into the Xilinx XACT6000™ tool to generate a corresponding bitstream file for the XC6200. Unfortunately, HIDE was not brought through the stage where the system runs on a commercially available FPGA board.

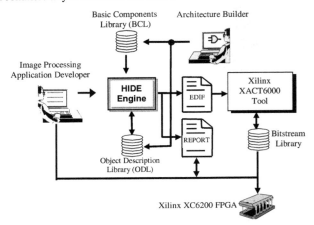

Figure 2.15 Overall HIDE system

2.3.3.3 Qualitative evaluation

In [Alo99], Alotaibi gave a qualitative comparison of HIDE with other relevant notations. The main criteria used in this comparison are (see table 2.2):

- Convenience criteria:
  - *Automatic port matching*: Is the environment able to automatically match corresponding ports, or has the user to define the interconnection explicitly even for the ports that can be connected exactly?
  - *Scaleability*: Is the circuit description scaleable?
  - *Automatic placement*: How little information needs to be supplied by the user to perform placement?
  - *Automatic routing*: Does the environment have its own routing capability? (If not, the routing process would rely on the vendor's routing tools). This

---

[1] HIDE exploits local routing resources only. In real world applications, this can be a serious limitation.

criterion is important for size predictability and for the speed of the process of generating a configuration with full information.

- Expressive power criteria:
  - *Gate level*: Is it possible to describe a circuit right down to the gate level?
  - *Overlapping*: Can non-rectangular blocks overlap to save space?
- Environment criteria:
  - *Portability*: How easily can designs be ported to a different FPGA? If the environment is chip-specific, this would require the whole environment to be re-implemented.
  - *Coding size*: As a benchmark, how many lines of hardware description code are needed to describe a generic PxQ convolver? (The number of lines does not include the description of basic library blocks).
  - *Time to generate EDIF*: How long does the environment take to generate an EDIF description from a higher level convolution description?
  - *Time to load EDIF into the placement and routing tool (XACT tool)*: How long does it take to load the generated EDIF for convolution into the XACT tool?

(Note: High score is the best, and '-' is zero score)

Comparison Criteria	Schematic	VHDL	Lola	Pebble	HIDE
Automatic Port Matching	-	-	-	☆	☆☆☆☆
Scaleability	-	☆☆☆	☆☆☆	☆☆☆	☆☆☆☆
Automatic Placement	☆	☆☆	☆☆	☆☆	☆☆☆☆
Automatic Routing	-	-	☆☆☆☆☆	-	☆☆
Gate Level	☆☆☆☆☆	☆☆☆☆☆	☆☆☆☆☆	☆☆☆☆☆	☆
Overlapping	☆☆☆☆☆	☆☆☆☆☆	☆☆☆☆☆	☆☆☆☆☆	-

Portability	☆☆☆☆	☆☆☆☆☆	☆	☆☆☆	☆☆
Coding Size (in lines)	N/A	☆ (300)	☆☆ (180)	☆☆☆ (90)	☆☆☆☆☆ (7)
Time to generate EDIF	☆☆☆☆	☆☆☆ (1.76 sec)	N/A	☆☆ (2.30 sec)	☆☆☆☆☆ (0.85 sec)
Time to Load EDIF into the XACT tool	☆☆☆ (24.5 sec)	☆☆☆ (24.5 sec)	☆☆☆☆☆ (5 sec)	☆☆☆ (24.5 sec)	☆☆☆ (8.5 sec)

Table 2.2 Comparison between HIDE and other HDL environments.

Overall, Alotaibi concluded that HIDE comes out well from this comparison (even doing a crude score summation). This is partly because the criteria for comparison reflect the objectives of the research presented in this book. He noted that HIDE gains in the convenience criteria and the conciseness criterion whereas it loses in low level control over the layout (e.g. *Overlapping* and *Gate level*) and portability.

2.4 Objectives of this project

The previous work conducted in the School of Computer Science at QUB has demonstrated the following strengths:

- The HIDE system has proved very efficient in generating FPGA architectures from generic and parameterised descriptions [Alo99]. Features like the automatic port matching, floating ports and dynamic line buffers allow for very concise descriptions alleviating the FPGA user from the low level hardware details.
- The automatic generation of low level EDIF descriptions directly from a HIDE notation speeds up the hardware design cycle by bypassing the lengthy and costly general purpose HDL tools (e.g. VHDL synthesisers).
- The use of Prolog as a basis of a hardware description notation has proved beneficial. The concept of *unbound variables* was very useful in describing blocks with uncommitted factors such as size and port positions (floating ports). *Rules* were useful for capturing heuristics for first time place and route, and for expressing flexible block condition.

However, both Donachy's and Alotaibi's work still suffer from some limitations. Specifically, the limitations that neither Donachy nor Alotaibi addressed are:

- All the FPGA architectures were based on a fixed data representation: radix-2 digit, SDNR system, and 16 bits per pixel. These decisions were made to cope with all the IP operations provided. This *"one solution fits all"* approach usually comes at a considerable hardware price. For instance, a 16 bit per pixel wordlength might be very inefficient when implementing some less demanding IP operations.

- Though HIDE allows the generation of FPGA architectures automatically and dynamically from a high level, it is still a hardware description notation. HIDE has not bridged the gap between the image processing application level and the FPGA hardware. The ultimate goal is to program in a Tulip-like environment.

- The HIDE system implementation was dedicated to XC6200 FPGAs. As mentioned in chapter 1, Xilinx has discontinued its support to this FPGA family. Moving to another target FPGA requires the re-implementation of the HIDE system.

- Alotaibi's library of basic components was entirely based on Donachy's ones. The range of the IP operations generated from HIDE was only sufficient to match Donachy's architecture (e.g. no median filter implementation).

- Alotaibi's objectives did not include producing a practical working system running on a commercial FPGA based board. Practical aspects which he did not address are:
    - Multiple clock domain management.
    - I/O connections to the package pins.
    - Possible interface to an off-chip RAM for line or frame buffering.

- Following on the previous remark, Alotaibi did not address the issue of optimising the generated architectures' speed. His routing strategy was exclusively based on local routing resources. This becomes a major limitation when architectures are not highly regular such as *compound* operators.

The desire to overcome these limitations is the underlying motivation for the research presented in this book. The latter aims to support Image Processing application developers with a software environment which hides the FPGA hardware details and allows them to exploit the performance of a direct hardware solution while programming at an application oriented environment. More specifically, the following objectives were set for the research presented in this book:

- The new environment should provide an *IP application oriented* environment (Tulip-like) for FPGA based Image Processing. This environment would ideally *hide the FPGA hardware details completely* from the user's point of view. The user would, ideally, describe the IP operation to be executed on FPGA from a very high level (e.g. Local and Global operators and window template, for simple neighbourhood operations) or even interact with a GUI.

- The IP application oriented environment should be able to generate a *customised* and *efficient* FPGA configuration for each high level description. Our system's task should not consist in merely assembling blocks together like in HIDE or most of the other HDLs. It should act as *an optimising silicon compiler*, which looks at the high level code and from this optimises the resulting FPGA configuration.

- Alternative implementation techniques should be considered when necessary. For instance, the system should not be tied to a unique number system (e.g. SDNR) or arithmetic type (e.g. bit-serial).

- The IP operations library should be extended to new operations other than those provided by Donachy (e.g. median filtering).

- The system will target Xilinx 4000 series, which was the most successful product family in the FPGA market at the time in which the research presented in this book was conducted. A prototype working system running on a commercially available FPGA board should be produced.

Chapter | 3 |

Bit Serial implementation of the FPGA based Image Processing Coprocessor

Chapter 3

Bit Serial implementation of the FPGA based Image Processing Coprocessor

In this chapter, we present one possible way of implementing the Image Processing Coprocessor (IPC) instruction set outlined in section 2.3.2.

We first review the design objectives for an FPGA based implementation of the IPC. From these, certain design decisions follow (e.g. Bit serial arithmetic). The chapter then presents the architecture designs of the standard set of Image Algebra (IA) neighbourhood operations. Finally, conclusions will be drawn.

3.1 Hardware implementation objectives

Before implementing the FPGA-based IPC, we have set the following objectives for our implementation:

Scaleability: In order to increase reuse of architecture descriptions, the architectures should be scaleable in terms of the following parameters:
- Window size
- Coefficients wordlength
- Processing wordlength
- Image size

Reuse of High Level design: The IPC's instruction set should contain a small number of powerful, general instructions (e.g. Image Algebra neighbourhood operations) rather than a large set of specialised instructions (e.g. one for Laplace, one for Erode, one for Dilate etc.).

High Level design generation and optimisation: Although we wish to provide a high level programmer's instruction set, we cannot afford to sacrifice the efficiency of the hardware implementation. Our system should be able to generate an *optimal* and *custom* FPGA architecture, automatically, for each particular IP operation (e.g. the system should take into account the window coefficient values). This is a major difference between our approach and Donachy's [Don96] approach. In the latter, FPGA architectures were fixed and designed to cope with a variety of IP operations (e.g. fixed processing wordlength).

First Time Right Place and Route: Ultimately, it would be very desirable to be able to generate bitstream directly from a high level architecture description. However, at present, details of Xilinx 4000 bitstream are not publicly available, so this goal is not currently achievable. Nevertheless, to retain this option in future, our architecture designs should guarantee first time right place and route, with no user intervention (space permitting).

3.2 Hardware implementation of template neighbourhood operations

Neighbourhood operations involve using the pixels in a neighbourhood of the source image to calculate the new result pixel. They form the basis of most low level image processing algorithms [Pra91][Teu93]. Most common neighbourhood operations can be split in two stages: a *local* operator applied between each image pixel in the neighbourhood and the corresponding window coefficient, and a subsequent *global* operator applied to the set of local operation results to generate a result image pixel.

Consider the set of IA operations presented in Table 2.1 (i.e. Convolution, Multiplicative Maximum/Minimum, Additive Maximum/Minimum). Each of these operations can be performed in the four template modes: *template*, *tile*, *splice* and *isplice* (see section 2.3.1). We will first start by presenting the design of a convolution operation in template mode. The design of other neighbourhood operators (e.g. Multiplicative Maximum/Minimum and Additive Maximum/Minimum) using other window template modes (*tile, splice* and *isplice*) will be based on this convolution template operation.

3.2.1 Architecture of a general 2D convolution

Consider a convolution operation with the generic PxQ window template shown in Figure 3.1.

Figure 3.1 A generic PxQ window template

Generalising the convolver architecture given in chapter 2 (see section 2.3.2.2) for a PxQ template, and assuming a vertical scan of the input image, Figure 3.2 shows the corresponding hardware architecture.

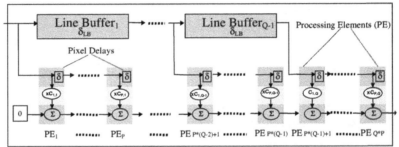

Figure 3.2 Architecture of a general 2-D, PxQ convolution operation

Note that each PE is characterised by a latency δ_{PE}, which is in fact the latency of the global operator ('Σ' in a convolution case). In order to synchronise the supply of data, this delay should be compensated both in the pixel and line buffers. In other words, δ_{PE} delays should be added to the pixel delay δ and $P*\delta_{PE}$ delays must be added to each line delay. The additional line delay is dependent on the window size. It is more appropriate to add this delay to the processing elements as shown in Figure 3.3 [Don96].

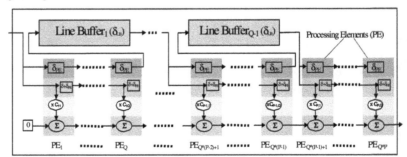

Figure 3.3 Revised architecture of a generic 2-D, PxQ convolution operation

Note that the only difference between convolution and other neighbourhood operations is the local and global operators.

3.2.2 Architecture of a Processing Element

Before deriving the architecture of a Processing Element, we first have to decide which type of arithmetic to be used- either bit parallel or bit serial processing.

While bit parallel designs process all of data bits simultaneously, bit serial ones process input data one bit at a time. Bit serial architectures, usually, require less hardware resources than their equivalent bit parallel ones. In addition, the resulting layout in a serial implementation is fairly regular due to the reduced number of interconnection needed between PEs (less routing stress). This regularity feature would allow us to generate FPGA architectures from a high level specification, with first time right place and route. Moreover, a serial architecture is not tied to a particular processing wordlength. It is relatively straightforward to move from one wordlength to another with very little extra hardware (if any). For these reasons, our first choice was to implement the IPC hardware architectures using serial arithmetic.

Given a decision to use bit serial processing, the same reasoning process as followed by Donachy [Don96] (see section 2.3.2.2) results in the following overall design decisions:

- Bit serial arithmetic
- Most Significant Digit First processing
- Signed Digit Number Representation (SDNR)

Note that there will be various situations where the circumstances will enable different design choices (especially the number representation) to be made for greater efficiency. These circumstances will be discussed in the next chapter.

3.2.3 Online arithmetic

Online arithmetic was first introduced in 1977 by Ercegovac and Trevidi [ET77][ERC84]. During online computations, the operands and the results flow through the arithmetic units serially, digit by digit, starting from the most significant digit. After an initialisation phase in which the online unit receives δ digits, each new input digit will then produce a new output digit. This δ is known as the *online delay*.

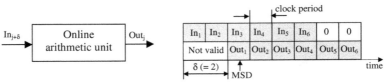

Figure 3.4 An online arithmetic unit with an online delay δ

This ability to perform successive operations in digit pipelined fashion makes it possible to compute large expressions in an efficient manner. In such a case, the global online delay will be the sum of the individual online delays as shown in Figure 3.5.

Figure 3.5 An online pipeline

Although online arithmetic would have been possible using carry-save representation of numbers, the number systems used in the literature are Avizienis' Signed Digit Number systems [Mul91].

3.2.4 Signed Digit Number Representation

The Signed Digit Number Representation (SDNR) was first introduced by Avizienis [Avi61]. In this system, numbers are represented in radix r using a digit set $\{-a, -a+1, ..., 0, ..., a+1, a\}$ $(a \leq r -1)$, instead of the classical digit set $\{0, 1, ..., r-1\}$. A signed digit number is defined by a digit chain $d_{-n}d_{-n+1} ...d_{-1}d_0d_1 ... d_md_{m-1}$ and represents the number:

$$\sum_{i=-n}^{m} d_i r^{-i} .$$

At least r different digits are needed to represent a number in radix r. Since $-a \leq d_i \leq a$, the inequality $2a+1 \geq r$ must be satisfied. Moreover, if $2a+1 > r$, then some numbers have several representations and the system is said to be *redundant*. For instance, in radix 2, with $a=1$, the number 7 can be represented as 0111, 1$\bar{1}$11, 100$\bar{1}$ etc. where $\bar{i}$ denotes the digit $-i$. This added redundancy can be very beneficial. Indeed Avizienis [Avi61] has proved that if $2a \geq r+1$, then it is possible to perform a *parallel addition without carry propagation*.

The advantage of carry free addition with Signed Digit Number Representation does not come without cost. Indeed, the introduction of redundancy requires more digit values than in non-redundant systems, which means that more signals will be used to implement a single digit. This increases the bandwidth of interconnects between arithmetic units and ultimately the physical chip area [PK94][WMcC92]. For this reason, we have decided to use the smallest radix, i.e. a radix 2 system. This is also well suited to the 4-input LUT structure of the XC4000 CLB.

It is worth noticing that the two conditions $2a \geq r+1$ and $a+1 \leq r$ cannot be simultaneously satisfied unless $r \geq 3$. This means that Avizienis's carry free parallel addition algorithm is not applicable in radix 2 ($r=2$). Fortunately, it is still possible to perform a carry free parallel addition in radix 2 with $a=1$ using a slightly different approach. In this approach, a digit d, $d \in \{\bar{1}, 0, 1\}$ will be represented by two bits d^+ and d^- such that $d = d^+ - d^-$. This representation is called *Borrow Save (BS)* by analogy to *Carry Save (CS)* representation [Mul91].

3.2.5 Revised architecture of a Processing Element

With the above decisions, a revised PE architecture is given as follows:

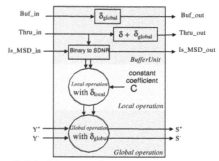

Figure 3.6 Architecture of a standard Processing Element.

Note that a Radix-2 SDNR number needs twice as much storage area as its 2's complement equivalent. Hence, the basic storage format for on-chip image data is in 2's complement format rather than in SDNR. This, in particular, reduces the chip area required for the line buffers. Therefore, processing elements first convert their incoming image data (see 'Thru_in' in Figure 3.6) to SDNR. A final unit to convert a SDNR result into 2's complement will be needed before any result can be returned to the host system.

Note that a special case of PE arises when a window position is not used ('~'). In such cases, the PE reduces to a simple pixel delay unit as shown in Figure 3.7.

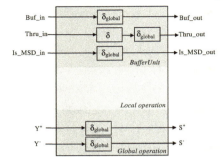

Figure 3.7 Architecture of an unused Processing Element

In the following section, we will present the hardware architecture of all the necessary basic building blocks for simple IA operations on the XC4000.

3.3 Design of the basic building blocks

This section will present the design of the basic hardware components necessary for the implementation of all simple IA operations:

- Line buffers
- Buffer unit
- 2's complement to SDNR converter
- Online adder (global operation)
- Online multiplier (local operation)
- Addition (local operation)
- Maximum and Minimum selectors (global operations)
- SDNR to 2's complement converter

Note that these components have been carefully designed in order to fit together with as little wastage area as possible. Considerable time has been spent to floorplan those components on the FPGA for that purpose.

All the basic components presented in this chapter have been designed in schematic using the Xilinx Foundation™ software package [Fnd98]. This is an integrated environment which has been used throughout this project, and combines a variety of tools such as Schematic Editor, HDL Editor, State Diagram Editor, Logic Simulator, Timing Analyser and FPGA floorplanner.

3.3.1   Line Buffer

Shift registers are implemented efficiently on XC4000 using on-chip distributed synchronous RAMs and a small address counter [XAP52]. As mentioned in chapter 1 (see section 1.3.2), the CLB's 4-input LUTs can be configured as 16x1 or 32x1 synchronous RAMs. The RAM address should be generated by a separate counter. Since any repetitive pattern is acceptable, there is no need for a conventional binary counter. Instead, a more compact and scaleable counter design is used in the form of LFSR counters. A 32x1 shift register design requires two CLBs for the ÷16 LFSR address counter, in addition to one CLB for the 32 bit RAM as shown in Figure 3.8. Longer shift registers can be implemented using the same concept by dividing the required length into equal parts of up to 16 bits each and use a common LFSR counter to address all the 16x1 RAMs. An N-bit long line delay uses N/32 CLBs for RAM storage plus two extra CLBs for the LFSR counter. For instance, a 256 16-bit pixel line buffer consumes 130 CLBs. In order to reduce the propagation delay of the address bus, multiple LFSR counters can be used to address small sets of RAMs.

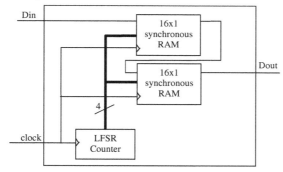

Figure 3.8 A 32-bit shift register design on XC4000

3.3.2   2's complement to SDNR converter

Note that 2's complement system is a subset of the SDNR system. In order to convert a 2's complement number to SDNR, the most significant bit is inverted. For example, the 2's complement representation 1111, is converted to the SDNR $\bar{1}$111. Similarly, 2's complement 0111 remains 0111 in SDNR. Therefore, there is a need for an extra control signal 'Is_MSD', which is set to one during the Most Significant Digit (MSD) clock cycle of the 2's complement input. The circuit diagram of the 2's complement to SDNR unit is thus given in Figure 3.9. The unit operates with a latency of 1 cycle.

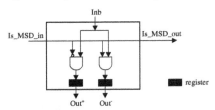

Figure 3.9 Binary to SDNR converter

3.3.3   Buffer unit

As described earlier, the buffer unit synchronises the supply of pixels within image columns. It also compensates for the PE's online delay.

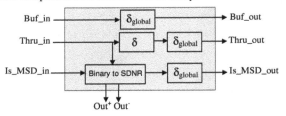

Figure 3.10 Buffer unit

The pixel delay δ depends on the pixel processing wordlength. This is implemented using the on-chip distributed synchronous RAM and an LFSR counter as explained in section 3.3.1. Moving from one wordlength to another simply implies supplying the proper LFSR counter. All the delays have been designed using on-chip distributed synchronous RAM and LFSR counters making the area of this unit independent of the pixel delay δ, and the global delay δ_{global}. The buffer unit consumes 8 CLBs.

3.3.4   An online adder unit (accumulate global operation)

If X and Y are to be added using online arithmetic, i.e. $X = \{0.x_{1...}\ x_{n-1}x_n\}$ and $Y = \{0.y_{1...}\ y_{n-1}y_n\}$ are presented to the online adder unit serially and Most Significant Digit First (MSDF), the following algorithm [Mul91] computes the corresponding sum $S = \{s_0.s_{1...}\ s_{n-1}s_n\}$:

- *Initial state*

$$c_0^- = s_{-1}^+ = y_0^- = 0;$$

$$x_{n+2}^+ = x_{n+2}^- = y_{n+2}^+ = y_{n+2}^- = 0;$$

$$x_{n+1}^+ = x_{n+1}^- = y_{n+1}^+ = y_{n+1}^- = 0;$$

- For $i \in \{1, 2, \ldots, n+2\}$ compute:

  - c_{i-1}^+ and c_i^- such that: $x_i^+ + y_i^+ - x_i^- = 2c_{i-1}^+ - c_i^-$

  - s_{i-1}^+ and s_{i-2}^- such that: $y_{i-1}^- + c_{i-1}^- - c_{i-1}^+ = 2s_{i-2}^- - s_{i-1}^+$

The two steps of the addition stated above need the same basic computation: the evaluation of two bits t and u from three bits x, y and z, such that $x+y-z=2t-u$. The values of t and u are given by the following boolean functions:

$$\begin{cases} u = x \oplus y \oplus z \\ t = xy + x\overline{z} + y\overline{z} \end{cases}$$

The cell implementing these equations is called PPM (Plus Plus Minus). It is very similar to a *full adder* cell as shown in Figure 3.11.

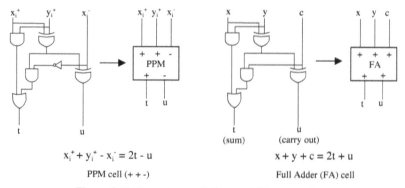

$$x_i^+ + y_i^+ - x_i^- = 2t - u$$

PPM cell (+ + -)

$$x + y + c = 2t + u$$

Full Adder (FA) cell

Figure 3.11 Elementary cells for an addition operation

By using 2 PPM cells and 3 latches, we obtain the online adder shown in Figure 3.12a. The online delay δ is equal to 2. Note that this adder unit needs two zero digits after each processed word before another word is to be input. This will ensure that the operands do not interfere with each other's results. Thus 'N+2' digits will be used for an 'N' digit addition with two extra leading zeros in each input operand.

An additional delay has been added to the adder unit in the FPGA implementation (see Figure 3.12b). This decreases the propagation delays and thus increases the maximum operating frequency. The new online delay is equal to 3. The online adder unit consumes 3 CLBs as laid out in Figure 3.12c.

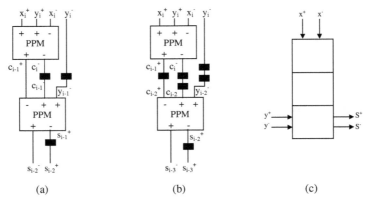

(a)   (b)   (c)

Figure 3.12 (a) Original online adder unit   (b) Modified online adder unit
(c) FPGA layout of an online adder unit

3.3.5 Online multiplier unit

The multiplier unit used is based on a hybrid serial-parallel multiplier outlined in [MRM94][EL90]. It multiplies an MSDF serial SDNR input with a 2's complement parallel coefficient $C = C_0 C_1 ..... C_{N-2} C_{N-1}$ as shown in Figure 3.13 for N=6. Compared to the original design, an additional 1-bit delay has been added to the outputs (out$^+$ and out$^-$) to decrease the propagation delay.

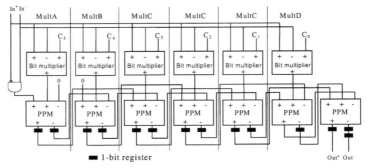

Figure 3.13 Multiplier unit with 6-bit coefficient $C=C_0C_1C_2C_3C_4C_5$

The bit multiplier block is defined as follows:

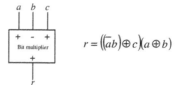

Figure 3.14 Bit multiplier unit

The multiplier has a modular, scaleable design, and comprises four distinct basic building components [Don96]: *MultA*, *MultB*, *MultC* and *MultD*. An N bit coefficient multiplier is constructed by:

$$MultA \rightarrow MultB \rightarrow (N\text{-}3)^* \ MultC \rightarrow MultD$$

The coefficient wordlength may be varied by varying the number of type C units. The minimum coefficient wordlength, however, is 3 and occurs when no type C unit is used.

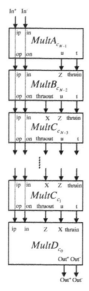

Figure 3.15 Design of an N bit hybrid serial-parallel multiplier

There are two possible implementations for each block type depending on the value of the corresponding coefficient bit (either 1 or 0). This results in 8 basic multiplier building blocks: *MultA₀*, *MultA₁*, *MultB₀*, *MultB₁*, *MultC₀*, *MultC₁*, *MultD₀* and *MultD₁*, where the index (0 or 1) indicates the value of the corresponding coefficient bit. Fixing the value of the multiplier coefficient bits results in many optimisations, and shrinks the required hardware resources. The XC4000 CLB's two 4 input lookup tables are sufficient to implement the combinatorial part of each block. Hence, *MultA*, *MultB* and *MultC* unit types occupy one CLB only, whereas *MultD* unit type occupies 2 CLBs. Therefore, an 'N' bit coefficient multiplier occupies 'N+1' CLBs. The corresponding online delay is 'N+2'.

The multiplication of an 'M' digit multiplicand by an 'N' digit multiplier gives an 'M+N' digit result. Hence, 'N' leading zeros should be added to the multiplicand, which is then coded on 'M+N' digits. Note that, for a convolution (Multiply-Accumulate), the input to the multiplier requires 'M+N' digits and a further two zero digits to ensure the proper operation of the addition (accumulation). Therefore, for a convolution, the 'M' digit input multiplicand will be coded on 'M+N+2' digits with 'N+2' leading zeros.

3.3.6   The 'Addition' local operation unit

This unit is used in Additive Maximum and Additive Minimum operations. It takes a single SDNR input value and adds it to the corresponding window coefficient. The coefficient is stored in 2's complement format to reduce the required storage hardware. It is stored into RAM addressed by a counter whose period is the pixel wordlength. The coefficient bits are preloaded into the appropriate RAM cells according to the counter output sequence. The input SDNR operand is added to the coefficient in bit serial MSDF using the online adder outlined in section 3.3.4.

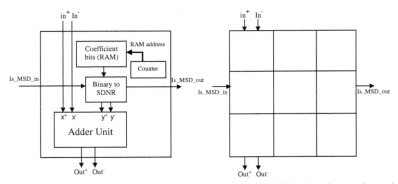

Figure 3.16 Block diagram and FPGA floorplan of an 'Addition' local operation unit

The adder unit occupies 3 CLBs. The whole addition unit occupies 9 CLBs laid out in a 3x3 array. The online delay of this unit is 3 clock cycles.

3.3.7   The Maximum global operation unit

The Maximum selector is used as a global operator in Additive Maximum and Multiplicative Maximum operations. Since $\text{Max}(P_0, P_1, ..., P_{n-2}, P_{n-1}, P_n) = \text{Max}(P_0, \text{Max}(P_1, ..., \text{Max}(P_{n-2}, \text{Max}(P_{n-1}, P_n))))$, the global Maximum operator can be implemented as a chain of two input maximum selectors in the same manner as in the accumulation unit.

The serial online Maximum unit selects the maximum of two SDNR serial inputs, MSDF. Figure 3.17 shows the transition diagram of the Finite State Machine (FSM) performing the maximum 'O' of two SDNRs 'X' and 'Y' [MRM94]. Note that the start state is indicated by a '*' superscript. The control signal 'Is_MSD' is used to reset the initial state of the FSM to state 'A' indicating the start of two new operands. The unit can be performed with an online delay of 0 but with a high clock period. Three pipeline stages have been introduced to speed up the FPGA implementation.

The physical implementation of this machine occupies an area of 13 CLBs laid out in 3 CLBs high by 5 wide. Note that this will allow this unit to fit conveniently with the previous local addition unit in an Additive Maximum neighbourhood operation.

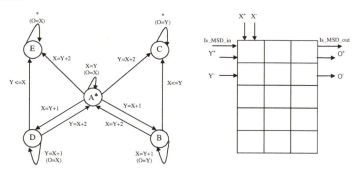

Figure 3.17 State diagram and FPGA floorplan of a Maximum unit

3.3.8   The Minimum global operation unit

The minimum of two SDNRs can be determined in a similar manner knowing that $\text{Min}(X,Y) = -\text{Max}(-X,-Y)$. Inverting an SDNR number $SD=SD^+-SD^-$ is simply done by inverting the order of its BS representation i.e. $-SD=SD^--SD^+$. This does not require any additional hardware. Thus, an FPGA implementation of a Minimum unit is the same as a Maximum unit one, with only input/output inversion. Similarly, the online delay is equal to 3.

3.3.9   SDNR to 2's complement converter

The conversion of a number from an SDNR representation to a 2's complement one is not as straightforward as its reverse. Suppose the task is to convert a redundant signed digit number P represented in a normalised fraction $p = \sum_{i=1}^{W} p_i 2^{-i}$ (with $p_i \in \{-1, 0, 1\}$), into its 2's complement representation equivalent:

$$q = -q_0 + \sum_{i=1}^{W} q_i 2^{-i} \text{ (with } q_i \in \{0,1\})$$

A simple online algorithm would be to form $q[k]$ such that:

$$q[k] = q[k-1] + p_k 2^{-k}$$

which results in q= $q[w]$.

In calculating $q[k]$ given $q[k-1]$, there are three possible cases depending on the value of the incoming SDNR digit p_k:

- $p_k = 0$: $q[k]$ is derived from it previous state by a left shift with its LSB set to 0 $(q[k] = q[k-1])$.

- $p_k = 1$: $q[k]$ is derived from it previous state by a simple left shift with its LSB set to $p_k=1$ $(q[k] = q[k-1] + 2^{-k})$.

- $p_k = -1$: in this case $q[k]$ is derived from it previous value by a simple left shift first, the result is then decremented by 1 $(q[k] = q[k-1] - 2^{-k})$.

In contrast with the two first cases, the third case requires carry propagation. On the XC4000, fast carry logic is used for the decrementation operation [XAP13]. A two bit slice decrementer can be implemented in one CLB. A 'W' digit SDNR word conversion consumes W/2+1 CLBs laid out as shown in Figure 3.18. The control signal 'Is_MSD' is used to reset $q[k]$ indicating the start of a new operand.

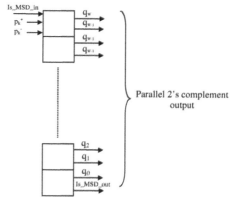

Figure 3.18 Cell layout of an W-bit word SDNR to 2's complement converter

The unit has an online delay of W cycles. If the output data is needed serially MSDF, a W-bit parallel to serial converter should be used. The latter consumes W/2 CLBs. The whole unit would then occupy W+1 CLBs. Another implementation of this unit based on an algorithm outlined in [EL87] would occupy 3*W/2+1 CLBs. This latter algorithm has also been used to target the Xilinx XC6000 in [Don96]. As a result, we see that an implementation based on the algorithm presented above saves W/2 CLBs for a W-digit SDNR word converter. Timing simulation shows that it is even slightly faster.

3.4   Processing wordlength

In image processing applications, 256 grey level images are typically used. This means that pixels are represented by an 8-bit word. However, internal word precision may require more than 8 bits. Increasing the internal wordlength requires more clock cycles to process one pixel word and thus reduces the throughput rate. One possible implementation way is to choose a fixed word precision which is large enough for all possible operand values. Note that in practice, a 16-bit precision is generally sufficient for most IP applications. However, this is not an optimal solution for less demanding IP applications. A more efficient solution is to use knowledge of pixel range and coefficient values to find the minimum necessary wordlength for each particular IP operation. We can do this because our architectures have been designed to be either independent of, or scaleable in terms of, the pixel wordlength. Indeed, in the core units, the wordlength information is necessary only in the LFSR counters in the local addition unit and in the pixel delay in the PE's buffer unit. Using a specific wordlength means then, supplying the corresponding LFSR counter to these units. The appropriate wordlength is the minimum number of digits necessary to represent the maximum positive or the minimum negative intermediate value.

3.5   Implementation of a generic PxQ convolution

In this section, we will present the architecture of a generic PxQ convolution operation applied in template mode. However, before describing the architecture of a complete convolver, there is one remaining problem to address, namely, redundancy reduction.

Redundancy reduction

Because of the redundancy property of Signed Digit arithmetic, an intermediate result could be represented by many more bits than are necessary. For example $\bar{1}111$ is actually equivalent to 0001. This is particularly dangerous in the case of a convolution operation where a chain of online adders is used to accumulate the partial pixel results. Indeed, this redundancy may grow continuously in an adder chain resulting in a longer wordlength. In order to reduce this redundancy (or *representation* overflow as opposed to a *real* overflow), a conversion to a limited representation is necessary. The redundancy reductor unit we have used is based on a unit outlined in [MRM94]. The truth table and block diagram of this unit is shown in Figure 3.19. The Online delay of this unit is 1 cycle. It consumes 2 CLBs.

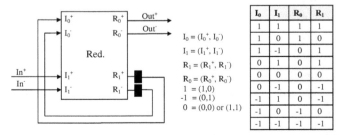

Figure 3.19 Block diagram and truth table of a redundancy reductor unit

$I_0 = (I_0^+, I_0^-)$
$I_1 = (I_1^+, I_1^-)$
$R_1 = (R_1^+, R_1^-)$
$R_0 = (R_0^+, R_0^-)$
$1 = (1,0)$
$-1 = (0,1)$
$0 = (0,0)$ or $(1,1)$

I_0	I_1	R_0	R_1
1	1	1	1
1	0	1	0
1	-1	0	1
0	1	0	1
0	0	0	0
0	-1	0	-1
-1	1	0	-1
-1	0	-1	0
-1	-1	-1	-1

We have used this redundancy reduction unit at the output of each adder in the convolver adder chain. This results in a new adder unit with a redundancy reduced output. This new unit occupies 4 CLBs laid out vertically as shown in Figure 3.20. It operates with an online delay of 4.

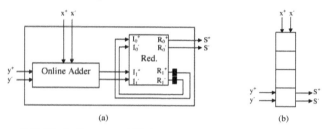

(a)   (b)

Figure 3.20 Block diagram and FPGA layout of an adder unit with redundancy reduction.

We can now proceed to the architecture of a generic PxQ convolver. Since both the multiplication and the new accumulation units are 1 CLB wide, the PE's buffer unit has been laid out vertically as shown in Figure 3.21.

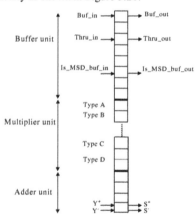

Figure 3.21 A convolution PE layout

The height of the multiplier unit depends on the maximum wordlength of the window coefficients 'N' and is equal to 'N+1'. The height of a whole PE unit is 'N+13' CLBs.

Using PxQ of these combined units, the overall convolution circuit layout is given by Figure 3.22 for a PxQ window size case.

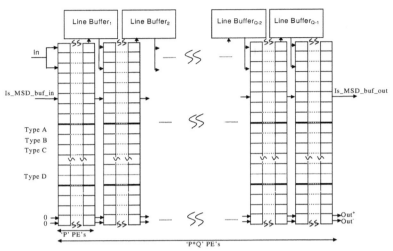

Figure 3.22 A convolver layout for a 3x3 window

The minimum necessary intermediate wordlength depends on the actual values of the window coefficients and the input pixel wordlength (W_{in}). In general, it is given by:

$$W_{proc.} = W_{conv.} = maximum(W_{in}+N+2, W_{max}+2) \quad \text{(Equation 3.w1)}$$

where:

'W_{in}' is the input pixel wordlength.

'N' is the window's maximum coefficient wordlength.

'W_{max}' is the maximum intermediate wordlength determined from the maximum/minimum possible intermediate pixel values (in 2's complement). This will depend on the actual window coefficients' values.

The first term ($W_{in}+N+2$) ensures the proper functioning of the array of multipliers, with two leading zeros (at least) at the output of each one. The second term ($W_{max}+2$) ensures that each input operand of any adder unit within the adder chain has at least two leading zeros. The latter is an essential condition for an online adder to function properly (see section 3.3.4 above).

For instance, let us take the case of a Laplace filter which is a 3x3 convolution filter given by the following window:

~	-1	~
-1	4	-1
~	-1	~

Suppose the input wordlength is 8 (i.e. 256 grey-level image). The maximum intermediate value is 4*(127+128). In general, it will be:

Σ max. grey level * (positive coefficients) + Σ min. grey level * (negative coefficients)

Similarly, the minimum intermediate value is -4*(127+128) and more generally:

Σ min. grey level * (positive coefficients) + Σ max. grey level * (negative coefficients)

For Laplace, 11 bits are sufficient to represent both extreme values. Hence the minimum processing wordlength is given by Equation 3.w1 with $W_{in} = 8$, $N = 4$ ($4 = 0100_2$) and $W_{max} = 11$:

$$W_{Laplace} = maximum(8+4+2,\ 11+2) = 14$$

This means that a 14-bit wordlength guarantees a proper functioning of the circuit, which results in a 14% throughput rate increase compared to a fixed 16-bit wordlength implementation. This also reduces the area of the line buffers. For a 512x512 image, a 512x14 bit line buffer consumes ~32 CLBs less than a 512x16 bit one.

Since $W_{conv.} > W_{in}$, the W_{in}-bit input pixel bits should be preceded by ($W_{conv.}$ – W_{in}) zeros. If 'Is_MSD' is the MSD control signal of the full '$W_{conv.}$'-bits input pixel, then 'Is_MSD_buf_in' control signal is a delayed version of 'Is_MSD' by δ = ($W_{conv.}$ – W_{in}) bits as shown in Figure 3.23.

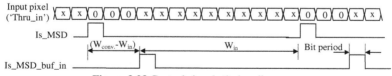

Figure 3.23 Control signals timing diagram

3.6 Other template neighbourhood operations

This section presents the full implementation of the four remaining neighbourhood operations, which will be similar to the convolution operation.

3.6.1   Multiplicative Maximum/Minimum

In this neighbourhood operation, the local operation is a multiplication whereas the global one is a Maximum (or Minimum) selector. Since the Maximum (Minimum) unit is 3 CLBs wide, the buffer unit has been laid out in a 3x3 rectangle. Moreover, the multiplication unit has also been laid out 3 CLBs wide as shown in Figure 3.24. The height of the latter unit depends on the window coefficient wordlength.

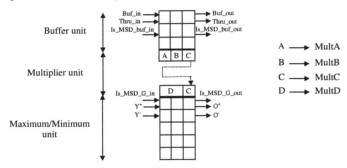

Figure 3.24 A Multiplicative Maximum PE layout

The design layout of a PxQ Multiplicative Maximum operation is then given in Figure 3.25.

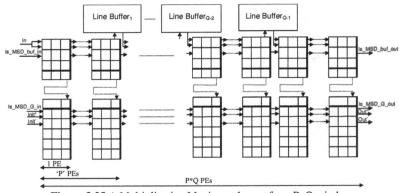

Figure 3.25 A Multiplicative Maximum layout for a PxQ window

Note that the value of Init=(Init$^+$, Init$^-$) is equal to (1,0) for a Multiplicative Minimum operation and (0,1) for a Multiplicative Maximum one.

The minimum processing wordlength is given by:

$$W_{proc.} = W_{\text{Multiplicative Maximum/Minimum}} = W_{in} + N \qquad \text{(Equation 3.w2)}$$

As in a convolution case, 'Is_MSD_buf_in' control signal is a delayed version of 'Is_MSD' by $\delta = (W_{proc.} - W_{in})$ bits (see Figure 3.23). Note that 'Is_MSD_G_in' input signal of the global operation (Maximum/Minimum) is a delayed version of the input 'Is_MSD' by $\delta = \delta_{sdnr2tc} + \delta_{local} = 1+N+2 = N+3$, where N is the maximum coefficient wordlength.

3.6.2 Additive Maximum/Minimum

In this neighbourhood operation the local operation is an addition, whereas the global one is a Maximum (Minimum) selector. Since both Maximum (Minimum) and local adder units are 3 CLBs wide, the buffer unit has been laid out in a 3x3 rectangle as in the previous operation. The corresponding PE layout is then given as follows:

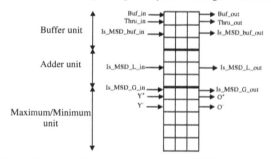

Figure 3.26 Additive Maximum/Minimum PE unit layout

The Overall neighbourhood operation is then given in Figure 3.27.

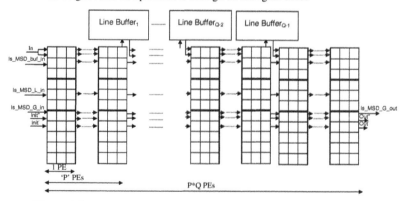

Figure 3.27 An Additive Maximum/Minimum layout for a PxQ window

Here again Init=(Init$^+$, Init$^-$) is equal to (1,0) for an Additive Minimum operation and (0,1) for an Additive Maximum one.

The minimum processing wordlength is given by:

$$W_{proc.} = W_{Additive\ Maximum/Minimum} = maximum(W_{in}, N)+2 \qquad (Equation\ 3.w3)$$

As in a convolution case, 'Is_MSD_buf_in' control signal is a delayed version of the 'Is_MSD' one by $\delta = (W_{proc.} - Win)$ bit cycles (see Figure 3.23). Note that the window coefficients are coded on ($W_{proc.}$-2) bits plus two leading zeros. This ensures the proper functioning of the local online adder. As a result 'Is_MSD_L_in' control signal is a delayed version of 'Is_MSD' by 2 bit cycles. Note also that 'Is_MSD_G_in' control input signal of the global operation (Maximum/Minimum) is a delayed version of the input 'Is_MSD' by $\delta = \delta_{sdnr2tc} + \delta_{local} = 1+3 = 4$.

3.7   Overall online delay of a complete neighbourhood operation

Input image pixels are fed to the FPGA in 2's complement bit parallel format. The resulting image data should be produced also in 2's complement bit parallel. An overall neighbourhood operation includes a parallel to serial converter at the input and a serial to a parallel converter at the output. The signed digit to 2's complement converter automatically outputs bit parallel 2's complement data.

The overall online delay is given by:

$$\delta_{overall} = \delta_{input} + \delta_{neighbourhood\_operation} + \delta_{sdnr2tcp}$$

and is expressed in bit clock cycles. The input and output supply, however, operates at the word level (in lower pixel clock cycles). Since the result data has to be stored on a pixel clock cycle, it is then necessary to make $\delta_{overall}$ a multiple of the processing wordlength, i.e. add an extra delay δ_{extra} to $\delta_{overall}$, if necessary, to make the new overall online delay $\delta_{new\_overall}$ a multiple of the processing wordlength $W_{proc.}$. This condition can be expressed as:

$$(\delta_{overall} + \delta_{extra})\ MOD\ W_{proc.} = 0$$

$$\delta_{overall\_new} = (\delta_{overall} + \delta_{extra})$$

This should be satisfied for both image data and 'Is_MSD' control signal. The additional extra online delay can be implemented using XC4000 synchronous RAM as described in section 3.3.1.

3.7.1   Convolution case

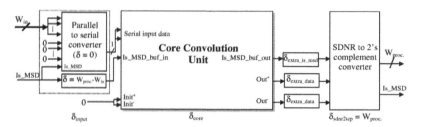

Figure 3.28 Overall neighbourhood operation

The data online delay of a general PxQ neighbourhood operation is given by:

$$\delta_{data\_delay}(Local\_operation, Global\_operation)= \delta_{local} +\delta_{sdnr2tc}+ P*Q*\delta_{global}$$

Since $\delta_{sdnr2tc} =1$, it is then given by:

$$\delta_{data\_delay}(Local\_operation, Global\_operation)= \delta_{local} +1+ P*Q*\delta_{global}$$

In a convolution case, $\delta_{local} = \delta_{mult} = N+2$, where N is the window's maximum coefficient wordlength, and $\delta_{global} = 4$. Thus:

$$\delta_{data\_convolution} = \delta_{data\_delay}(mult, accum)= N+3+P*Q*4 \qquad \text{(Equation 3.d1)}$$

The data extra delay δ_{extra_data} should hence satisfy:

$$(\delta_{data\_convolution} + \delta_{extra\_data})\ MOD\ W_{proc.} = 0$$

The delay of 'Is_MSD_buf' signal through the convolution core unit is however, given by:

$$\delta_{is\_msd\_buf} = P*Q*\delta_{global} = P*Q*4 \qquad \text{(Equation 3.d2)}$$

The control extra delay $\delta_{extra\_is\_msd}$ should hence satisfy:

$$(W_{proc.}-W_{in} + \delta_{is\_msd\_buf} + \delta_{extra\_is\_msd})\ MOD\ W_{proc.} = 0$$

For instance, let us consider the case of a Laplace filter applied on an 8-bit/pixel image. As seen above: P=Q=3, N=4 (4 = 0100_2) and $W_{proc.}$=14. This gives:

$$\delta_{data\_convolution} = 43 \text{ and } \delta_{is\_msd\_buf} = 36$$

The data and control extra delay should satisfy:

$$(43 + \delta_{extra\_data})\ MOD\ 14 = 0 \text{ and } (6 + 36 + \delta_{extra\_is\_msd})\ MOD\ 14 = 0$$

Thus:

$$\delta_{extra\_data} = 13 \text{ and } \delta_{extra\_is\_msd} = 0$$

3.7.2　Multiplicative Maximum/Minimum

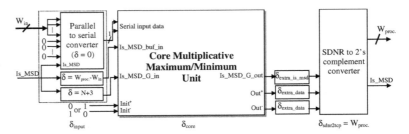

Figure 3.29 Overall Multiplicative Maximum/Minimum neighbourhood operation

Since $\delta_{local} = \delta_{mult} = N+2$, where N is the window's maximum coefficient wordlength, and $\delta_{global} = \delta_{maximum} = 3$, the data online delay of a PxQ Multiplicative Maximum (Minimum) operation is:

$$\delta_{data\_delay}(mult, maximum/minimum)= N+3+P*Q*3 \qquad \text{(Equation 3.d3)}$$

The data extra delay δ_{extra_data} should hence satisfy:

$$(N+3+P*Q*3+ \delta_{extra\_data}) \text{ MOD } W_{proc.} = 0$$

Note that 'Is_MSD_G_out' is synchronised with the output data (Out⁺, Out⁻) and hence has the same delay as the output data. As a result:

$$\delta_{extra\_is\_msd} = \delta_{extra\_data}$$

3.7.3　Additive Maximum/Minimum

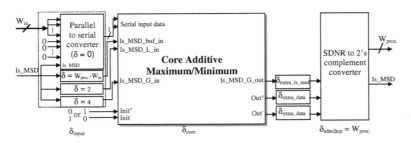

Figure 3.30 Overall Additive Maximum/Minimum neighbourhood operation

Since $\delta_{local} = \delta_{add} = 3$ and $\delta_{global} = \delta_{maximum} = 3$, the data online delay of a PxQ Additive Maximum(Minimum) operation is:

$$\delta_{data\_delay}(add, maximum/minimum)= 4+P*Q*3 \qquad \text{(Equation 3.d4)}$$

The data extra delay δ_{extra_data} should hence satisfy:

$$(4+P*Q*3 + \delta_{extra\_data})\ MOD\ W_{proc.} = 0$$

Note that 'Is_MSD_G_out' is synchronised with the output data (out⁺, out⁻) and hence has the same delay as the output data. As a result:

$$\delta_{extra\_is\_msd} = \delta_{extra\_data}$$

3.8 Other neighbourhood operation modes

In the previous sections, we presented the hardware implementation of Image Algebra operations in standard, non recursive mode (*template* mode). In the following, we will discuss the implementation of these operations in the other modes i.e. *tile* mode, and the two recursive modes *splice* and *isplice*.

3.8.1 Tile neighbourhood operations

In *tile* neighbourhood operations, result pixels are generated from *non-overlapping* regions in which the PxQ window is applied to the input image with a step size of <P,Q> instead of <1,1>. For an MxN input image size, the result image size is $\frac{M}{P} \times \frac{N}{Q}$. This is the only difference between *tile* neighbourhood operations and *template* ones. A possible way to implement *tile* operations is thus, to perform a complete template operation using the same window size, coefficient values and neighbourhood operation and produce the $\frac{M}{P} \times \frac{N}{Q}$ image by sub-sampling the stream of MxN result pixels. Note that this solution does not suffer from any pixel throughput rate decrease since each pixel is still supplied only once to the FPGA.

3.8.2 Recursive neighbourhood operations: *splices* and *isplices*

Recursive neighbourhood operations are another type of neighbourhood operations, in which the result pixel of each neighbourhood operation is conceptually stored back in the original image. Thus, each result pixel is generated from the combination of original image pixels and pixels from the result image as shown in Figure 3.31 for a 3x3-window size.

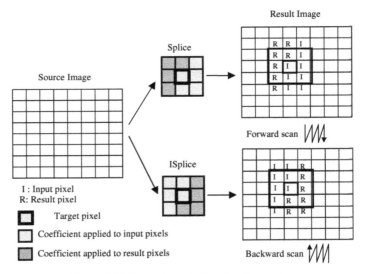

Figure 3.31 Recursive neighbourhood operations

Note that there are two recursive modes, depending on the direction of image scan. If the input image is scanned from top left corner to bottom right one (forward scan), this defines a *splice* mode. In the opposite case (backward scan), we define an inverse splice mode (*isplice*). This terminology for recursive image processing was put forward by Brown [Bro92].

The *isplice* operation can be performed using a *splice* operation by re-ordering the window coefficients and image data according to the following formula [Don96]:

$$\text{ISplice(image, window)} = \text{Splice(image}^{t_1 t_2}, \text{window}^{t_1 t_2})^{t_1 t_2}$$

where t_1 and t_2 are transposes about the falling and rising diagonals respectively as shown for a 3x3 window case in Figure 3.32.

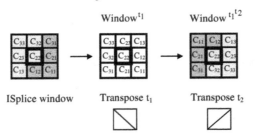

Figure 3.32 ISplice window transpose

Once the window coefficients are transposed, the rest (transposing the input image and the result one) can be performed by changing the order in which the pixels are supplied and retrieved from the FPGA. Hence, we will concentrate from now on *splice* mode.

A recursive neighbourhood operation can be seen as the composition of two windows, one applied to the result image and another to the source one, *spliced* together as shown in Figure 3.33.

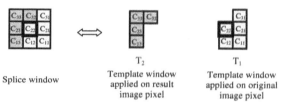

Splice window   Template window applied on result image pixel   Template window applied on original image pixel

Figure 3.33 Splice window decomposition

The template T_2 will be applied to the pixels resulting from template T_1 as shown in Figure 3.34 for a generic 3x3 neighbourhood operation, defined by a local operation L and a global one G with a central target pixel [Don96].

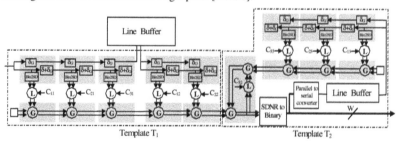

Template T_1 Template T_2

Figure 3.34 Splice operation layout for a 3x3 window

3.8.3   Splice hardware implementation limitations

Donachy's *splice* hardware implementation presented above suffers from a serious problem at the image borders. Indeed, the architecture presented above actually calculates boundary pixel result values, which strictly should not be calculated. These invalid values are then propagated in the scanning direction: a result generated for the bottom row of an image may be passed onto the next calculation at the top row of the next column. This may give the wrong result as seen in Figure 3.35 for an Additive Maximum *splice* operation.

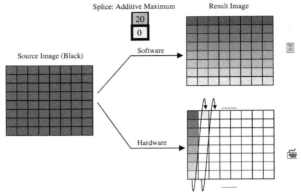

Figure 3.35 Splice operation hardware limitation

The reason for this is that our hardware implementation essentially processes the image data as 1-D vector as shown in Figure 3.36.

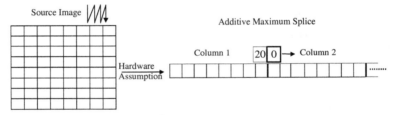

Figure 3.36 Drawback of a 1-D model of an image

Donachy's solution relied on border image being zero, and was limited to template operations where this problem does not occur.

To produce a general purpose solution, an extra control signal should be provided to inhibit the propagation of result pixels from the bottom rows to the top rows of the next columns. This control signal will indicate whether or not the target pixel is in a border region.

For implementation reasons (including the above limitation, and the irregularity of the *splice* operation for a general window size and shape), and more importantly, because the *splice* operation is only useful for a small number of algorithms, we have not generated a general framework for this type of neighbourhood operations. However, we have used this window type in a special recursive algorithm (Connected Component Labelling), which will treated separately in chapter 8.

3.9   Summary and conclusions .

In this chapter, we have presented a bit serial implementation of the basic instruction set of the FPGA-based IPC on the Xilinx XC4000. Serial implementation has been chosen for its compactness and regularity. The standard set of Image Algebra neighbourhood operations was designed using a small set of parameterisable basic building blocks. These basic components were carefully designed in order to fit together with as little wastage area as possible (the *design to fit* approach). This approach, plus the regularity and parameterisability features of the designs, will be particularly useful when we are to design the high level architecture generator, as will be shown in Chapter 6.

This chapter has been a useful exercise in porting a number of major architectures from an FPGA series (XC6000) to another (XC4000). Three lessons in particular which have emerged are:

- The *high level* design of neighbourhood operation architectures has been retained due largely to the abstract algebraic approach to neighbourhood operations which has been followed.

- The basic building blocks are much less portable than the high level designs, if we require an efficient implementation. The fine grain structure of the sea-of-gates XC6000 is totally different from the coarse grained LUT-based XC4000 structure. An efficient implementation should take advantage of the particular features of the target FPGA architecture (e.g. fast carry logic in the XC4000). Before implementing a particular design, it is better to go back to the original problem rather than merely remap the same algorithm. At times, it is necessary to make some algorithmic changes to take advantage of the target FPGA architecture. As something of a warning, we would note that many algorithms in the literature have been specifically optimised for software or VLSI implementation, or even for a particular FPGA architecture. Implementing the same algorithm on another FPGA might be very inefficient. This is particularly true in the case of the *signed digit to 2's complement converter* block, where the use of a different algorithm from the one advocated in literature [EL87] (also used in [Don96] for XC6000) has resulted in a much compact and even faster implementation on XC4000.

- We have shown that it is possible to perform certain optimisations at the low level hardware architectures (e.g. limiting the processing wordlength to its minimal necessary value according to the template coefficient values) while keeping the same high level framework.

The latter point will be further consolidated in the following chapter in which alternative design decisions to the ones presented in this chapter (i.e. bit serial SDNR, MSBF) will be made in certain special cases, for greater efficiency.

The following table summarises the basic building blocks presented in this chapter:

Block name	Input type	Output type	Function
Line buffer	2's complement bit serial	2's complement bit serial	Image width/height buffer
2's complement to SDNR converter	2's complement bit serial MSBF	Radix-2 SDNR digit serial MSDF	Converts a bit serial 2's complement MSBF input into radix-2 SDNR digit serial MSDF
Online adder	Radix-2 SDNR digit serial MSDF	Radix-2 SDNR digit serial MSDF	Adds two input operands using online arithmetic
Online multiplier	Radix-2 SDNR digit serial MSDF	Radix-2 SDNR digit serial MSDF	Multiplies a radix-2 SDNR digit serial MSDF input with a 2's complement bit parallel coefficient
Online adder (Local operation)	Radix-2 SDNR digit serial MSDF	Radix-2 SDNR digit serial MSDF	Adds a radix-2 SDNR digit serial MSDF input to a constant coefficient
Online maximum	Radix-2 SDNR digit serial MSDF	Radix-2 SDNR digit serial MSDF	Selects the maximum of two radix-2 SDNR digit serial MSDF inputs
Online minimum	Radix-2 SDNR digit serial MSDF	Radix-2 SDNR digit serial MSDF	Selects the minimum of two radix-2 SDNR digit serial MSDF inputs
SDNR to 2's complement converter	Radix-2 SDNR digit serial MSDF	2's complement bit parallel	Converts a radix-2 SDNR digit serial MSDF input into 2's complement bit parallel
Redundancy reductor	Radix-2 SDNR digit serial MSDF	Radix-2 SDNR digit serial MSDF	Reduces the redundancy of a radix-2 SDNR digit serial MSDF input
Parallel to serial converter	2's complement bit parallel	2's complement bit serial MSBF	Converts a 2's complement bit parallel input into a 2's complement bit serial MSBF output

Table 3.1 Summary of the basic building blocks presented in this chapter

Chapter 4

Optimised solutions for special cases

Chapter 4

Optimised solutions for special cases

In the previous chapter, we presented a bit serial implementation of the proposed FPGA based IPC instruction set. This implementation was based on online arithmetic (Signed Digit, Most Significant Bit First). We have also noted that there are various situations where it is possible to make different design decisions for greater efficiency (area and speed). In this chapter, we will present two such cases:

(i)   When the input image to be processed is *binary*.

(ii)   When the operations involve only simple convolutions.

4.1   Binary image processing

Binary images are images in which just two grey levels are used to represent the pixels' brightness. They are usually the result of a threshold operation performed on ordinary grey level images, in order to separate features from background, so that counting, measurement, or matching operations can be performed. We assume that the two only possible grey levels are either 1 or 0. Therefore, each pixel can be represented by one bit.

4.1.1   Review of design decisions

Image Algebra operations applied to binary images present an enormous potential for simplification. Note that though the input image is binary, the output image might not be so, as we do not impose any restriction on the window coefficient values.

The implications for simplifications for processing binary input images include the following:

(i)   Multiplication of a binary pixel by a coefficient value 'C' is obsolete, since the result will be either 0 or 'C'.

(ii)   'Local' addition of a binary pixel and a coefficient 'C' produces either 'C' or
        'C+1' (an increment operation).

If 'increment' and all the global operations ('Σ', 'Max' and 'Min') can be implemented
in bit parallel, there are further advantageous implications:

(iii)   The line buffer needs to hold only one bit per pixel, thus drastically reducing
        the area.

(iv)   A complete result pixel can be generated every clock cycle, thus increasing the
        throughput rate (provided the clock period does not have to be increased by a
        factor of more than the wordlength).

Using the dedicated fast carry logic on the XC4000, fast bit parallel implementations
of 'increment', 'Σ', 'Max' and 'Min' can readily be achieved [XAP13][XCL23].
Therefore, for processing binary input images, we have made the following design
decisions:

• Bit parallel arithmetic rather than bit serial

• 2's complement number representation rather than SDNR

With these considerations, a standard binary Processing Element architecture is as
follows:

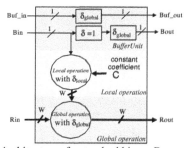

Figure 4.1 Architecture of a standard binary Processing Element

4.1.2   Binary convolution neighbourhood operation

In a convolution operation, the local and global operations are Multiply-Accumulate
respectively. Each PE performs the following equation (see Figure 4.1):

$$Rout = C*Bin+Rin$$

If the incoming binary pixel value 'Bin' is zero, then 'Rin' is added to zero, otherwise
the window coefficient $C = C_w C_{w-1} \ldots C_2 C_1$ is added. Hence, the multiplication is

reduced to simple multiplexing. Therefore, the PE's Multiply Accumulate (MAC) operation reduces to a multiplexed addition as shown in Figure 4.2.

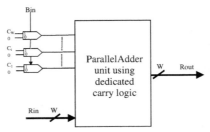

Figure 4.2 A block diagram of a Multiply Accumulate unit for Binary Images

The accumulator is implemented in XC4000 FPGAs using dedicated fast carry logic and is composed from 1-bit and/or 2-bit 2's-complement addition slices plus a carry initialisation stage. Figure 4.3 shows a 1-bit MAC slice.

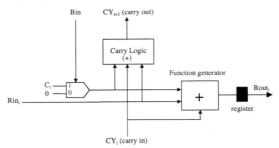

Figure 4.3 Convolution 1-bit slice

A two-bit MAC slice occupies 1 CLB. Therefore, a W-bit MAC unit occupies $\lceil W/2 \rceil + 1$ CLBs. The local operation (multiplication) operates with no latency i.e. δ_{local} = 0, whereas the PE's latency $\delta_{PE} = \delta_{global}$ = 1 cycle. The buffer unit (see Figure 4.1) is then reduced to 3 flip-flops.

The line buffer unit is very compact since it holds just 1-bit pixels. One CLB can implement up to 34 bit pixel delays.

The latency of a general PxQ binary neighbourhood operation is given by:

$$\delta_{binary\_nop}(Local\_operation, Global\_operation) = \delta_{local} + P*Q*\delta_{PE}$$

Since, for a convolution, δ_{local}=0 and δ_{PE} = 1, then:

$$\delta_{binary\_nop}(mult, accum) = P*Q \qquad \text{(Equation 4.d1)}$$

Note that this latency is evaluated in pixel cycles as the unit operates in bit parallel.

The minimum processing wordlength depends on the window coefficients and is given by:

$$W_{proc.} = W_{max} \qquad \text{(Equation 4.w1)}$$

where W_{max} is the maximum possible result pixel wordlength.

For instance, consider binary convolution with the following window:

10	2	10
2	1	2
10	2	10

The maximum result pixel value is equal to 49, and occurs when the image pixels' values within the window neighbourhood are all equal to 1. Hence, the minimum pixel wordlength is 7 ($49 = 0110001_2$).

4.1.3 Multiplicative Maximum/Minimum

In this operation, the local and global operations are Multiply and Maximum/Minimum respectively. Each PE performs the following equation:

$$Rout = Max/Min(C*Bin, Rin)$$

The multiplication again reduces to a multiplexer. The maximum/minimum is performed by carrying out the subtraction: $C*Bin-Rin$, and examining the sign of the result, i.e. the most significant bit (MSB) of the subtraction result:

-   If MSB=1, then $C*Bin<Rin$ and hence:

    $Max(C*Bin, Rin) = Rin$ and $Min(C*Bin, Rin) = C*Bin$.

-   If MSB=0, then $C*Bin>Rin$ and hence:

    $Max(C*Bin, Rin) = C*Bin$ and $Min(C*Bin, Rin) = Rin$.

Fast carry logic in each CLB is set for a $C*Bin-Rin$ subtract function, while the function generators are used to implement a 2:1 multiplexer. The multiplexer is controlled by the MSB of the whole subtraction as shown in the following figure.

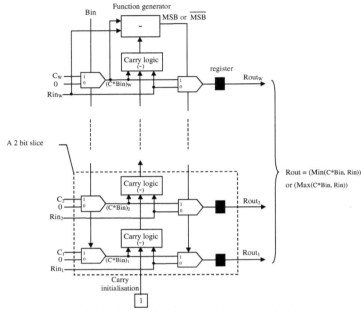

Figure 4.4 A Multiplicative Maximum/Minimum unit for binary images

The Multiplicative Maximum/Minimum unit is composed from 2-bit Mult-Max/Min slices. Each fits in one CLB. A 'W' bit Mult-Max/Min unit occupies $\lfloor W/2+1 \rfloor$ CLBs. As in the case of convolution, the local operation (multiplication) operates with no latency i.e. $\delta_{local} = 0$, whereas the PE's latency $\delta_{PE} = \delta_{global} = 1$ cycle. Hence, the latency of a PxQ multiplicative maximum (minimum) operation is:

$$\delta_{binary\_op}(\textit{mult, maximum/minimum}) = P*Q*\, \delta_{PE} = P*Q \qquad \text{(Equation 4.d2)}$$

The minimum processing wordlength is given by:

$$W_{proc.} = C_{max} \qquad \text{(Equation 4.w2)}$$

where C_{max} is the window's maximum coefficient wordlength.

4.1.4   Additive Maximum/Minimum

In this case, the window coefficient has to be added to its corresponding image pixel rather than multiplied. This makes this type of neighbourhood operations more difficult to implement compared to the previous ones.

Note that each PE has to evaluate:

$$Rout = Max/Min(Bin+C, Rin) \qquad \text{(Equation 1)}$$

As explained in the previous section, a Max/Min(A,B) operation is implemented by doing A-B, and uses the MSB of the result to multiplex the maximum/minimum to the output. A subtraction operation A-B is carried out in XC4000 as an addition A+(-B). Multiplication by –1 is performed by logically inverting the operand B and adding one:

$$A\text{-}B = A + \overline{B} + 1 \qquad \text{(Equation 2)}$$

The operand B is inverted within the CLB whereas the one is added by forcing the carry into the adder chain to be high. So in order to evaluate (Equation 1), we perform the following subtraction:

$$Rin - (Bin + C) = (Rin\text{-}C)\text{-}Bin$$
$$= Rin + \overline{C} + 1 \text{-} Bin$$
$$= Rin + \overline{C} + \overline{Bin} \quad (\text{since } 1\text{-} Bin = \overline{Bin} \text{ in binary})$$

We now implement this as a normal subtraction Rin-C, using $\overline{Bin}$ as the carry initialisation of the whole subtracter (instead of '1'). This subtraction will generate the MSB signal, which will multiplex 'Rin' and 'C+Bin' to the output.

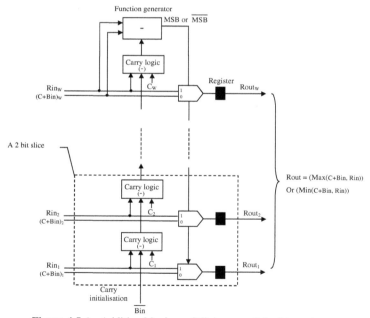

Figure 4.5 An Additive Maximum/Minimum unit for binary images

Another problem arises now, which is the evaluation of 'C+Bin'. By knowing the value of C at 'compile time', we can work out the value of 'C+Bin' in terms of 'Bin'. For instance, if C=1011, then C+Bin will be either:

$$\begin{array}{ccccl} & 1 & 0 & 1 & 1 & \text{(if Bin=0)} \\ \text{or} & 1 & 1 & 0 & 0 & \text{(if Bin=1)} \end{array}$$

$$\text{i.e. C+Bin} = 1 \quad \text{Bin} \quad \overline{\text{Bin}} \quad \overline{\text{Bin}}$$

These expressions at each bit position (0, 1, Bin or $\overline{\text{Bin}}$) will of course depend on the value of C; but they can be calculated in software at compile time. Hence, no extra hardware is needed.

The Additive Maximum/Minimum PE unit is composed from 2-bit Additive Maximum/Minimum slices. A 'W' bit Additive Maximum/Minimum PE unit occupies $\lfloor W/2+1 \rfloor +1$ CLBs. The local operation (addition) operates with no latency i.e. $\delta_{local} = 0$, whereas the PE's latency $\delta_{PE} = \delta_{global} = 1$ cycle. Hence, as in the two previous cases, the latency of a PxQ Additive Maximum/Minimum operation is:

$$\delta_{binary\_nop}(add, maximum/minimum) = P*Q* \delta_{PE} = P*Q \quad \text{(Equation 4.d3)}$$

The minimum necessary processing wordlength depends on the window coefficients and is given by:

$$W_{proc.} = \max_{i,j} \{ \ max(word\_length\_of(C_{ij}+1), word\_length\_of(C_{ij})) \ \}, \ 1<i<P, \ 1<j<Q$$

$$\text{(Equation 4.w3)}$$

where C_{ij} is a window coefficient.

A classical operation using this type of neighbourhood operation is 'Erode' which is an Additive Minimum operation with either of the two following windows:

~	0	~
0	0	0
~	0	~

or

0	0	0
0	0	0
0	0	0

where '~' stands for an unused window coefficient. Note that an unused PE unit, in this case as well as in all the other cases, reduces to simple bit delays.

4.2   Simple convolution

The choice of MSBF processing made in chapter 3 was dictated by the use of maximum and minimum operations. These operations are naturally performed MSBF, and using LSBF would make their implementation dependent on the wordlength and would increase the latency. Similarly, *absolute* and *division* operations are also performed naturally MSBF.

In situations where these operations are not involved, however, the choice of MSBF processing is no longer justified. Consequently, the use of SDNR is also unjustified. Using 2's complement instead would result in significant area saving as only one signal is used to represent a digit (instead of two in SDNR). Such situations include doing simple convolution. In the following, we will build up the design of a 2D convolution based on *2's complement bit serial LSBF* arithmetic.

4.2.1   Basic building block architectures

The architecture of a generic PxQ convolver has been already presented in section 3.2.1. The following will present the design of the convolver basic building blocks. These are based on 2's complement bit serial LSBF arithmetic.

4.2.1.1   Bit serial adder

Figure 4.6 presents the architecture of a traditional bit serial adder, where the two input operands are supplied bit serially LSBF (called a *carry save adder*- CSA) [Omo94]. Because the initial state of the carry flip-flop should be zero, an extra signal 'Is_MSB' is provided to clear it synchronously.

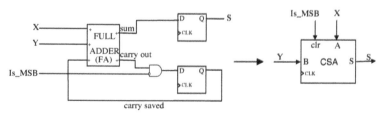

Figure 4.6 Architecture of a carry save adder (CSA)

The unit occupies one CLB and operates with one bit latency.

4.2.1.2   Negating a bit serial LSBF number

This 'Negate' unit will be required for the bit serial multiplication given below. The bit serial LSBF 2's complement negating design is given by Figure 4.7 [OMO94]. It is based on the following simple paper-and-pencil method:

1.   Copy each incoming bit up to and including the first '1'.

2.   After the first '1', invert each subsequent incoming bit.

Note that the initial state of the '1' detect flip-flop ('detect_1') should be zero. This is performed synchronously by using 'Is_MSB' signal as in the carry save adder. The unit occupies one CLB and operates with one bit latency.

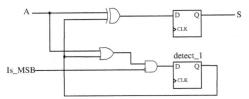

Figure 4.7 Architecture of a bit serial LSBF 'Negate' unit

4.2.1.3   2's complement serial parallel multiplier

Although there is a variety of multiplier architectures to choose from in the literature [Kor93][Cav84], the multiplier architecture that we have chosen is based on a unit outlined in [And93] and is shown in Figure 4.8. The multiplier (coefficient) is presented in parallel while the multiplicand (the pixel value) is presented bit serial LSBF. The multiplier coefficient 'C' multiplies, in turn, each bit of the serial multiplicand using the logical ANDs. Each of the resulting partial products is added to the shifted accumulation of the previous products using the carry save adders chain. The serial output is then taken from the output of the least significant bit adder with 1-bit latency. Note that if the multiplier coefficient 'C' is negative (i.e. $C_N = 1$), then the sign extension 'C_N' should negate the multiplicand. This is performed by the 'Negate' stage (which performs 2's complement of the input number) placed at the most significant bit.

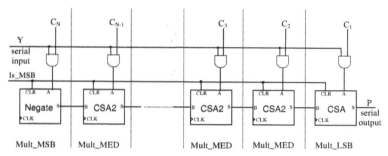

Figure 4.8 Architecture of a signed serial (LSBF) by parallel multiplier

The serial multiplier must be cleared before each new input word to prevent errors. Since it operates with one bit latency, the sum output flip-flop in all the carry save adders (CSA2s) is cleared synchronously (by 'Is_MSB') except the least significant bit adder (CSA) since the latter will hold the last bit (the MSB) of the result at the end. The carry save adder CSA2 is then slightly different from CSA since the sum output should be cleared synchronously (as well as the carry) by 'Is_MSB'. The 'Negate' stage is also slightly different from the one presented above since its output should also be cleared. Both 'CSA2' and 'Negate' architectures are given in Figure 4.9.

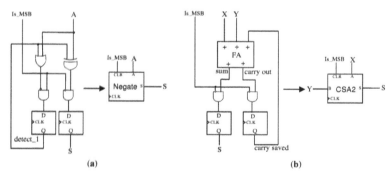

Figure 4.9 Architecture of: **(a)** A modified 'Negate' block
                                   (b) A modified carry save adder (CSA2)

This actually divides our multiplier into three parts: Mult_MSB, Mult_MED and Mult_LSB (see Figure 4.8). An N bit multiplier is constructed by:

$$\text{Mult\_MSB} \rightarrow (N-2) \text{ Mult\_MED} \rightarrow \text{Mult\_LSB}.$$

Note that since the multiplier value is constant, there are two variants of each of these three sub-blocks corresponding to a coefficient bit value C_i equal to '1' or '0'. This gives a set of six sub-blocks: $Mult\_MSB_1$, $Mult\_MSB_0$, $Mult\_MED_1$, $Mult\_MED_0$, $Mult\_LSB_1$ and $Mult\_LSB_0$. In the case where the coefficient C_i is '0', the carry save adders use only one flip-flop and hence occupy a half CLB. In the opposite case (i.e. C_i='1'), the corresponding block occupies one CLB. Hence an N bit multiplier block consumes at most 'N' CLBs.

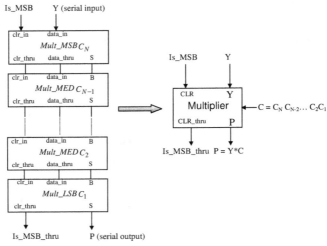

Figure 4.10 Design of an 'N' bit LSBF serial-parallel 2's complement multiplier

4.2.2 A generic PxQ 2's complement LSBF convolver

Figure 4.11 presents the architecture of a Multiply-Accumulate PE based on the above basic building blocks.

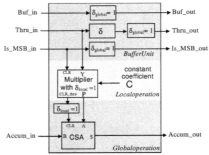

Figure 4.11 A bit serial 2's complement Multiply-Accumulate PE

The pixel delay δ is implemented using XC4000 on-chip distributed synchronous RAMs as explained in section 3.3.1. The buffer unit occupies 4 CLBs.

The whole convolution PE has been laid out vertically on the FPGA as shown in Figure 4.12.

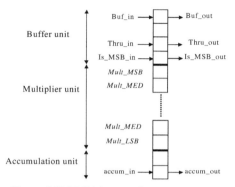

Figure 4.12 FPGA layout of a convolution PE

The PE unit occupies 'N+6' CLBs where 'N' is the multiplier coefficient wordlength. This is 7 CLBs less than the equivalent PE unit based on SDNR (see section 3.5). Figure 4.13 gives the FPGA layout of a 3x3 convolution.

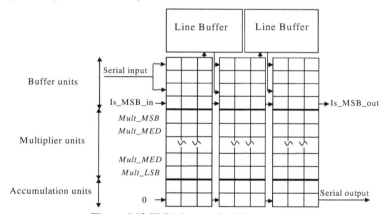

Figure 4.13 FPGA layout of a 3x3 convolver

The latency of a general PxQ convolution operation is given by:

$$\delta_{convolution\_2's\ complement} = \delta_{local} + P*Q*\delta_{Global} \quad \text{(Equation 4.d4)}$$

Since $\delta_{local} = 1$ and $\delta_{Global} = 1$:

$$\delta_{convolution\_2's\ complement} = 1 + P*Q$$

The minimum processing wordlength depends on the window coefficients. In general, it is given by:

$$W_{convolution\_2's\ complement} = \text{maximum}(W_{in}+N,\ W_{max}) \quad \text{(Equation 4.w4)}$$

where:

'W_{in}' is the input pixel wordlength.

'N' is the window's maximum coefficient wordlength.

'W_{max}' is the maximum intermediate wordlength (in 2's complement) determined from the maximum/minimum possible intermediate pixel values. This depends on the actual window coefficient values.

The first term ($W_{in}+N$) ensures the proper functioning of the multiplier array, while the second (W_{max}) ensures the minimum precision required. For instance, let us consider the case of a Laplace filter (see section 3.5). Suppose the input wordlength is 8 (i.e. 256 grey-level image), we have then:

-   $W_{in} = 8$
-   $N = 4$
-   $W_{max} = 11$

Hence, the minimum processing wordlength is:

$$W_{laplace\_2's\ complement} = \text{maximum}(8+4,\ 11) = 12 \text{ bits.}$$

This is 2 bits less than an equivalent SDNR based implementation. Hence, a 2's complement based implementation gains in the PE's area (7 CLBs less than an online arithmetic based implementation) and the line buffers area (since the processing wordlength is 2 bits less).

4.3   High level environment

Although the FPGA designs presented both in this chapter and the previous one are different (e.g. SDNR, binary input image and 2's complement), they have all the same high level framework. All that a user has to supply is:

-   Local and Global neighbourhood operator.
-   The template (shape, size and coefficients).
-   Input image size (The line buffer size is equal to the image height for a vertical scan direction)
-   Input pixel wordlength

This information should be sufficient for a high level environment to work out automatically the most appropriate implementation. This can be done by a rule-based system with no user intervention.

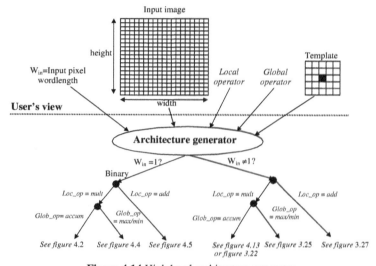

Figure 4.14 High level architecture generator

4.4   Summary

In this chapter, we have presented architectures for special cases where the design decisions made in chapter 3 (i.e. bit serial, SDNR, MSDF) can be replaced by alternative decisions leading to better performance.

First, we presented architectures for the special case where the input image data is binary. The bit serial choice is no longer justified in this particular case. A bit parallel architecture becomes more attractive as it generates one result pixel per cycle and, with greater reduced buffer space, consumes less area compared to its equivalent serial implementation.

Secondly, we have presented an alternative implementation for simple convolution based on LSBF 2's complement arithmetic. The choice of MSBF processing (and hence SDNR) made in chapter 3 was dictated by the presence of Maximum and Minimum operations. These operations along with Division, Absolute are more efficiently performed MSBF. When these operations are not involved (e.g. simple convolution), an alternative LSBF 2's complement based implementation consumes less area, operates with a smaller latency and word precision compared to a SDNR based implementation.

We have also shown that, given a high level abstract description of the required operation, the most appropriate implementation can be selected automatically by examining a small set of user-supplied parameters (e.g. input wordlength).

The following chapter will present the high level environment from which the designs presented in this chapter and the previous one are generated. The performance of the resulting architectures will be presented and discussed in chapter 6.

The following table summarises the basic building blocks presented in this chapter:

Block name	Input type	Output type	Function
Multiply-Accumulate unit	(binary, 2's complement bit parallel)	2's complement bit parallel	Multiplies a binary input with a 2's complement, bit parallel, constant coefficient and adds the result with a 2's complement bit parallel input
Multiply-Maximum unit	(binary, 2's complement bit parallel)	2's complement bit parallel	Multiplies a binary input with a 2's complement, bit parallel, constant coefficient and outputs the maximum between this result and another 2's complement bit parallel input
Multiply-Minimum unit	(binary, 2's complement bit parallel)	2's complement bit parallel	Multiplies a binary input with a 2's complement, bit parallel, constant coefficient and outputs the minimum between this result and another 2's complement bit parallel input
Add-Maximum unit	(binary, 2's complement bit parallel)	2's complement bit parallel	Adds a binary input to a 2's complement, bit parallel, constant coefficient and outputs the maximum between this result and another 2's complement bit parallel input
Add-Minimum unit	(binary, 2's complement bit parallel)	2's complement bit parallel	Adds a binary input to a 2's complement, bit parallel, constant coefficient and outputs the minimum between this result and another 2's complement bit parallel input
Carry save adder	2's complement Bit serial LSBF	2's complement Bit serial LSBF	Adds two input operands in 2's complement bit serial LSBF
Negate unit	2's complement Bit serial LSBF	2's complement Bit serial LSBF	Negates a 2's complement bit serial, LSBF input
Serial parallel multiplier	2's complement Bit serial LSBF	2's complement Bit serial LSBF	Multiplies a 2's complement bit serial LSBF input with a 2's complement bit parallel coefficient

Table 4.1 Summary of the basic building blocks presented in this chapter

Chapter 5

A Hardware Description Environment-
HIDE4k

Chapter 5

A Hardware Description Environment- HIDE4k

The previous chapters have presented FPGA designs for the set of Image Algebra operators. These designs were fairly regular and scaleable in terms of the window size and the pixel wordlength. In order to convert those designs into actual FPGA architectures, this chapter presents a high level hardware description environment which will capture these designs in a parameterised notation from which actual FPGA architectures are automatically synthesised. Rather than inventing a new environment, we decided to design our new environment based on a previous hardware description environment developed at Queen's University called HIDE. The latter was specific to Xilinx XC6000 series and was presented in section 2.3.3. In addition to the obvious historical reason, this choice was also driven by the strengths demonstrated by HIDE environment, which were identified in section 2.4.

Our hardware description environment targets the Xilinx XC4000 series and is called HIDE4k (Hardware Intelligent Description Environment for Xilinx 4000 series) as opposed to HIDE6k. The latter name will be used in the remaining of this chapter to refer to the previous environment. Central to HIDE4k environment is a high level hardware description notation which allows for parameterised and very concise circuit descriptions to be made. This is particularly suitable for regular and highly scaleable architectures as those encountered in Image Processing.

After a brief overview of HIDE4k environment, this chapter will first start by presenting the HIDE4k notation. Then, some simple illustrative examples are given (more will be developed in chapter 6). After that, the structure of the overall HIDE4k environment is outlined. The implementation of each part of this system is then considered.

5.1 HIDE4k environment: an overview

Rather than invent a brand new environment, we decided to design our hardware description environment based on the previous HIDE6k system. The latter has been designed specifically for Xilinx XC6000 and offered a simple way of describing XC6000 based hardware architectures. The HIDE6k implementation by Alotaibi has been completely reworked and extended to give our HIDE4k implementation.

The HIDE4k environment consists of:

- A high level hardware notation, similar to HIDE6k, particularly suited to describing regular architectures such as those encountered in IP neighbourhood operations.

- A Prolog-based translator which automatically and dynamically generates hardware configurations, in either EDIF or VHDL formats, from HIDE4k descriptions.

5.2 Essentials of HIDE4k notation

As mentioned above, HIDE4k notation is similar to HIDE6k one. The main component in a HIDE4k description is a block, which can be either a basic block or a compound block. Each block has a set of input/output *ports* to communicate with other blocks (see section 2.3.3.1).

5.2.1 Block composition

A compound block is obtained by hierarchical composition of sub-blocks using a simple set of five constructors:

- **vertical([B$_1$, B$_2$, ..., B$_n$])** used to compose the supplied sub-blocks (B$_1$, B$_2$, ...B$_n$) together vertically.

- **horizontal([B$_1$, B$_2$, ..., B$_n$])** used to compose the supplied sub-blocks (B$_1$, B$_2$, ..., B$_n$) together horizontally.

- **v_seq(N, B)** used to replicate the supplied block 'B', N times vertically.

- **h_seq(N, B)** used to replicate the supplied block 'B', N times horizontally.

- **offset(B, X, Y)** used to offset the supplied block 'B' by 'X' CLBs positions horizontally and 'Y' CLBs positions vertically.

These perform exactly the same function as their equivalent in HIDE6k and were described in section 2.3.3.1.

In addition to these constructors, we provide a facility for generalising **v_seq** and **h_seq** constructors: we provide a constructor (***p_b_seq***), which describes a sequence of parameterised blocks:

$$p\_b\_seq(i, init, step, final, B(i))$$

where

i : represents a variable with an initial integer value ***init***, a final integer value ***final*** and an integer index ***step***.

B(i) : is a parameterised block description (function of the variable ***i***).

This describes a list of $\lfloor(final-init)/step+1\rfloor$ blocks ***B(i)*** for values of ***i*** starting from ***init*** with an increment value equal to ***step***, such that $i \leq$ ***final***.

This can be useful for generating systolic architectures (see Figure 5.1).

a) vertical([p_b_seq(i,1,1,4,h_seq(5-i , B))])   *b) vertical([p_b_seq(i,1,1,4,offset(h_seq(4 ,B), i-1,0))])*

Figure 5.1 Examples of parameterised block composition

5.2.2 Block interconnection

On the Xilinx XC6000, it was possible in an EDIF description to specify exact routing paths. Unfortunately, there is no equivalent access to routing on the Xilinx XC4000 series. This is particularly because the XC4000 series are commercial, while the XC6000 are intended mainly for research purposes. Therefore, we do not perform routing in HIDE4k. This task is left to Xilinx routing tools. Placement of basic components is however performed by HIDE4k. The following facilities for block interconnection are all novel to HIDE4k and did not exist in HIDE6k.

Ports matching and manipulation

As a result of not performing routing, the block interconnection consists merely in assigning each input port to its proper output port and vice versa. Note also that in the XC4000, the routing resources (e.g. Programmable Switch Matrices) are separate logic resources unlike in XC6000 where actual logic cells are used for routing. The concept of a network block introduced in HIDE6k, is hence replaced by a network connection which is *conceptually* seen as a dummy block with *zero* width and height. The input/output ports of this dummy block are floating (see section 2.3.3.1).

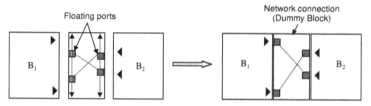

Figure 5.2 Network connection for ports matching

The following network connection constructor is provided for that purpose:

$$nc([(i, j), ...]) \quad i,j > 0$$

i : is a port sequence number on the first side.

j: is a port sequence number on the second side.

In certain circumstances, connections may be defined by a formula. A smarter description of these cases would use a parameterised sequence (*p_seq*) within the network connection as follows:

$$nc([..., p\_seq(i, init, step, final, [...(f(i), g(i)),...]), ...]) \quad f(i),g(i) > 0$$

i   : represents a variable with an initial integer value *init*, a final integer value *final* and an integer index step *step*.

f(i), g(i) : functions of the variable *i*.

As in *p_b_seq*, this describes a list of $\lfloor (\text{final-init})/\text{step}+1 \rfloor$ connections *(f(i), g(i))* for values of *i* starting from *init* with an increment value equal to *step*, such that $i \leq final$.

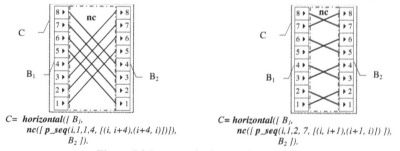

$C= horizontal([B_1,$
$\quad nc([p\_seq(i,1,1,4, [(i, i+4),(i+4, i)])]),$
$\quad B_2]).$

$C= horizontal([B_1,$
$\quad nc([p\_seq(i,1,2, 7, [(i, i+1),(i+1, i)])]),$
$\quad B_2]).$

Figure 5.3 Parameterised network connection

At times, some block ports need to be connected to non-adjacent blocks through an adjacent block. The fact that a port is to be extended through an adjacent block is indicated by putting '**thru**' at the position where we would normally put the corresponding port sequence number in the '**nc**' 2-tuple. The extended ports will take the higher ports' positions as shown in Figure 5.4.

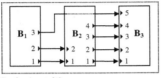

C = horizontal([
horizontal(B1,nc([(1,1), (2,2), (3,thru)]), B2]),
B3])

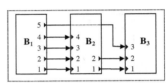

C = horizontal([B1,
horizontal([B2,nc([(1,1), (2,2), (thru,3)]), B3])
])

Figure 5.4 'Thru' connection

Often, when combining components, it is desirable to specify the outer ports of a particular block. The unmentioned ports will not be considered for connection. HIDE4k provides the following constructor for that purpose:

> *outer_ports([North_list, South_list, East_list, West_list, NE_list, NW_list, SE_list,*
> *SW_list], B)*

where each sub-list contains the sequence number of the ports that are put on the outer interface of a particular block side (see Figure 5.5).

However, it is sometimes more convenient to specify which ports of a block **B** are not to be considered for connection (rather than those to be considered for connection). HIDE4k provides the following constructor for that purpose:

> *open_ports([North_list, South_list, East_list, West_list, NE_list, NW_list, SE_list,*
> *SW_list], B)*

where each sub-list contains the sequence number of the ports to be left unconnected (see Figure 5.5). Note that, in both *outer_ports* and *open_ports*, if the outer ports of a whole side are wanted to be kept unchanged, the user would simply put '~' in the corresponding sub-list.

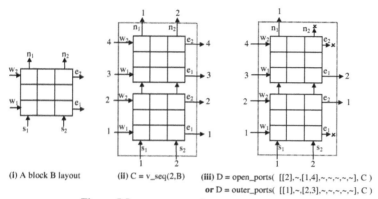

(i) A block B layout   (ii) C = v_seq(2,B)   (iii) D = open_ports([[2],~,[1,4],~,~,~,~,~], C)

or D = outer_ports([[1],~,[2,3],~,~,~,~,~], C)

Figure 5.5 *open_ports* and *outer_ports* constructors

Note that the block that is at the top of the hierarchy should be connected to the FPGA package pins. This is performed in HIDE4k by the following constructor:

connect2pin([North_list, South_list, East_list, West_list, NE_list, NW_list, SE_list, SW_list], B)

where each list contains the I/O ports with their corresponding pins and is given as follows:

[...,(i, pin_name),.....]

i is a port sequence number on a particular side.

pin_name is a particular pin name on the FPGA chip pins package (e.g. 'P11', 'P24' etc.).

5.2.3 Control signals

Control signals (e.g. Clocks and Clears) are different from ports in that they are potentially broadcast to all components in a block. That explains why in HIDE6k, they were represented by a separate object *signal_list* in the block properties. This list contains the logical names of all control signals used in that particular block. When combining sub-blocks to give a new block, the set of control signals for the new block is the union of the sets of all the sub-blocks. However, because the signal names in a block definition are local to the sub-block, two cases may arise:

1. The same logical name may be used in two sub-blocks, but they actually represent two different control signals for the new block.

2. Sub-blocks may use different names for what will be the same signal in the combined block.

The solution to this problem in HIDE4k is the same as the one adopted in HIDE6k [Alo99]. We provide the following constructor for renaming control signals:

rename_signals(signal_list_renaming, Block)

where *signal_list_renaming* is a list representing the mapping between old logical names and new logical names as follows:

signal_list_renaming = [...., ([List_of_old_control names], new_control_name),...]

C_1 = rename_signals([(Clk, Clk1), (Clr1, Clr)],B_1) C_2 = rename_signals([(Clk, Clk2), (Clr2, Clr)],B_2)

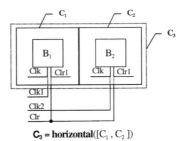

C_3 = horizontal([C_1 , C_2])

Figure 5.6 Signals renaming

The assignment of these logical signals to physical signals can be then performed by the following constructor:

drive_signals(signal_list_mapping, Block)

where *signal_list_mapping* is the list that maps the logical control signals to the physical ones. Unlike HIDE6k where the logical control signals could be assigned only to global routing resources in the FPGA chip, HIDE4k offers the possibility of driving logical signals by the outputs from on-chip control generator blocks. These can be even generated dynamically in HIDE4k notation. The structure of the supplied *signal_list_mapping* is:

signal_list_mapping = [..., (Glob_resources, Control_generator,
Controls_logical_names, X, Y), ...]

where:

- ***Control_generator*** is the block that generates the physical control signal(s) which are assigned to the logical controls ***Controls_logical_names***. This can be either a pin name or a logic block: simple or compound (i.e. generated by HIDE4k). The block can be placed relative to the driven block if desired by giving its relative 'X' and 'Y' co-ordinates.

- ***Control_logical_names*** is a list of lists in which each sub-list contains the logical control names associated with a particular port (physical signal) of ***Control_generator***. If only one port is used to drive all logical controls, then ***Control_logical_names*** reduces to a simple list.

- ***Glob_resources*** is a list containing optional global buffers used to drive the physical control signals (e.g. ***BUFGP***, ***BUFGS***). If no global buffer is used to drive the physical control signals, then ***Glob_resources*** is left unbound ('_').

5.2.4 Dynamic line buffers

As presented in section 3.2.1, image line buffers are used in order to supply each image pixel only once to the FPGA. A line buffer is a soft block, as its parameters (number of pixels in an image column -or row-, and its pixel wordlength) and its input/output ports positions, are all variables. The generation of this block should hence be dynamic. HIDE4k provides the following constructor for the generation of a set of 'M' adjacent dynamic line buffers, all having the same size:

lb(Type, M, Size, Width_or_Height)

Type: the line buffers' position relative to the adjacent block- either *top*, *bottom*, *right*, or *left*.

M: The number of adjacent line buffers.

Size: Size of each individual line buffer.

Width_or_Height: width or height of the rectangular area enclosing the line buffers. The width (or hight) of each individual line buffer is *(Width_or_Height/M)*. The other variable value will be automatically determined by the system. If the user leaves this variable unbound, the system would take the width of the adjacent block (for *top* or *bottom* buffers' positions) as the actual width of the line buffer; it would, however, take the height of the adjacent block for *right* or *left* line buffers' positions.

This constructor has a similar format to HIDE6k's one. The internal implementation is, however, substantially different. Indeed, while HIDE6k used 1-bit registers as a basic building block, the XC4000-based implementation is based on the CLB's two 16x1 synchronous RAMs. As explained in section 3.3.1, a shift register is implemented on XC4000 using on-chip distributed synchronous RAMs and a small address counter. We have also mentioned that in order to reduce the address bus delay, multiple counters should be used to address smaller parts of the distributed RAMs. Each one of these counters consumes 2 CLBs. Consider the case of just one line buffer (M=1) and let us focus on the case where the line buffer is placed on the top of a logic block. Other cases will be generated by simple transformation as shown in Figure 5.7.

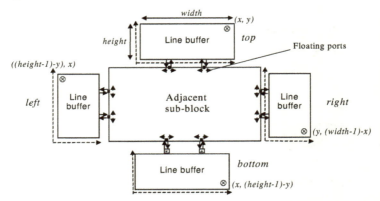

Figure 5.7 Transforming a line buffer location from *top* to other relative positions

The algorithm for building the line buffer on the top of a block is as follows:

- The input and output ports of the line buffer are floating ports. They have the same position as the corresponding adjacent block I/O ports.
- The line buffer delays start from the input port and ends at the output port.
- Multiple LFSR counters are used to address separate parts of the distributed synchronous RAMs. The counters placement heuristic is to allocate an LFSR counter for each two (or three) rows of RAMs. This should make the generated circuits speed less dependent on the image size. The LFSR's are placed vertically (for *top* and *bottom* cases), each consuming 2 CLBs, and placed on either sides of the core of the line buffer.
- The line buffer size is first computed in bits by multiplying the image height (or width according to the scan direction) by the pixel wordlength. The result is divided by 16 in order to get the number of RAM16x1 needed to hold the image

height (or width). The rest of this division (less than 16) is implemented using some CLBs flip-flops and hence does not consume extra CLBs.

- Having determined the number of RAM16x1 (and hence the number of CLBs), the missing dimension (height or width) can then be deduced. It is first approximated by dividing the total number of CLBs by the line buffer width minus one (or height minus one). Two cases are to be distinguished: a) the height is *even*, in which case the buffer chain is first driven from the start point to the *left* direction, b) the height is *odd*, in which case the buffer chain is first driven from the start point to the *right* direction (see Figure 5.8). The maximum size of the resulting line buffer is then computed (for height either *odd* or *even*). If the latter is greater than the required buffer size, then this choice is retained. Otherwise, the height is incremented.

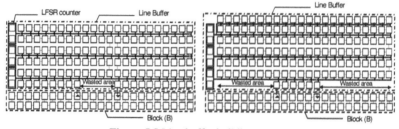

Figure 5.8 Line buffer building process

Figure 5.9 gives an example of HIDE4k code for generating a line buffer in *top* position (the pixel wordlength is 16).

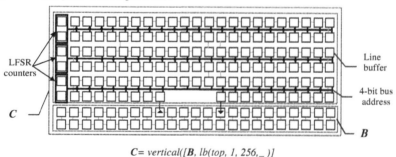

$$C= vertical([\boldsymbol{B}, \, lb(top, \, 1, \, 256,\_\,)]$$

Figure 5.9 Example of dynamic line buffer generation

5.2.5 Placement

During block composition (horizontal or vertical), HIDE4k adds automatically placement information to the sub-blocks in the generated netlist. In such way, the whole circuit can be placed automatically without any user intervention.

If the user does not want to rely on the automatic placement of a particular compound block, he or she can switch the latter off by **undo_auto_placement** constructor:

$$C = undo\_auto\_placement(B)$$

This will remove any placement directive within the block hierarchy. The placement of this block will then be left to the automatic placer.

Note that the FPGA chip origin is assumed to be at the top left hand corner by Xilinx XC4000 PAR tools. A CLB location is given by a row number and a column one. Row and column numbers increase from top to bottom and from left to right respectively (see Figure 5.10).

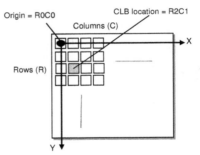

Figure 5.10 CLB co-ordinates on XC4000

5.3 Examples

In the following, we will present two simple HIDE4k code examples in order to demonstrate some of its capabilities.

Example 5.1

A bit parallel adder is constructed in XC4000 using dedicated fast carry logic. An N-bit parallel adder is composed of at least two sections: A main section of 1-bit or 2-bit adder slices each consuming one CLB, and a carry initialisation section at the start of the carry chain. Optionally, the adder may have a third section at the most significant end in order to create a carry output or detect overflow [XAP13]. An N-bit adder is given by:

- N even:

Adder = vertical([init_0, v_seq(N//2, add_2), add_carry_out])

- N odd:

Adder = vertical([init_0, v_seq((N-1)//2, add_2),add_1, add_carry_out])

where **init_0** is a block which forces the initial carry to zero, **add_1** and **add_2** are 1-bit and 2-bit adder slices respectively, with carry-in and carry-out and **add_carry_out** is a block that outputs the carry-out of the whole addition.

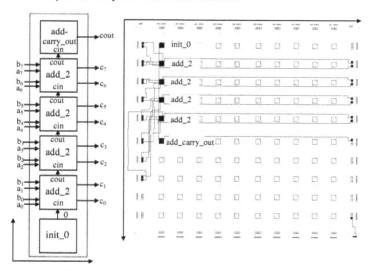

Figure 5.11 8-bit parallel adder on XC4003E (N=8).

Example 5.2

This example shows the use of *lb* constructor in order to implement large shift registers (buffers). It also shows the use of *offset* constructor. The buffer is placed in the *right* position as shown in Figure 5.12.

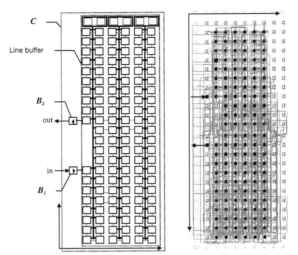

$C= horizontal([offset (vertical([B_1, offset(B_2, 0, 4)]), 0, 7), lb(right, 1, 256, 23)])$

Figure 5.12 Dynamic line buffer generation

5.4 Implementation of HIDE4k environment

In the previous sections, HIDE4k concepts and notation were introduced. In this section, we will present the HIDE4k environment and its implementation. Figure 5.13 presents a block outline of the HIDE4k environment.

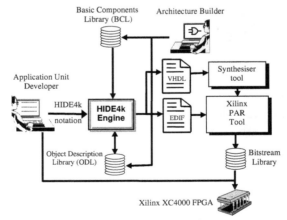

Figure 5.13 Overall HIDE4k environment

The _application unit developer_ describes his/her IP architecture in HIDE4k notation. The basic components in the library are first built by the _architecture builder_ and stored in a _Basic Component Library_ (BCL) in EDIF and/or VHDL formats. Note that HIDE6k system does not generate VHDL (see Figure 2.15).

In order to assemble the basic building blocks, HIDE4k engine needs a short description of each block properties (e.g. width, height, I/O ports etc.) which has the following format:

_is_basic_block(name, width, height, signals_list , ports_list)_

This header description is stored in an _Object Description Library_ (ODL). The following is an example of such description for **_multa0_** sub-block (see section 3.3.5).

---

is_basic_block(multa0,1, 1, [clk, clr] ,[[(inp,in,0,0), (inm,in,0,0)],[(outp,out,0,0), (outm,out,0,0)],[],[],[],[],[]])

The HIDE4k engine generates the final circuit architecture in two possible formats:

EDIF format: which is a low level (FPGA target dependent) netlist describing the circuit assembled from low level basic building blocks. These were optimised, for area and speed, for a particular FPGA target architecture (XC4000 in our case). Schematic design entry, which contains all the placement information, has been used for the design of the basic components. These schematic descriptions were then converted into EDIF netlist. Xilinx Foundation™ [Fnd98] software has been used for that purpose. The basic building blocks were optimised in order to fit together with as little wastage area as possible (_the design to fit approach_).

VHDL: The basic building blocks are described using VHDL at RTL level (see section 1.2.1.2). The following is an example VHDL description of 'binary_to_sdnr' sub-block (see section 3.3.2).

```
entity bin_to_sdnr is                                    process(clk,clr)
    port(   clk, clr   : IN std_logic;                   begin
            INB        : IN std_logic;                       if(clr='1') then
            Is_MSD_in  : IN std_logic;                          Outplus <='0';
            Is_MSD_out : OUT std_logic;                         Outmin <='0';
            Outplus    : OUT std_logic;                      else
            Outmin     : OUT std_logic);                        if(clk='1' and (not clk'stable)) then
    end bin_to_sdnr;                                               Outplus <=temp1;
                                                                  Outmin <=temp2;
    architecture arch_bin_to_sdnr of bin_to_sdnr is           end if;
    signal temp1, temp2 : std_logic;                         end if;
    begin                                                end process;
        temp1 <= ( INB and (not Is_MSD_in));
        temp2 <= ( INB and Is_MSD_in);                   end arch_bin_to_sdnr;
        Is_MSD_out <= Is_MSD_in;
```

The resulting circuit description contains just the connectivity between the sub-blocks; no placement or other FPGA technology dependent information is included. It is hence portable across different FPGA platforms. Synopsys FPGA Express™ 2.0 [Syn99] has been used to synthesise the resulting VHDL code. This is a tool within Foundation integrated environment.

Note that it is also possible to generate structural VHDL with FPGA target specific optimisations and placement directives. However, the resulting code would ultimately be synthesised into EDIF by a synthesiser tool; hence there is no need for it since we can generate EDIF directly from HIDE4k. The main reason for us to generate VHDL from basic building blocks described at RTL level, however, is that the basic blocks are more portable (across different FPGA architectures) and can be designed much more quickly and easily since no mapping or placement are involved. This also addresses the issue of portability raised in HIDE6k (see section 2.3.3.3). The following will describe the HIDE4k engine in more detail.

5.4.1 The HIDE4k engine

As in HIDE6k, the HIDE4k engine has been written in Prolog [CM94]. It has retained most of HIDE6k structure. As shown in Figure 5.14, HIDE4k engine takes a circuit description written in HIDE4k notation and produces an EDIF or VHDL configuration file.

First, the HIDE4k circuit description is transformed into a *configuration data structure* (CDS) containing the hierarchy of the circuit with all the connectivity and placement information. Then, the CDS is used to generate a configuration file (EDIF or VHDL). These two processes are presented in more details in the following two sections.

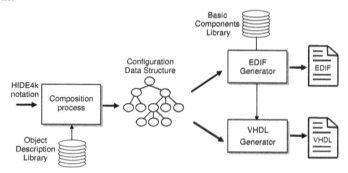

Figure 5.14 The HIDE4k engine structure

5.4.2 The Composition Process

This process consists in going through the input HIDE4k notation in order to generate a configuration data structure representing the detailed hierarchy of the circuit in terms of the basic building components. This is based mainly on the *horizontal/vertical composition process.* Other sub-processes, needed during the processing of the input HIDE4k notation, include the dynamic line buffer sub-process, offsetting sub-process, control signals management sub-process, altering ports sub-process (see section 2.3.3.1) and the notation expansion sub-process. The latter consists in expanding concise high level descriptions such as parameterised block sequence (see *p_b_seq* in section 5.2.1 above) and parameterised block interconnection (see *p_seq* in section 5.2.2 above). Besides the circuit hierarchy, the configuration data structure should also contain the sub-block interconnection. These are performed by the *port matching and manipulation* sub-process.

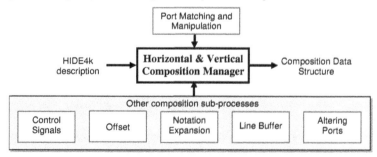

Figure 5.15 The composition sub-processes

Port Matching and Manipulation Sub-Process

This sub-process consists in performing the desired connectivity between adjacent sub-block ports. It can be summarised in the following points:

- Perform the actual port matching between adjacent sub-block ports, from a network connection description.

- Determine the outer ports of a block (see *outer_ports* and *open_ports* in section 5.2.2 above).

- Altering ports position and manipulating hinged ports. Both these techniques were inherited from HIDE6k (see section 2.3.3.1).

- Ports naming.

The last point is extremely important to avoid the duplication of port names within a compound block. The solution to that problem, also inherited from HIDE6k, is based on assigning new sequential numbers for all ports in the following order of port sub-lists: N, S, E, W, NE, NW, SE and SW (see Figure 5.16). As a result, a port is always characterised by an old name (its name in the lower level of hierarchy) and a new name (its name in the actual level of hierarchy).

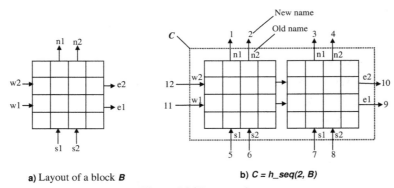

a) Layout of a block **B**   b) C = h_seq(2, B)

Figure 5.16 Ports naming

5.4.2.1 Configuration Data Structure

As explained above, the composition process of HIDE4k engine generates a Configuration Data Structure (CDS) that holds the details of the FPGA configuration. This data structure is a *tree* structure whose *root* represents the complete circuit configuration and whose *terminal nodes* represent the basic building blocks.

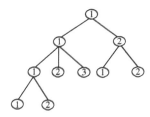

Figure 5.17 Configuration Data Structure tree model

Each HIDE4k constructor (e.g. *horizontal*, *vertical*) generates a new node in the circuit hierarchy. Each intermediate node represents the structure of a sub-block of the whole circuit and holds all its characteristics (block name, width, height, placement, intermediate interconnection, outer ports etc.). The CDS is held in a Prolog data object (similar to HIDE6k's one). The structure of a CDS node B_i representing a sub-block B has the following formats:

- If the CDS node B_i has been generated by:

    horizontal([..., Child_block, ...]) **or** *vertical([..., Child_block, ...])*, then:

    B_i = **cds_node**(Label, Locx, Locy, Width, Height, Child_blocks, Controls, Links, Ports, Rloc_flag)

- If the CDS node B_i has been generated by:

    h_seq(Rep_no, Child_block) **or** *v_seq(Rep_no, Child_block)* then:

    B_i = **cds_node**(Label, Rep_no, Locx, Locy, Width, Height, Child_block, Child_Locs,

    Controls, Links, Ports, Rloc_flag)

- If the CDS node B_i represents a basic building block **B**, then:

    B_i = **cds_node**(Label, B, Locx, Locy, Rloc_flag)

Label is the sub-block's label in the CDS tree (see Figure 5.17).

Locx and *Locy* are the X and Y co-ordinates (Column and row number respectively) of the block B_i relative to its parent block origin.

Width and *Height* define the size of the sub-block B_i.

Child_blocks is a list which contains the structure of B_i own sub-blocks. Each sub-block structure description has one of the above descriptions.

Controls is a list of control signals (e.g. clocks) for the block B_i.

Links is a list which holds the internal links between the sub-blocks of the block B_i.

Ports is a list of outer ports of the block B_i.

Child_locs is a list of co-ordinates of the child blocks in a replicated block composition. For a block B replicated *rep_no* times, ***Child_locs*** object holds the placement position of each copy of B and has the following structure:

> Child_locs = **Child_locs**([**copy_loc**(label, locx, locy), **copy_loc**(...), ...])

Rloc_flag is a flag which can take two values:

- ***auto_placement***: In this case, the automatic placement will be kept.

- ***undo_auto_placement***: the automatic placement is ignored.

The following will explain some of the above objects in more details.

- **Controls**

The ***Controls*** object holds information about a block's controls signals. In order to avoid the duplication of controls names when combining sub-blocks, each control signal is given two names: an internal name which corresponds to its name in the lower level of hierarchy and an external name in the actual level of hierarchy (see section 5.2.3 above). The ***Controls*** object contains two sub-objects:

- *external_signals_view* object: which assigns each external signal name to its corresponding internal signal(s) name(s). Each assignment is represented by *assign_signal* object.

- *internal_signals_view* object: which associates each internal signal name with its corresponding sub-block's label. Each association is represented by *reference_signal* object.

The control object structure is as follows:

> Controls = **controls**(
>   *external_signals_view*([...,***assign_signal***(external_name, internal_name),...],
>   *internal_signals_view*([....,***reference_signal***(sub_block_label, internal_name), ...]
>   )

- **Ports List**

A list of a block's ports, for all sides (i.e. N, S, E, W, NE, NW, SE and SW), is represented by ***port_list*** object which is composed of 8 sub-lists corresponding to the eight sides of the block. Each port in these sub-lists is represented by a ***port*** object, which holds all its properties (i.e. label of port's block, port's internal name, port's external name, type (in or out) and co-ordinates positions). The following structure represents the format of a Ports list:

```
Ports = port_list(
          [[ .., port(label, internal_port_name, external_port_name, type, locx, locy), ... ],
          [S sub-list], [E sub-list], [W sub-list], [NE sub-list], [NW sub-list],
          [SE sub-list], [SW sub-list] ])
```

Note that, for the top-block of the hierarchy (i.e. the one representing the whole circuit), the outer ports are the FPGA chip pins. The external port name is hence replaced by a pin identifier (e.g. 'P12').

- **Links List**

The list of internal interconnection is represented by a **link_list** object. Each item of this list (represented by **link** object) describes *one* relation (i.e. link) between corresponding ports. This link could be from one input/output port to one output/input port, from one output port to many input ports or from many input ports to one output port. A **link** object holds a list of ports that makes up this particular link. Each port is represented by **port** object, which holds all the ports' properties (i.e. port's label, port's name (only the internal port name is relevant here), type, position). The following structure represents the format of a link list:

```
Links = link_list([
          .........., link([...., port(label, port_name, _, type, locx, locy), ....]), link([ ..........
                   ])
```

A complete configuration data structure is given in Appendix I, for the bit parallel adder given in Figure 5.11.

5.4.3 Netlist Generator

As mentioned above, HIDE4k allows for the generation of two types of netlist: EDIF and VHDL (RTL level). The following will describe how both EDIF and VHDL are generated from the configuration data structure.

5.4.3.1 EDIF generator

EDIF (Electronic Data Interchange Format) is a standard format for the interchange of electronic design information [Cra84]. It is generated by virtually all FPGA vendors' tools as a netlist containing the FPGA configuration information (including placement information optionally). The resulting EDIF file needs, however, to be converted into an FPGA configuration bitstream using a Placement And Routing (PAR) tool.

By generating FPGA configurations in EDIF format, the design flow cycle is reduced compared with generating VHDL. The latter would need an extra synthesiser tool to convert VHDL first into EDIF.

As presented in Figure 5.18, an EDIF description is expressed in the form of a hierarchy. The top level of an EDIF file contains all the information required for a design and is represented by one cell. This top-level cell is made up from more basic cells which must be defined before their use so that the define-before-use rule is not broken. An EDIF file contains one or more libraries which contain information about technologies and cells.

A cell definition may be segmented into one or more views. These views classify the types of information that are needed to fully describe a cell, and include NETLIST view for defining cells connectivity, SCHEMATIC view for both connectivity and associated diagrammatic information and LOGICMODEL for describing the logic simulation model of a cell. In our case, cell's view is NETLIST. A cell's '_interface_' defines its outer ports. A cell's '_contents_' section consists of a detailed implementation of a view of a cell. This section contains a list of _instances_ i.e. the child cells (sub-blocks) making up the cell, and nets i.e. the intermediate links between these child cells in addition to the interface ports.

Note that EDIF has different versions and levels (0,1 and 2). We generate EDIF version 2.0.0 in level 0. This is the standard format accepted by FPGA vendors' tools.

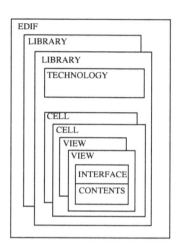

```
(edif edif_name  // name of edif file for external use
  (edifVersion edif_version)
  (edifLevel edif_level)
  (keywordMap (keywordLevel keyword_level)
  ........
  (library library_name // library description
    (edifLevel edif_level)
    (technology  technology_info )
         .........    // A cell description
    (cell cell_name
      (cellType cell_type)
      (viewRef view_name (ViewType view_type)
      (interface   // List of outer ports
          (port port_name (direction dir_type))
          (port port_name (direction dir_type))

      )
      (contents
          .....          // list of sub-blocks instances)
          (instance inst_name (property  property)
              (viewRef view_name (cellRef cell_name)))
              .....       // list of intermediate links
          (net net_name (joined
              (portRef port_name (instanceRef inst_name))
              (portRef port_name (instanceRef inst_name))
          ))
          ....   // list of interface links
          (net net_name (joined
              (portRef port_name)
              (portRef port_name (instanceRef inst_name))
          ))
      )
  )
  .....
)
  .....

(design design_name
   (cellRef cell_name (LibraryRef Library_name) )
)
```

Figure 5.18 EDIF file structure

EDIF Generation Process

The EDIF generator parses the configuration data structure (CDS) described in the previous section. It goes through the hierarchy tree until it reaches the terminal nodes which represents the basic building blocks. These basic block configurations are stored in EDIF format in the BCL library. They are first included, by copying, into the generated EDIF file before they are wrapped in a new EDIF cell in order to show where the basic block is located in the hierarchical EDIF structure. The generator does a depth first traversal of the tree in order to assemble higher level blocks from lower level blocks.

Cell naming

A unique cell name is obtained for each node (representing a block) in the CDS tree by concatenating the labels from the root node to the actual node as follows (see Figure 5.19):

$BLK\_l_1l_2...l_n$ where l_i (i=1,2,..., n) are nodes' labels.

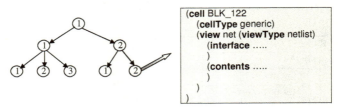

Figure 5.19 EDIF cell naming

Interface ports

A cell's interface ports represent the outer ports of the corresponding block. They are obtained from *port_ list* object in the CDS (see section 5.4.2.1). The property *external_name* of each *port* in *port_list* represents the interface port's name. The latter can either be a string (in the case of basic block) or a number x in which case the associated port name in EDIF will be *Port_x*.

```
Port_list([[],[], [port(3,old1,1, in,0, 8), port(3,old2,2, in,1, 8), port(3,old3,3,out,2,8)],[],[],[],[],[]])
```

```
(interface
        (port Port_1  (direction input))
        (port Port_2  (direction input))
        (port Port_3  (direction output))
)
```

Figure 5.20 Cell's ports naming

Contents part – Instances

This section of a cell description gives a list of all the sub-cells' instances. Here again, each instance name is generated by concatenating the labels from the root node to the corresponding instance node, and is given as follows:

$inst\_l_1l_2...l_n$ where l_i (i = 1,2,..., n) are nodes' labels.

Each instance has its own placement represented by the property RLOC (Relative LOCation) and is obtained from *locx* and *locy* properties of the corresponding CDS node. The following description shows three instances of a block B generated by $v\_seq(3, B)$:

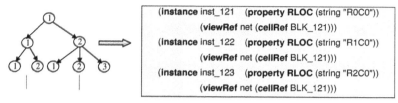

(**instance** inst_121   (**property RLOC** (string "R0C0"))
        (**viewRef** net (**cellRef** BLK_121)))
(**instance** inst_122   (**property RLOC** (string "R1C0"))
        (**viewRef** net (**cellRef** BLK_121)))
(**instance** inst_123   (**property RLOC** (string "R2C0"))
        (**viewRef** net (**cellRef** BLK_121)))

Figure 5.21 Cell's instances naming

Contents part – nets

This part of a cell description gives the connectivity of the sub-cells' ports both internally (sub-cells interconnection) and externally (connection to outer ports). The net name is generated by concatenating the labels from the root node to the corresponding instance node plus an increment index:

$$net\_l_1l_2...l_n\_j$$

where l_i (i=1,2,…, n) are nodes' labels and j is an increment index.

Interface ports are assigned to the corresponding sub-blocks ports using a net which has the same name as the interface port itself (i.e. Port_x).

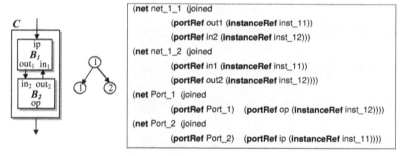

(**net** net_1_1 (joined
                (**portRef** out1 (**instanceRef** inst_11))
                (**portRef** in2 (**instanceRef** inst_12)))
(**net** net_1_2 (joined
                (**portRef** in1 (**instanceRef** inst_11))
                (**portRef** out2 (**instanceRef** inst_12))))
(**net** Port_1 (joined
                (**portRef** Port_1)   (**portRef** op (**instanceRef** inst_12))))
(**net** Port_2 (joined
                (**portRef** Port_2)   (**portRef** ip (**instanceRef** inst_11))))

Figure 5.22 Cell's nets naming

5.4.3.2 VHDL generator

In addition to generating FPGA configurations in EDIF format, HIDE4k can generate FPGA configurations in VHDL at RTL level. The VHDL generated is independent of the target FPGA architecture. The generator merely links the sub-blocks with no FPGA dependent information (e.g. placement). The task of mapping the VHDL code into a particular FPGA architecture is left to the synthesiser.

Note that generating VHDL does not use the placement information contained in the previously described CDS, and thus a simpler data structure could have been used. However, instead of generating a specific CDS for VHDL, the same CDS is being used to generate either EDIF or VHDL.

The structure of VHDL has been already presented in section 1.2.1.2. The following will present the VHDL generation process.

VHDL Generation Process

As in EDIF generation, the VHDL generator does a depth first traversal of the configuration data structure (CDS). Since no placement information is included in the generated VHDL file, the basic building blocks need not to be copied first, then wrapped by a new design entity. Rather, each basic building block's VHDL description is stored in two separate files: one holding its entity declaration part and another holds its architecture. Figure 5.23 shows how a basic block (a full adder) is included in the generated VHDL code. The entity and architecture naming scheme is similar to the one used for EDIF cell naming. Note that if a basic building block is used more than once, there is no need for replicating its architecture part after the first instance. Instead, the first instance will be declared as a component in the architecture body of each subsequent instance.

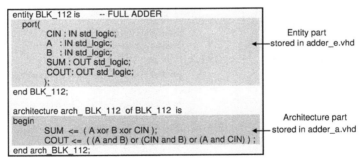

Figure 5.23 Basic design entity

Before describing the architecture of a compound block, its sub-blocks are first declared in the architecture body as components (see Figure 5.24). All interface ports of a component should be explicitly declared. This latter information is taken from *Port_list* of each child block. After including all component declarations, temporary signals necessary for child blocks interconnection should be declared. The number of these temporary signals is equal to the number of child blocks interlinks (i.e. link-list length). A unique temporary signal name for a link between two ports named *Pname1* and *Pname2,* of two blocks whose labels on the CDS are *Blk1* and *Blk2* respectively, is obtained as follows:

temp_Blk1_Blk2_Pname1_ Pname2

In the activity statement part of the architecture body, instances of the previously declared components are created. This is equivalent to instances declared in the content part of a cell in EDIF. The interface ports of these instances will be mapped to either temporary signals (these ports are member of *link_list* object in the CDS node) or to outer ports (these ports are member of *port_list* object in the CDS node). If neither of the previous two cases is true, the corresponding ports will be left *open.* Figure 5.24 gives an example of a VHDL compound block description.

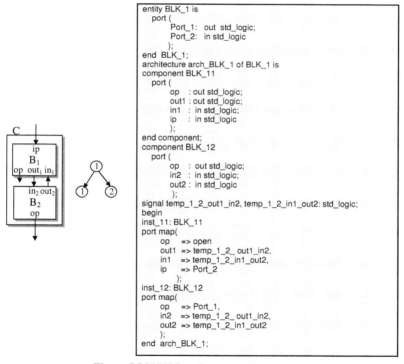

Figure 5.24 VHDL code generated by HIDE4k

5.6 Summary

In this chapter, we have presented a hardware description environment targeting Xilinx XC4000 FPGAs, called HIDE4k. This environment allows for simple and very concise descriptions of *parameterised* and *scaleable* architectures such as those encountered in Image Processing. It is an adaptation of a previous environment (HIDE6k) which was designed specifically for the XC6000 series. The HIDE6k implementation by Alotaibi has been completely reworked and extended to give our HIDE4k implementation. The main features of HIDE4k, which were not existent in HIDE6k, are:

- Increased facilities for block interconnection
- A more flexible control management scheme
- A more flexible placement scheme
- HIDE4k generates FPGA configurations in VHDL format as well as EDIF. An interesting discussion of the advantages and disadvantages of the generation of each netlist type will be presented in the next chapter.

In addition, the new environment has been used much more extensively than the HIDE6k and has ultimately been tested on a real working (as it will be seen later in this book). In order to achieve that, practical considerations (e.g. speed and multiple clock domain) have been addressed during the design of HIDE4k. These considerations were not carefully addressed in HIDE6k since the system was not brought to the point where it is actually used to target a real FPGA based system.

In the next chapter, we will demonstrate how HIDE4k is used to describe and generate the FPGA architectures corresponding to the Image Algebra neighbourhood operations designs presented in chapter 3.

Chapter **6**

HIDE4k descriptions of Image Algebra neighbourhood operations

Chapter 6

HIDE4k descriptions of Image Algebra neighbourhood operations

In the previous chapter, a hardware description environment (HIDE4k) was introduced. Simple examples were given to illustrate the capabilities of HIDE4k in describing hardware architectures. In this chapter, we will show how full architectures of the Image Algebra (IA) operators presented in chapter 3 can be described using HIDE4k. In order to achieve that, a library of arithmetic components is provided. Using HIDE4k system, these components are assembled by the application unit developer to generate full architectures (e.g. IA operations). At the top level, the application developer uses those full architectures to target the FPGA in an application oriented environment.

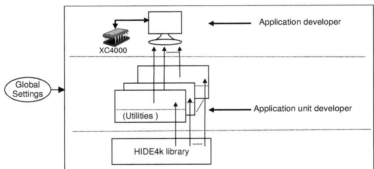

Figure 6.1 Design environment

What the rest of this chapter will present will be:

- The 'core' HIDE4k library structure.
- The development of full HIDE4k descriptions for IA neighbourhood operations.
- A discussion on EDIF and VHDL generation approaches
- The potential use of HIDE4k for core generation

6.1 Layered model of the HIDE4k library

The HIDE4k library contains a range of components with different levels of abstractions (e.g. from a 1-bit section of a multiplier to a full parameterised multiplier unit). To clarify the user's view of this library, we will organise the library with a set of layers, as illustrated in Figure 6.2.

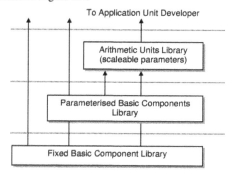

Figure 6.2 A layered model of the HIDE4k library

6.1.1 Fixed basic components layer

At the bottom level, fixed (non-parameterised) basic hardware components (e.g. adder, multiplier parts) are designed by the architecture builder. These could be described either in schematics and then converted into EDIF, or in VHDL at RTL level. They are stored in the Basic Components Library. As mentioned in section 5.4, the properties of these components should also be provided and stored in the Object Description Library (ODL). For instance, an online accumulator component (see Figure 3.12) is described as:

```
is_basic_block(online_accum,1, 3, [clk, clr] ,[[ (xp,in,0,2),(xm,in,0,2)],[ ],
      [(sm,out,0,0),(sp,out,0,0)],[(ym,in,0,0),(yp,in,0,0)],[ ],[ ],[ ],[ ]])
```

6.1.2 Parameterised basic components Layer

This layer contains generalised block descriptions for more convenient access to the bottom layer. Those descriptions include:

• **Multiplier sections**

As explained in chapter 3, an online multiplier can be built from 4 basic sections, in which each section can have two implementations- one for each coefficient bit value (0 or 1). The necessary basic blocks are: multA0, multA1, multB0, multB1, multC0, multC1, multD0 and multD1. A generalised block (B) is defined by the following rule:

> **is_mult_section(Section_type, Bit_value, B)**

where **Section_type** is a, b, c or d and **Bit_value** is 0 or 1.

For example: **is_mult_section**(c, 1, Mult_section) will result in Mult_section = multC1.

The role of the parameterised basic components builder is to implement such rules.

- **Delay units**

Delay units are often used in order to synchronise the supply of data. We provide a library of single input delays and dual input delays.

- **Single input delays**

A block (B) to delay a signal by 'N' clock cycles (where 0≤N≤16) is defined by the following rule:

> **is_single_delay(N, B)**

An LFSR counter is used to address a 16x1 synchronous RAM. For 0<N≤4, however, simple flip-flops are used instead. For N=0, the unit is a simple *one-2-one* network connection.

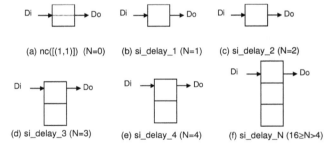

Figure 6.3 Single input delay units

- **Dual input delays**

These are used to delay a Radix-2 SDNR input In = (In$^+$, In$^-$) as shown in Figure 6.4. A block (B) to delay an SDNR signal by 'N' clock cycles (where 0≤N≤16) is defined by the following rule:

> **is_dual_delay(N, B)**

The implementation of this will select, depending on the value of 'N', one of three different implementations:

- 2<N≤16: Two 16x1 synchronous RAMs are used. These are addressed by the same LFSR counter.

- 0<N≤2, simple flip-flops are used instead.

- N=0, the unit is a simple *one-2-one* network connection.

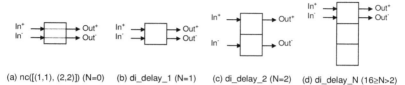

(a) nc([(1,1), (2,2)]) (N=0)   (b) di_delay_1 (N=1)   (c) di_delay_2 (N=2)   (d) di_delay_N (16≥N>2)

Figure 6.4 Dual input delay units

6.1.3 Arithmetic units layer

This layer contains parameterised descriptions of a range of full arithmetic units. They include:

- **Online multiplication by a K-bit coefficient**

A K-bit serial-parallel, vertically aligned, online multiplier block (B) is obtained by invoking the following rule:

> **is_online_multiplier(Coeff_value, K, B)**

Although we will not be presenting the implementation of all the components in this section, we present one here for illustration. The following gives the implementation of this vertically aligned online multiplier block:

```
is_online_multiplier(Coeff_value, K, B):-
integer_to_binary(Coeff_value, K, Binary_list), % convert 'Coeff_value' into
% its binary equivalent (in 2's complement), on K bits.
is_online_multiplier_description(Binary_list, B).

is_online_multiplier_description([Head|Tail], vertical([MultD|Mult_list])):-
is_mult_section(d, Head, MultD), % gets MultD name
is_online_multiplier_description_x(Tail, Mult_list).

is_online_multiplier_description_x([B_bin, A_bin], [MultB, MultA]):-
is_mult_section(b, B_bin , MultB),
is_mult_section(a, A_bin, MultA).
is_online_multiplier_description_x([Head|Tail], [MultC|MultC_tail]):-
is_mult_section(c, C_bin , MultC),
is_online_multiplier_description_x(Tail, MultC_tail).
```

For instance, invoking **is_online_multiplier**(8, Mult8) will result in:

Mult8 = vertical([multD0, multC1, multC0, multB0, multA0])

- **Special version of online multiplication by a K-bit coefficient**

In Multiplicative Maximum/Minimum neighbourhood operation, we have seen that the local multiplication unit is laid out in a special layout (snake-like shape) as shown in Figure 3.24. The following special rule is provided for generating such units:

> **is_special_online_multiplier(Coeff, K, W, B)**

where **W** is the width of the unit (in CLBs) as illustrated in Figure 6.5.

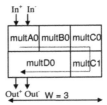

Figure 6.5 Special online multiplier constructor:
is_special_online_multiplier(8, 5, 3, Mult_Block)

- **Online Local Adder Unit**

This unit adds its SDNR input to a given coefficient using a specified wordlength. The unit stores its coefficient into a CLB RAM16x1 addressed by a counter (as explained in section 3.3.6). An online local adder unit is obtained by invoking the following rule:

> **is_online_local_adder(Coeff_value, Wordlength, B)**

- **Online buffer unit**

This unit synchronises the supply of successive pixels within a Processing Element array as described in section 3.3.3. A buffer unit (B) used for online arithmetic based architectures is obtained by invoking the following rule:

> **is_online_buffer_unit(Global_op, B)**

where **Global_op** is the global operation identifier i.e. *accum*, *maximum* or *minimum*.

- **Parallel to serial conversion unit**

This unit is used to convert a W_{in}-bit parallel 2's complement input word into W_{proc} bit serial MSBF 2'complement output. In addition, the unit outputs the necessary initial control signals for the core neighbourhood operation unit as seen in section 3.7.

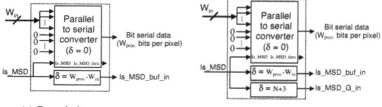

(a) Convolution case   (b) Multiplicative Maximum/Minimum case

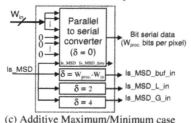

(c) Additive Maximum/Minimum case

Figure 6.6 Parallel to serial unit

A W-in bit parallel to serial converter (B) is constructed by:

> **is_parallel_2_serial_converter(W-in, B)**

Given a local and a global operation, an input wordlength (W-in), a processing wordlength (Wproc) and the maximum coefficient wordlength within the neighbourhood operation window (N), a full parallel to serial unit (B) is constructed by:

> **is_parallel_2_serial_unit(Local_Op, Global_Op, W-in, Wproc, N, B)**

- **Signed Digit to 2's complement unit**

As described in section 3.3.9, this unit converts a Radix-2 digit serial SDNR input into a bit parallel 2's complement number. The unit is based on the four basic components shown in Figure 6.7.

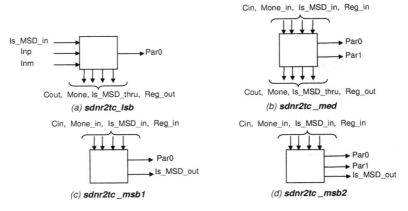

Figure 6.7 SDNR to 2's complement converter components

The HIDE4k constructor of a W-bit unit is given by:

- For W even:

    Sdnr2tc = vertical([sdnr2tc_msb1, v_seq((W-2)//2,sdnr2tc_med),sdnr2tc_lsb])

- For W odd:

    Sdnr2tc = vertical([sdnr2tc_msb2, v_seq((W-3)//2,sdnr2tc_med),sdnr2tc_lsb])

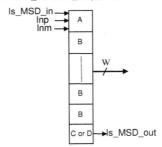

Figure 6.8 Layout of W-bit SDNR to 2's complement converter.

This can be expressed by the following Prolog rule:

```
is_sdnr2tcp(W, Sdnr2tcp):-
(
W // 2 =:= 0, % W even
Sdnr2tcp = vertical([sdnr2tc_msb1, v_seq((W-2)//2,sdnr2tc_med),sdnr2tc_lsb])
; % ELSE
Sdnr2tcp = vertical([sdnr2tc_msb2, v_seq((W-3)//2,sdnr2tc_med),sdnr2tc_lsb])
)
```

6.2 Development of the application unit for image processing

In this section, we will demonstrate how a library of application-specific architectures can be built using the HIDE4k library of arithmetic units. We will focus on the description of a generic PxQ convolution operation. The remaining IA neighbourhood operation descriptions (Additive-Maximum/Minimum and Multiplicative Maximum/Minimum) will be deduced from this. For each online arithmetic based IA operation, we will derive a suitable instance of the constructor predicate:

> **is_online_IA_nop(Local_Op, Global_Op, Window, Buffer_size, Input_wordlength, Processing_Wordlength, Latency, B)**

However, we will first start by describing a number of reusable utilities, which it is convenient to describe first.

6.2.1 Utilities library

A library of utilities is offered to the IP application unit developer. This includes:

- **Maximum coefficients wordlength**

A rule is provided for computing the maximum coefficient wordlength within a window, and is given by:

> **is_maximum_coeff _wordlength(Window, Max_Coeff_wordlength)**

where **Window** is a list of lists containing the coefficient values. For instance, invoking:

> **is_maximum_coeff_ wordlength([[~,-1,~],[-1,4,-1],[~,-1,~]], Max_Coeff_ wordlength).**

will result in **Max_Coeff_ wordlength** = 4 (= $word\_length\_of(4) = 0100_2$).

- **Window coefficient rearrangement**

The direction of scan of the input image will affect the order in which the window coefficients are matched to the PEs array. A rule is provided for rearranging the original elements accordingly, and is given by:

> **is_rearranged_window(Original_window, Rearranged_window)**

For instance, if **Original_window** = [[-1, 0,1], [-2, 0, 2], [-1, 0, 1]] and if the input image is scanned vertically, then invoking the above rule will result in:

> **Rearranged_window** = [[1, 2, 1], [0, 0, 0], [-1, -2, -1]].

- **Processing wordlength**

A rule is provided for computing the minimum necessary wordlength for a particular neighbourhood operation. It is given by:

> **is_online_processing_wordlength(Local_Op, Global_Op, Window,**
> **Input_wordlength, Processing_wordlength)**

This rule implements equations 3.w1, 3.w2 and 3.w3.

- **Online delay of a neighbourhood operation**

Another rule is provided for computing the online delay of both data and 'Is_MSD' control signal of a core neighbourhood operation unit. It is given by:

> **is_online_core_delay(Data_or_Control, Local_Op, Global_Op, Window, Delay)**

Data_or_Control is a flag indicating whether the required online delay is for data or the control signal 'Is_MSD'. This can be either *data* or *control*.

This rule implements equations 3.d1, 3.d2, 3.d3 and 3.d4.

6.2.2 HIDE4k description of a generic PxQ convolution core unit

The core unit of a neighbourhood operation consists of an array of Processing Elements (PEs) plus line delays (see Figure 3.3). Each processing element consists of a *local* operation unit (e.g. Multiply) with a particular window coefficient and a *global* operation unit (e.g. accumulator), in addition to a *buffer unit*. The latter consumes 8 CLBs and is placed vertically for a convolution case (see Figure 3.21). The corresponding ports are stored in the HIDE4k ODL as shown in Figure 6.9.

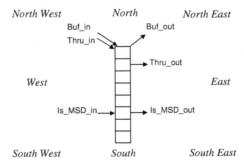

Figure 6.9 Layout of a buffer unit for a convolution operation (buffer1)

The resulting PE is shown in Figure 6.10.

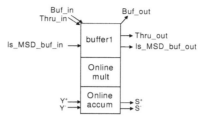

Figure 6.10 Layout of convolution PE

A generic PE (based on online arithmetic) would be fully described in terms of a *local* and *global* operation, a coefficient value and finally the maximum coefficient wordlength:

is_online_PE(Local, Global, Coeff, Max_Coeff_ wordlength, PE)

For instance, the definition of a PE for convolution would be:

is_online_PE(mult, accum, Coeff, Max_Coeff_wordlength, PE):-
is_online_multiplier(Coeff, Max_Coeff_wordlength, Mult),
is_online_buffer_unit(accum, Buffer_unit),
PE = vertical([online_accum, Mult, Buffer_unit]).

Note that an unused PE (corresponding to **Coeff** = ~) is implemented using a special case predicate.

Given a row of window coefficients (**Row_Coefficient_List**) and a maximum coefficient wordlength (**MCWL**), a row of PEs can then be constructed by a horizontal composition of each specific PE. The corresponding HIDE4k constructor is:

is_row_of_PEs(Local, Global, Row_Coeff_list, MCWL, B):-
is_row_of_PEs_list(Local, Global, Row_Coeff_list, MCWL, List_of_PEs),
B = horizontal(List_of_PEs).

is_row_of_PEs_list(_, _, [], _,[]).
is_row_of_PEs_list(Local, Global, [PE_Coeff|Coeff_Tail], MCWL, [PE|Tail_Row]):-
is_online_PE(Local, Global, PE_Coeff, MCWL, PE),
is_row_of_PEs_list(Local, Global, Coeff_Tail, MCWL, Tail_Row).

The result of this constructor is illustrated in Figure 6.11 for a row of 3 elements.

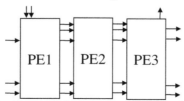

Figure 6.11 Resulting layout of a horizontal composition of processing elements

The direction of the *hinged ports* is determined automatically using the algorithm presented in section 2.3.3.1. The whole PE array is then obtained by a horizontal composition of rows of PEs. The corresponding HIDE4k constructor is:

```
is_array_of_PEs(Local, Global, Window, MCBL, B):-
is_array_of_PEs_list(Local, Global, Window, MCBL, PEs_list),
B = horizontal(PEs_list).


is_array_of_PEs_list(_, _, [], _,[]).
is_array_of_PEs_list(Local, Global, [Row|Wind_Tail], MCBL, [Row_of_PEs|Array_Tail]):-
is_row_of_PEs(Local, Global, Row, MCBL, Row_of_PEs),
is_array_of_PEs_list(Local, Global, Wind_Tail, MCBL, Array_Tail).
```

The result of this constructor is illustrated in Figure 6.12 for a 3x3 window.

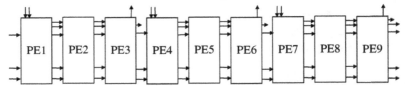

Figure 6.12 Resulting layout after a horizontal composition of all window PEs

Note that the two first inputs in the north side of the PE array correspond to the input pixel of the whole operation. These directions need to be overridden (altered) to the west (using *alter_ports* constructor) before any subsequent composition.

The entire neighbourhood core unit can now be given by a vertical composition of the PE array and 'Q-1' line delays, where 'Q' is the number of columns in the window (or rows depending on the scan direction) as illustrated in Figure 6.13 for a 3x3 window case.

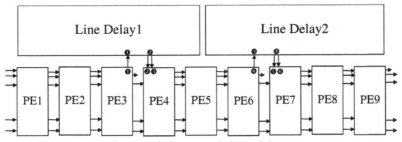

Figure 6.13 Core convolution unit layout

The corresponding HIDE4k constructor is:

```
is_online_core_unit(Local, Global, Window, Buf_size, MCWL, Core_unit):-
is_rearranged_window(Window, Rearranged_window),
is_array_of_PEs(Local, Global, Rearranged_window, MCWL, PEs_Array),
PEs = alter_ports(north,west, [1, 2], PEs_Array),
length(Rearranged_window, Q),
LBs = lb(top, Q-1, Buf_size, _ ), % Replace '_' by a particular line buffers width
% (in CLBs) if  desired (e.g. The width of the target FPGA chip)
Core_unit = vertical([PEs_Array,  nc([p_seq(i,1, 1, Q-1, [(3*i-2, 2*i-1), (3*i-1, 2*i),
                                      (3*i, 2*i)])])]), LBs]).
```

Finally, a number of low level details must be added to produce a complete, convolution circuit. Firstly, a parallel to serial unit is needed at the input, plus a zero block (ground) to initialise the accumulation chain. The SDNR output and the control signal 'IS_MSD_out' of the neighbourhood core unit need to be delayed in order to align with the pixel clock (see equation 3.d1...3.d4). Finally, an SDNR to 2's complement converter is needed (see Figure 6.14).

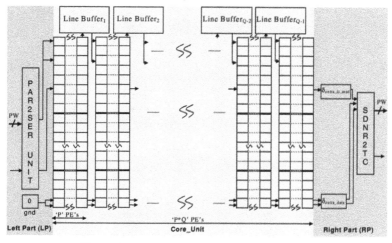

Figure 6.14 Complete layout of a PxQ convolution

The HIDE4k constructor of the whole PxQ convolution architecture is then given by:

```
is_online_IA_nop(mult, accum, Window, Buf_size, W-in, Wproc, Latency, B):-
is_maximum_coeff_ wordlength(Window, MCWL),
is_online_processing_wordlength(mult, accum, Window, W-in, Wproc),
is_parallel_2_serial_unit(mult, accum, W-in, Wproc, _, Par2SerUnit),
LP = vertical([gnd, Par2SerUnit]),
```

```
is_online_core_unit(mult, accum, Window, Buf_size, MCWL, Core_Unit),
is_online_core_delay(data, mult, accum, Window, Data_Delay),
Extra_data_delay is (Wproc - Data_Delay MOD Wproc) MOD Wproc,
is_dual_delay(Extra_data_delay, Di_delay),
is_online_core_delay(control, mult, accum, Window, Control_Delay),
Extra_contol_delay is (Wproc - Control_Delay MOD Wproc) MOD Wproc,
is_single_delay(Extra_contol_delay, Si_delay),
is_sdnr2tcp(Wproc, Sdnr2tcp),
RP= horizontal([vertical([Di_delay, Si_delay]), Sdnr2tcp)]),
B = horizontal([Lp, nc([(1,1),(1,2),(2,3),(3,4),(3,5)]), Core_Unit, Rp]),
Latency is Data_delay+Extra_data_delay+Wproc.
```

6.2.3 A generic PxQ Multiplicative Maximum/Minimum neighbourhood operation

A Multiplicative-Maximum processing element is represented as follows:

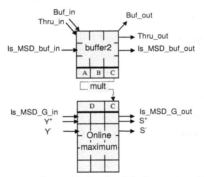

Figure 6.15 Layout of a Multiplicative-Maximum processing element

The following constructs a Multiplicative-Maximum PE:

```
is_online_PE(mult, maximum, Coeff, Max_Coeff_wordlength, PE):-
is_special_online_multiplier(Coeff, Max_Coeff_wordlength, 3, Loc_mult),
is_online_buffer_unit(maximum, Buffer_unit),
PE = vertical([online_maximum, Loc_mult, Buffer_unit]).
```

The only difference with a Multiplicative-Minimum PE description is the global unit which is *minimum* instead of *maximum*. The architecture of a PxQ Multiplicative-Maximum neighbourhood operation is shown in Figure 6.16.

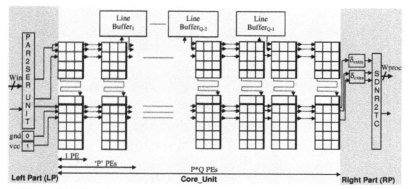

Figure 6.16 Complete layout of a PxQ Multiplicative-Maximum neighbourhood operation

The HIDE4k description of the core neighbourhood operation unit is exactly the same as in a convolution case, with *mult* as local operation and *maximum* (or *minimum*) as a global one (instead of *accum*).

The HIDE4k description of the whole Multiplicative-Maximum operation is then given as follows:

```
is_online_IA_nop(mult, maximum, Window, Buf_size, W-in, Wproc, Latency, B):-
is_maximum_coeff_ wordlength(Window, MCWL),
is_online_processing_wordlength(mult, maximum, Window, W-in, Wproc),
is_parallel_2_serial_unit(mult, maximum, W-in, Wproc, MCWL, Par2SerUnit),
LP = vertical([vcc, gnd, Par2SerUnit]),
is_online_core_unit(mult, maximum, Window, Buf_size, MCWL, Core_unit),
is_online_core_delay(data, mult, maximum, Window, Data_Delay),
Extra_data_delay is (Wproc - Data_Delay MOD Wproc) MOD Wproc ,
is_dual_delay(Extra_data_delay, Di_delay),
is_online_core_delay(control, mult, maximum, Window, Control_Delay),
Extra_contol_delay is (Wproc – Control_Delay MOD Wproc) MOD Wproc,
is_single_delay(Extra_contol_delay, Si_delay),
is_sdnr2tcp(Wproc, Sdnr2tcp),
RP= horizontal([vertical([Di_delay, Si_delay]), Sdnr2tcp)]),
B = horizontal([LP, nc([(1,1),(2,2),(3,3),(4,4),(5,5),(5,6)]), Core_Unit, RP]),
Latency is Data_delay+Extra_data_delay+Wproc.
```

Note that the only difference between Multiplicative-Maximum operation and Multiplicative-Minimum, in addition to the global operation unit, is the initialisation of the maximum (minimum) chain. Indeed instead of Init = (0,1) for the maximum chain, 'Init' is equal to (1,0) for a minimum chain. This influences the left part (LP) description only, which will be, for a Multiplicative-Minimum operation, as follows:

Lp = vertical([gnd, vcc, Par2SerUnit]).

6.2.4   A generic PxQ Additive Maximum/Minimum neighbourhood operation

The layout of an Additive-Maximum processing element is presented in Figure 6.17.

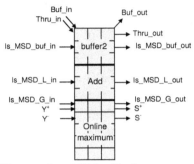

Figure 6.17 Layout of an Additive-Maximum processing element

The corresponding HIDE4k constructor is given by:

```
is_online_PE(add, maximum, Coeff, Processing_wordlength, PE):-
is_local_adder(Coeff, Processing_wordlength, Local_Add),
is_online_buffer_unit(maximum, Buffer_unit),
PE= vertical([online_maximum, Local_Add, Buffer_unit]).
```

The only difference with an Additive-Minimum description is the global unit which is *minimum* instead of *maximum*. The architecture of a PxQ additive Maximum neighbourhood operation is shown in Figure 6.18.

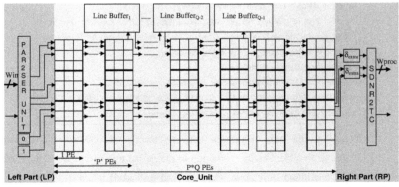

Figure 6.18 Complete layout of a PxQ Additive-Maximum neighbourhood operation

The HIDE4k description of the core neighbourhood operation unit is exactly the same as in a convolution case, with *add* as local operation and *maximum* (or *minimum*) as a global one (instead of *mult* and *accum* respectively).

The HIDE4k description of the whole Additive-Maximum operation is given as follows:

```
is_online_IA_nop(add, maximum, Window, Buf_size, Win,  Wproc, Latency, B):-
is_online_processing_wordlength(add, maximum, Window, Win, Wproc),
is_parallel_2_serial_unit(add, maximum, Win, Wproc, _, Par2SerUnit),
LP = vertical([vcc, gnd, Par2SerUnit]),
is_online_core_unit(add, maximum, Window, Buf_size, Wproc, Core_unit),
is_online_core_delay(data, add, maximum, Window, Data_Delay),
Extra_data_delay is (Wproc - Data_Delay MOD Wproc) MOD Wproc,
is_dual_delay(Extra_data_delay, Di_delay),
is_online_core_delay(control, add, maximum, Window, Control_Delay),
Extra_contol_delay is (Wproc - Control_Delay MOD Wproc) MOD Wproc,
is_single_delay(Extra_contol_delay, Si_delay),
is_sdnr2tcp(Wproc, Sdnr2tcp),
RP= horizontal([vertical([Di_delay, Si_delay]), Sdnr2tcp)]),
B = horizontal([LP, nc([(1,1),(2,2),(3,3),(4,4),(5,5),(6,6),(6,7)]), Core_unit, RP]),
Latency is Data_delay+Extra_data_delay+Wproc.
```

Note also that the only difference between Additive-Maximum operation and Additive-Minimum, in addition to the global operation unit, is the initialisation of the maximum (minimum) chain. Indeed instead of Init = (0,1) for maximum chain, Init =(1,0) for a minimum chain. This influences the left part description only, which would be:

$$Lp = vertical([gnd, vcc, Par2SerUnit]),$$

6.3 Global settings

Before generating full FPGA architectures from HIDE4k descriptions, the user has to specify some global settings. These are:

- **FPGA part**

In order to target a specific FPGA chip, the user needs to specify a particular FPGA part. Ultimately, this information is passed to the FPGA place and route tool. This is performed as follows:

> is_FPGA_part(FPGA_part)

where **FPGA_part** is a particular FPGA part within Xilinx XC4000 series (e.g. **XC4036EX-2-BG352**).

- **Scan direction**

The user has to specify the direction in which the input image is scanned. This could be either vertically or horizontally. Note that the scan direction will influence the way in which the window coefficients are rearranged. This is performed as follows:

> is_scan_direction(Direction)

where **Direction** is *horizontal* or *vertical*.

- **Netlist type**

The user has to specify the type of the netlist to be generated i.e. either EDIF or VHDL. This is performed as follows:

> is_netlist_type(Netlist_Type)

where **Netlist_Type** is either *edif* or *vhdl*.

- **Automatic placer usage**

The user has the choice between keeping the HIDE4k built-in placement or not. This is performed as follows:

> is_automatic_placement(Placement_flag)

where **Placement_flag** is either *true* or *false*.

- **Speed**

The user has also the possibility to specify the speed at which he or she wishes the circuit to operate at. Ultimately, this information is passed to the FPGA place and route tool as a timing constraint. This is performed as follows:

> is_required_Speed(Speed)

where **Speed** is the desired circuit speed in MHz (e.g. 70).

6.4   Performance of two generator approaches: EDIF vs. VHDL

FPGA configurations have been generated from the above HIDE4k descriptions in both EDIF and VHDL format for all five IA operators. Note that the EDIF netlist is generated from floorplanned basic building blocks, and contains all the placement information (*'design to fit'* approach). On the other hand, the VHDL is generated from basic components described at RTL level. No placement or FPGA target dependent information is specified. One exception is that the delay elements in the VHDL version of the HIDE4k library are implemented by synchronous RAM16x1 components. The synthesiser tool was not able to infer those components from RTL descriptions of delay elements. We could not afford to let the synthesiser implement delay elements based on simple flip-flops (huge area loss). This is the only architecture dependent instance in the VHDL code.

The resulting area and performance of examples of all five IA operators are summarised in the following tables for both EDIF and RTL-VHDL. The architectures were generated for 256x256 images of 8 bits per pixel and targeted XC4036EX-2. The FPGA floorplans of some of these architectures are presented in Appendix II.

- **Online Convolution (Laplace filter), with**

~	-1	~
-1	4	-1
~	-1	~

is_online_IA_nop(mult, accum, [[~,-1,~],[-1,4,-1],[~,-1,~]], 256, 8, OWL, Latency, B)

	EDIF	VHDL	EDIF:VHDL (%)
SPEED (MHZ)	75	63	119%
AREA(CLBS)	372	390	95%

- **Online Multiplicative Maximum/Minimum, with**

1	2	1
2	4	2
1	2	1

is_online_IA_nop(mult, maximum, [[1,2,1],[2,4,2],[1,2,1]], 256, 8, OWL, Latency, B)

	EDIF	VHDL	EDIF:VHDL (%)
SPEED (MHZ)	75	54	138
AREA(CLBS)	442	499	88

- **Online Additive Maximum/Minimum, with**

1	1	1
1	1	1
1	1	1

is_online_IA_nop(add, maximum, [[1,1,1],[1,1,1],[1,1,1]], 256, 8, OWL, Latency, B)

	EDIF	VHDL	EDIF:VHDL (%)
SPEED (MHZ)	75	61	122
AREA(CLBS)	458	496	92

From these tables, and many other examples, we can make the following observations:

- In EDIF versions, the critical path in all these circuits is determined by the delay of the RAM16x1s address bus used in the line buffer unit. The speed does not, significantly, vary with the window size and the image size.

- The design to fit (EDIF) approach consistently achieves higher throughput (between 19 and 38% higher in the above tables). A speed of the order of 75MHz for such operations on XC4036EX-2 is considered as a very good figure [And99]. The Laplace architecture, for instance, achieves a theoretical frame rate of 81 frames/sec. Note the difficulty in finding comparative timing results in the literature because of the variety of FPGA series used as well as their speed grades.

- The design to fit approach consistently achieves more compact designs (between 80 and 90% in the above tables). If the line buffers area is not counted, the ratios would be more pronounced in favour of the design to fit approach.

- Since it generates pre-placed architectures, the design to fit approach results in a reduced place and route time. Only a few minutes are necessary for the PAR tool to generate FPGA configurations from pre-placed architectures in EDIF format. The VHDL versions, however, need a relatively much longer time (>1hr on a Pentium 233 running Windows 95 with 32M of RAM). Note that this time includes the generation of a netlist from RTL-VHDL, added to the time needed by Xilinx PAR tools to generate an FPGA configuration from this netlist.

In the broader context, which includes the cost of setting up the HIDE4k libraries, the following comparison factors are also relevant:

- **Library design time**

The time needed to design the library of basic building blocks for the 'design to fit' (EDIF) approach is substantially longer than for the VHDL based one.

- **Portability of the library**

The EDIF library is optimised, for area and speed, for a particular target FPGA and hence is not portable across different FPGA platforms. An RTL-VHDL based approach is relatively target-independent though the design itself is surely influenced by the target architecture.

- **Maintainability**

To update or extend the library, the VHDL version is much easier to understand, and therefore more maintainable.

- **Cost**

In addition to the hardware cost, software tools cost should also be considered. The design to fit approach does not require VHDL synthesis tools and hence is cheaper.

- **Predictability**

It is desirable to be able to estimate accurately the area and the performance of the resulting circuit. This would allow making the necessary design decisions earlier and would hence reduce the design time. As hinted before, unlike an RTL-VHDL based approach, a design to fit approach gives highly predictable results (speed and area).

Note that *behavioural* synthesis tools were not sufficiently mature during this stage of the project to be used, and hence were not introduced in this comparison.

  Overall, the comparison shows that there is an argument for each method (EDIF vs. VHDL). As far as this project is concerned, speed and area are major constraints for us especially if we are to process data at video rate. We can see from the figures presented above that generating EDIF with proper floorplanning yields a significant area and speed improvement over VHDL at RTL level. The speed-area improvement is greater than 20% for all five neighbourhood operations. Note that since the basic units are to be re-used extensively, the cost of the lengthy time needed to carefully floorplan these units is worthwhile. Also, at the start of this project, the VHDL synthesiser tool (Synopsys FPGA compiler) was not able to infer certain special features of the XC4000 architecture automatically (e.g. synchronous RAMs for implementing delays and fast carry logic). That's why we have shifted toward the generation of EDIF netlist with careful floorplanning of the basic building blocks whenever possible.

  In the remainder of this book, this method will be used for generating FPGA architectures. However, as synthesiser tools become more sophisticated, relative merits of RTL level design, or even behavioural synthesis [ZB99], will increase.

6.5 Addendum- some special cases

This short section presents two constructors developed for the special case architectures presented in chapter 4. These have been developed using a similar approach to that presented in section 6.2:

- A bit serial 2's complement LSBF convolver is constructed by:

> **is_tc_lsbf_nop(mult, accum, Window, Buf_size, W-in, Wproc, Latency, B)**

The FPGA floorplan of the resulting configuration (from EDIF) for a Laplace filter is presented in Appendix III for a 256x256 image of 8-bit per pixels, on the XC4036EX-2 FPGA chip. The circuit occupies 283 CLBs and can run at 75MHz. This architecture operates at the same speed as an online-based convolution. However, since the processing wordlength is 12 bits (instead of 14 bits for the online arithmetic based architecture), the 2's complement LSBF architecture results in a higher pixel throughput (6.25MPixel/sec instead of 5.37MPixel/sec). Moreover, it consumes less area (89 CLBs less) as expected in chapter 4 (see section 4.2.2).

- The special architectures for binary images were also described in HIDE4k. The binary architectures can be constructed by:

> **is_binary_IA_nop(Local_Op, Global_Op, Window, Buf_size, Wproc, Latency, B)**

These can be considered as a special case of the Image Algebra architectures presented in section 6.2 when the input pixel wordlength is 1 (i.e. W-in = 1). An FPGA floorplan on XC4036EX-2 is presented in Appendix III, for a binary convolution with the following window:

10	1	10
1	2	1
10	1	10

The input image is 256x256. The circuit occupies 92 CLBs and can run at 95 MHz which is equivalent to a 90 MPixel/sec throughput. An equivalent 2's complement LSBF based architecture would have consumed 349 CLBs and run at 75MHz. In this case, the processing wordlength is 7 bits which gives a throughput of 10.7 MPixel/sec. Thus, we can see that the optimisation that we adopted in chapter 4 for binary images (use of bit parallel arithmetic instead of bit serial) leads to a much more compact circuit and even higher speed.

6.6 HIDE4k, a core generator

We have seen in section 6.2 that all IA architectures (based on online arithmetic) can be constructed by:

> is_online_IA_nop(Local_Op, Global_Op, Window, Buffer_size, Input_wordlength,
> Processing_Wordlength, Latency, B)

Given a filename, in which the resulting EDIF description is to be stored, the following generates the FPGA configuration of any of the five IA neighbourhood operations implemented (using online arithmetic) in either EDIF or VHDL format:

> is_online_IA_operations_core(Local, Global, Window, Buf_size, Win, Filename):-
> % Generate the HIDE4k notation
> is_online_IA_nop(Local, Global, Window, Buf_size, Win, Wproc, Latency, NOP),
> % Generate the corresponding FPGA configuration and store in file 'Filename'
> is_generated_netlist(NOP, Filename).

To demonstrate the ease with which a developer can build a new neighbourhood operation, a simple GUI has been constructed as shown in Figure 6.19.

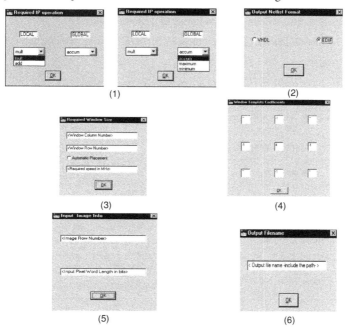

Figure 6.19 IA neighbourhood operations core generator based on HIDE4k

This demonstrates the potential use of HIDE4k as a core generator.

6.7 Summary

In this chapter, we have presented high level architecture descriptions for the set of IA operations presented in chapter 3, using HIDE4k. FPGA architectures have been generated in both EDIF (using a design to fit approach) and RTL-VHDL. A comparison between the two methods has been given. The design to fit approach achieves better performance (both in speed and area) compared to an RTL-VHDL based one. By generating FPGA configurations directly in EDIF format, the design cycle time is reduced as no synthesiser tool is involved. On the other hand, a design to fit approach involves careful floorplanning of the basic components. However, since the basic units are to be re-used extensively, the cost of the lengthy time needed to carefully floorplan these units is reduced. That's why we have chosen to generate FPGA configurations in EDIF format in the remaining of this project.

Lastly, we have illustrated the potential use of HIDE4k environment for core generation. This will be explored further in the next chapters.

The following table summarises the HIDE4k based constructors presented in this chapter:

Parameterised basic components	
Constructor name	**Function**
is_mult_section(Section_type, Bit_value, B)	Invokes a particular serial/parallel online multiplier section
is_single_delay(N, B)	Invokes a single input delay unit with a particular delay amount
is_dual_delay(N, B)	Invokes a dual input delay unit with a particular delay amount
Arithmetic units	
Constructor name	**Function**
is_online_multiplier(Coeff_value, K, B)	Constructs a vertically aligned serial/parallel multiplier based on online arithmetic
is_special_online_multiplier(Coeff, K, W, B)	Constructs a serial/parallel multiplier based on online arithmetic in a snake-like shape
is_online_local_adder(Coeff_value, Wordlength, B)	Constructs an online based local adder unit
is_online_buffer_unit(Global_op, B)	Constructs a buffer unit for online based neighbourhood operations

is_parallel_2_serial_converter(W-in, B)	Converts a bit parallel 2's complement input into a bit serial MSBF output
is_parallel_2_serial_converter(W-in, B)	Converts a 2's complement bit parallel input into a 2's complement bit serial MSBF output and outputs the necessary control signals for the core neighbourhood operation unit
is_sdnr2tcp(W, Sdnr2tcp)	Converts a radix-2 SDNR digit serial MSDF input into 2's complement bit parallel
Neighbourhood operations	
Constructor name	**Function**
is_online_core_unit(Local, Global, Window, Buf_size, MCWL, Core_unit)	Constructs the core unit of IA neighbourhood operations (the input is in 2's complement bit serial MSBF whereas the output is in online arithmetic)
is_online_IA_nop(Local_Op, Global_Op, Window, Buffer_size W-in, Wproc, Latency, B)	Constructs the full architecture of IA neighbourhood operations (Both input and output are in 2's complement bit parallel)
is_tc_lsbf_nop(mult, accum, Window, Buf_size, W-in, Wproc, Latency, B)	Constructs the full architecture of a convolution neighbourhood operation using 2's complement bit serial LSBF arithmetic (Both input and output are in 2's complement bit parallel)
is_binary_IA_nop(Local_Op, Global_Op, Window, Buf_size, Wproc, Latency, B)	Constructs the full architecture of IA neighbourhood operations for binary images

Table 6.1 Summary of the HIDE4k based constructors presented in this chapter

Chapter 7

Compound operations: towards the use of hardware skeletons

Chapter 7

Compound operations: towards the use of hardware skeletons

Practical image processing applications often comprise more than one single operation. Having presented optimised (area and speed-wise) FPGA architectures for the set of Image Algebra operators in the previous chapters, we will now present a generic framework for developing optimised FPGA architectures for a wider range of image processing applications. This framework should give the benefits of an application-oriented, high level programming model without sacrificing significantly the performance of the solution. Our approach to this is to use a concept which has proved relatively successful in developing parallel software, namely *skeletons* [Col89][DGT93][MSW95]. Skeletons are reusable, parameterised fragments or frameworks to which the user can supply components (e.g. functions). It is common for skeletons to include functions as parameters which are applied by the skeleton to a data set. The implementation of a skeleton is normally optimised for a specific target machine.

In this chapter, we introduce the concept of *hardware skeletons*. A hardware skeleton is a parameterised description of a task-specific architecture, to which the user can supply parameters such as values, functions or even other skeletons. In this sense, a skeleton is like a class, from which specific *instances* can be created. Hardware skeletons will be of two kinds: *primitives* (covering all the basic operations covered to date in this book) and *compound* (an assembly of more than one primitive - or compound- skeleton).

To develop a suitable library of skeletons, we will identify a suitable model for describing a subset of image processing operations. This model will be illustrated by two practical IP algorithms. Then, we outline the implementation strategy which we employ to generate efficient FPGA configurations from skeleton instances in section 7.3. Next, we will present optimised FPGA implementations, for speed and area, for a number of primitive skeletons and two compound skeletons. The proposed implementation strategy will then be applied to the two practical IP algorithms presented earlier for illustration. Finally, conclusions will be drawn.

7.1 An application oriented description model for IP operations

A useful subset of IP operations can be described by a *Directed Acyclic Graph* (DAG), where *vertices* represent IP tasks, and the *directed edges* represent the data flow.

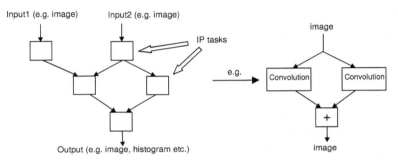

Figure 7.1 An image processing algorithm modelled as a DAG graph

There are three basic classes of primitive (non-compound) operations (or nodes): neighbourhood, point and global operations. These differ in the extent of their data access requirements. Edges can represent three different types of data: images, vectors (e.g. histograms) and scalars.

7.1.1   Neighbourhood operations

In neighbourhood operations, a new pixel value is calculated using the pixel values in the neighbourhood of the original pixel (e.g. convolution). This is done for all image pixels, and results in a new image. As explained in chapter 3, neighbourhood operations are defined by a *local* and *global* operation in addition to a template (window coefficients).

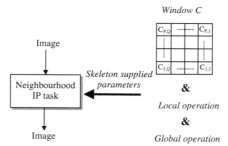

Figure 7.2 Neighbourhood operation IP task

We will provide skeletons in the form of Prolog predicates which describe parameterised frameworks, with operations (like functions) being passed as parameters. In fact, the Prolog predicates presented in chapter 6 are actually primitive skeletons. Therefore, any primitive neighbourhood operation based on online arithmetic is provided by the skeleton:

> **is_IA_online_nop(Local, Global, Window, Buf_size, W-in, W-proc, Latency, NOP)**

An instance of this will build a block (NOP) which implements the required neighbourhood operation.

7.1.2   Point operations

In point operations, the same operation is applied to each individual pixel of a source image(s) to produce a corresponding result pixel in the new image. We have identified six basic sub-classes of point operations, depending on the operands.

-   **Image-Image operations (I-I):** These produce a new image from *one* source image using a local (point to point) operation (e.g. Image negation, Absolute operation).

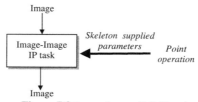

Figure 7.3 Image-Image (I-I) IP task

We provide a set of skeletons for I-I operations, to support different arithmetic types. The following skeletons implement I-I operations in online arithmetic and 2's complement bit parallel arithmetic respectively:

> **is_online_II_op(Point_op, IWL, Latency, B)**
>
> **is_tc_par_II_op(Point_op, IWL, OWL, Latency, B)**

where **Point_op** is a point operation identifier, **IWL** is the input wordlength, **OWL** is the output wordlength and **Latency** is the latency of the resulting unit.

For example, the following constructs a 'W_in' bit input absolute unit in online arithmetic and 2's complement bit parallel arithmetic respectively:

> **is_online_II_op(abs, W_in, Latency, B)**
>
> **is_tc_par_II_op(abs, W_in, OWL, Latency, B)**

- **Image-Scalar-Image operations (IS-I):** Given a scalar as a parameter, an IS-I operation produces a new image from *one* source image using a local point operation. A set of implemented point operations is: *relational operations* (e.g. '≥', '≤', '=') and *arithmetic operations* (e.g. '+', '-', '*', '/').

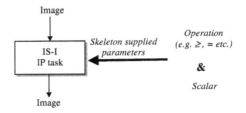

Figure 7.4 Image-Scalar-Image (IS-I) IP task

The following skeletons are provided to perform an IS-I task in online arithmetic and 2's complement bit parallel arithmetic respectively:

> **is_online_ISI_op(Point_op, Scalar, IWL, Latency, B)**
>
> **is_tc_par_ISI_op(Point_op, Scalar, IWL, OWL, Latency, B)**

- **Image-Multiple-Scalar-Image operations (IMS-I):** For operations which take more than one scalar parameter (e.g. multiple threshold), an array of scalars must be supplied.

Figure 7.5 Image-Multiple-Scalar-Image (IMSI) IP task

The following skeleton is provided to perform an IMS-I task in 2's complement bit parallel arithmetic:

is_tc_par_IMSI_op(Point_op, List_of_scalars, IWL, OWL, Latency, B)

where **List_of_scalars** is a list containing an array of scalars.

We have implemented instances of this skeleton for the following point operations (**Point_op**):

- **'between'** for a two level threshold in which the result is equal to 1 if the input value is between two threshold values and 0 otherwise.

- **'outside'** for a two level threshold in which the result is equal to 0 if the input value is between two threshold values and 1 otherwise.

The two threshold levels are sent as a list parameter (**List_of_Scalars**).

- **Image-Image-Image (II-I) operations:** produce a new image from *two* source images taking one pixel from each one and combining them to produce a result pixel in the new image. These include: *image-image addition, image-image subtraction, image-image maximum and image-image minimum.*

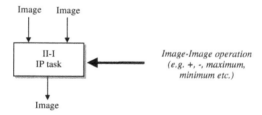

Figure 7.6 Image-Image-Image (II-I) IP task

We provide the following skeletons for constructing an II-I operation in online arithmetic and 2's complement bit parallel arithmetic respectively:

is_online_III_op(Point_op, IWL, Latency, B)

is_tc_par_III_op(Point_op, IWL1, IWL2, OWL, Latency, B)

For example, a 'W-in' bit image-image addition unit based on online arithmetic is constructed by:

is_online_III_op(+, W-in, Latency, B)

Similarly, in order to add two 'W-in' bit parallel operands (in 2's complement arithmetic), the following constructor is used:

is_tc_par_III_op(+,W-in, W-in, Wout, Latency, B)

We also provide the following skeleton for constructing an II-I operation in 2's complement bit serial LSBF:

> **is_tc_lsbf_III_op(Point_op, IWL, OWL, Latency, B)**

where **Point_op** is '+' for an addition operation and '-' for a subtraction operation.

Also provided is the following skeleton for constructing an II-I operation in 2's complement bit serial MSBF, and unsigned binary bit serial MSBF respectively:

> **is_tc_msbf_III_op(Point_op, IWL, OWL, Latency, B)**
>
> **is_unsigned_msbf_III_op(Point_op, IWL, OWL, Latency, B)**

where **Point_op** is '**max**' for a maximum operation and '**min**' for a minimum one.

We now present two further skeletons which have not yet been implemented but which are useful for expressing certain IP algorithms.

- **Multi-Image-Image (MI-I) operations:** produce a new image from *multiple* source images taking one pixel from each one and combining them to produce a result pixel in the new image. This is a generalisation of the previous case.

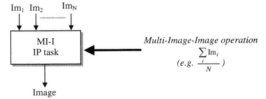

Figure 7.7 Multiple-Image-Image (MI-I) IP task

- **Image-Vector-Image (IV-I) operations**: Some operations use (or even generate) a *vector*. Given a vector as a parameter, an IV-I operation produces a new image from *one* source image by mapping one set of grey levels onto another set using a Look-Up Table (LUT). This is shown in Figure 7.8 where grey levels in the original image are used as indices into the LUT.

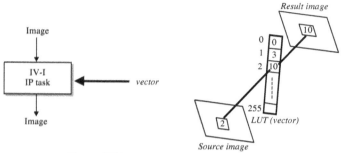

Figure 7.8 Image-Vector-Image (IV-I) IP task

7.1.3 Global operations

These have to process the whole image before a meaningful result is obtained. Depending on the nature of the operation, we distinguish:

- **Reduction to Scalar (RS)**: These operations operate on the whole image to produce a scalar as a result. They include *global maximum*, *global minimum* and *global accumulation* (Σ).

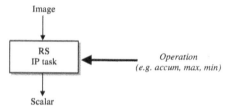

Figure 7.9 Reduction to Scalar (RS) IP task

We provide the following skeleton for constructing an RS operation based on bit parallel 2's complement arithmetic:

is_tc_par_RS_op(Point_op, IWL, OWL, Latency, B)

For instance, a 'W-in' bit input RS accumulation unit (B) producing an accumulation result with 'W-out' bits is constructed by:

is_ tc_par_RS_op(accum, W_in, Wout, Latency, B)

- **Reduction to Vector (RV)**: These operate on the whole image to produce a *vector* as a result. They include *histogramming* and *cumulative histogramming*. No skeleton has been implemented for these operations so far.

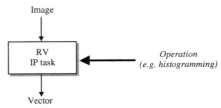

Figure 7.10 Reduction to Vector (RV) IP task

7.2 Simple examples using DAGs for representing practical compound IP operations

In this section, we will show how the above mentioned primitive operations are assembled into DAG representations for two practical IP compound operations.

7.2.1 Open and Close operators

'Open' and 'Close' are two standard morphological operators often applied to binary images [Pra91][Ros95]. An 'Open' operation is used for removing the borders of frayed regions, and for eliminating tiny regions. To do an 'Open' operation, an 'Erode' neighbourhood operation is first performed. Then, the resulting image is fed into a 'Dilate' neighbourhood operation as shown in Figure 7.11a. The 'Close' operator is used for filling internal gaps and gaps in fringes. It is obtained by applying a 'Dilate' operation first. Then, the resulting image is fed into an 'Erode' operation as shown in Figure 7.11b.

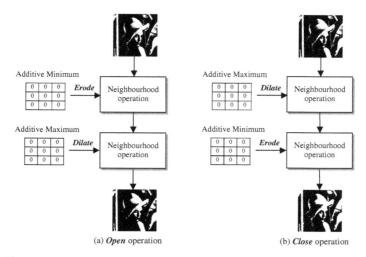

(a) *Open* operation   (b) *Close* operation

Figure 7.11 DAG representation of morphological operations: Open and Close

7.2.2 Sobel edge detection operation

Sobel edge detection algorithm is one of the most commonly used techniques for edge enhancement [Pra91][Ros95]. It can be performed (approximately) by adding the absolute results of two separate convolutions as shown in Figure 7.12.

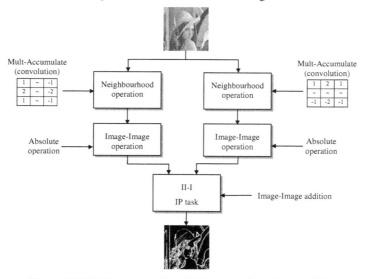

Figure 7.12 DAG representation of Sobel edge detection algorithm

7.3 Implementation strategy: generating an FPGA configuration from a DAG

A DAG like that presented in Figure 7.1 specifies the logical operations to be carried out. At this stage, it does not include all the information necessary for implementation e.g. type of *arithmetic* to be used. However, the skeletons presented above require this information to generate the corresponding FPGA configurations. Therefore, we need to consider the properties of the *edges* further. An item of data (represented by an edge in the DAG), has two properties:

1. **Logical data type:** This is defined by the following two properties:
-   **Structure:** could be an image, a vector or a scalar.
-   **Type:** which, for the purpose of this project, could be either an integer or a boolean.
2. **Data representation format:** A particular data representation format is defined by three properties:
-   The data could be in *bit serial*, *bit parallel* with a particular word size or in *digit serial* with particular digit and word sizes. For the purpose of this project, only bit serial and bit parallel have been considered.
-   If data is in bit serial (or digit serial), it can then be pipelined either *MSB (MSD)* First or *LSB (LSD)* First.
-   *Number Representation*: which, for the purpose of this project, can be either *2's complement* or *Signed Digit (SD)* number representation.

Binary representation (see chapter 4) corresponds to *bit parallel* with a word size *one* (denoted *Bit parallel(1)*). *Online arithmetic* is *digit serial SD MSD* First. For the purpose of this project, Radix-2 online arithmetic is used.

A node with a particular set of *logical* Inputs/Outputs could be implemented by a range of different possible primitive skeletons as illustrated in Figure 7.13.

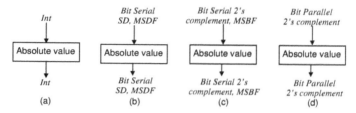

Figure 7.13 A DAG node (a) with several possible implementations (b), (c) and (d)

The user's first task will be to represent the algorithm in terms of a DAG, without initially being concerned with data representation considerations. Once this is done, an analysis of the properties of the input and output data formats of the nodes will identify a range of possible primitive skeletons for each node. For instance, the result of an N-bit integer image comparison operation could be either an N-bit integer image or a (1-bit) binary image. The choice will depend on subsequent processing of the result image, and on what skeletons are available. As a first step, the set of all possible skeletons should be considered by the user. The library of Hardware Skeletons (e.g. neighbourhood operations, point operations, etc.), in which each component has a set of different skeletons (e.g. bit serial, bit parallel), is the basis of this phase. The range of possible skeletons generated for a particular IP algorithm depends on the extent of this library.

To select the optimum skeleton from the set of possible choices, the cost of each choice of optional skeletons needs to be found (perhaps eventually using system tools), in terms of speed and area. This involves estimating the expected performance or effectively generating the FPGA configuration for each option, including the application of the optimisations associated with each skeleton. This *cost based analysis* enables the user to settle on a final DAG with all attributes (data types and representations) defined. The corresponding FPGA implementation is then generated, in the form of EDIF netlist, for the chosen solution using the HIDE4k system. The resulting EDIF file is finally fed to Xilinx Placement And Routing (PAR) tools to generate the FPGA configuration bitstream.

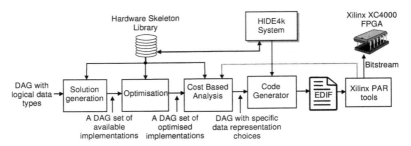

Figure 7.14 Implementation strategy

Note that during the process of implementing a DAG, the following issues arise:

- **Data representation conversion**

Since data in intermediate stages (DAG edges) can have different representations, *data representation converters* may therefore be needed to convert between different representations as illustrated in Figure 7.15.

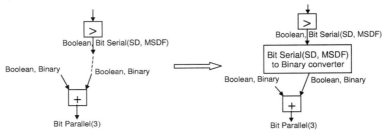

Figure 7.15 Example of data representation conversion

Table 7.1 shows the data formats used up to this point along with the corresponding data converters. The availability of a particular data converter is indicated by '✓'. In practice, there will be other data representations (e.g. unsigned bit serial: MSBF and LSBF, unsigned bit parallel etc.).

	Bit Serial (SD, MSDF)	Bit serial (2's C, MSBF)	Bit Serial (2's C, LSBF)	Bit Parallel (N, 2's C)	Bit Parallel(1)
Bit Serial (SD, MSDF)	–	✓	✓	✓	✓
Bit Serial (2's C, MSBF)	✓	–	✓	✓	✓
Bit Serial (2's C, LSBF)	✓	✓	–	✓	✓
Bit Parallel (N, 2's C)	✓	✓	✓	–	✓
Bit Parallel(1)	✓	✓	✓	✓	–

Table 7.1 Data representation converters

- **Data synchronisation**

When there are two or more inputs to a DAG vertex (e.g. II-I IP tasks), any branch that arrives earlier than the others should be forced to wait for the slowest branches. This is performed by adding appropriate delays to the fastest branches and can be implemented automatically. The latter requires knowledge of the latency of each vertex.

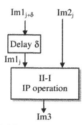

Figure 7.16 Data synchronisation

7.4 FPGA implementation of some additional primitive basic skeleton instances

In this section, we will present the design of some basic building blocks necessary to implement compound IP operations, which were not needed in previous chapters.

7.4.1 Online absolute value operator (I-I): is_online_II_op(abs, IWL, Latency, B)

The online absolute value operator takes a serial SDNR input MSDF and outputs its absolute value in SDNR. The following transition diagram presents the FSM which performs the absolute value 'Abs' of an SDNR input 'X' [MRM94]. Note that the start state is indicated by a '*' superscript.

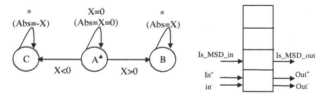

Figure 7.17 State diagram and floorplan of an online based Absolute unit

The control signal 'Is_MSD' is used to reset the initial state of the FSM to state 'A' indicating the start of a new operand. The physical implementation of this machine occupies 4 CLBs laid out vertically. The corresponding online delay is 1.

7.4.2   2's complement bit parallel Absolute operation (I-I):

is_tc_par_II_op(abs, IWL, OWL, Latency, B)

In order to generate the absolute value of a number in bit parallel, its 2's complement is generated unconditionally. The sign of the input is then used to choose between the input directly or its 2's complement. The 2's complement is generated by decrementing the input and inverting the result (which is equivalent to the usual way of inverting the input and incrementing the result). The decrementation is implemented using the dedicated fast carry logic [XAP13][XCL23]. Hence, each CLB can implement a two-bit slice of the absolute value. Figure 7.18 shows a one bit slice of the absolute unit. The result can be optionally registered within the CLB.

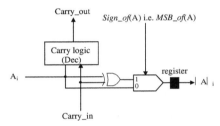

Figure 7.18 A one bit slice of an absolute unit

An 'N' bit Absolute unit occupies $\lceil N/2 \rceil$ CLBs.

7.4.3   Online thresholding (IS-I)

In this operation, the image pixel $X = (x^+, x^-)$ is compared to a constant value C. The serial SD MSDF output $R = (r^+, r^-)$ will be assigned 1 or 0 according to whether X is less than or greater than C. This defines two different operators:

- **Greaterthan operator ('>'): is_online_ISI_op(>, Thresh_value, IWL, Latency, B)**

In this case, the output $R = (r^+, r^-)$ is equal to '1' if the image pixel is greater than a constant C, otherwise, R will be set to 0. The coefficient C is stored in 2's complement format in a CLB RAM. It has the same wordlength as the incoming input pixel data, and is converted locally to an SDNR value. The input pixel $X = (x^+, x^-)$ is first subtracted from the coefficient C (converted to SDNR). The result $R = (r^+, r^-)$ will be determined by the sign of the subtraction result. If the leading non-zero digit of C-X is negative, then C-X is negative and hence $R = (r^+, r^-)$ will be set to 1 (i.e. $X > C$). Otherwise, R is set to 0 (i.e. $X \leq C$).

The negation of the input pixel X is done simply by inverting its BS notation as explained in section 3.3.8. The binary to SDNR converter and the online adder are based on the units outlined in section 3.3.2 and 3.3.4 respectively. The whole *greaterthan* unit occupies 10 CLBs laid out in a 2x5 rectangle as shown in Figure 7.19. The corresponding online delay is 4.

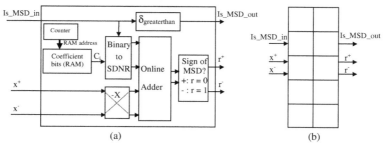

Figure 7.19 *Greaterthan* unit: (a) Block diagram (b) FPGA layout

- **Lessthan operator ('<'): is_online_ISI_op(<, Thresh_value, IWL, Latency, B)**

The *lessthan* operation can be performed in a similar way as the *greaterthan* one. Instead of subtracting the input pixel from the coefficient C, the coefficient C is subtracted from the input pixel. This implies the inversion of the BS notation of the coefficient C instead of the input pixel's one. If the leading non-zero digit of X-C is negative, then $R = (r^+, r^-)$ will be set to 1 (i.e. $X<C$). Otherwise, R is set to 0 (i.e. $X \geq C$). This does not imply any additional hardware compared to the *greaterthan* unit one. Hence the *lessthan* unit has exactly the same layout and online delay as *greaterthan*.

7.4.4   Online 'Equal' operator (IS-I):

is_online_ISI_op(=, Thresh_value, IWL, Latency, B)

The *equal* operation can be performed in a similar way as *greaterthan* and *lessthan* units presented above. The coefficient C is subtracted from the input pixel. However, instead of examining the sign of the subtraction result S, the boolean output $R = (r^+, r^-)$ is determined by the value of S. If the latter is zero, then the output R is set to 1. Otherwise, it is set to 0. The *equal* unit has exactly the same layout and online delay as *greaterthan* and *lessthan* units.

7.4.5   2's complement bit parallel threshold operator (IS-I):

This threshold block compares a bit parallel input pixel (in 2's complement) to a threshold value:

- **Greaterthan operator ('>'):**

  is_tc_par_ISI_op(>, Thresh_value, IWL, OWL, Latency, B)

This unit outputs '1' if the input pixel is greater than the threshold and '0' in the opposite case.

- **Lessthan operator ('<'):**

  is_tc_par_ISI_op(<, Thresh_value, IWL, OWL, Latency, B)

This unit outputs '1' if the input pixel is less than the threshold and '0' in the opposite case.

In both cases, a threshold block is implemented by subtracting the Threshold value from the input data and examining the *MSB* of the result:

- If $MSB = '0'$ then the subtraction result is positive. Thus, the input data is greater than or equal to the threshold value.
- If $MSB = '1'$ then the subtraction result is negative. Thus, the input data is less than the threshold value.

As a result *lessthan = MSB* whereas *greaterthan_or_equal = $\overline{MSB}$*. A *greaterthan* unit with a coefficient C is implemented by using *greaterthan_or_equal* with a coefficient $C+1$.

The subtraction block is implemented efficiently using dedicated carry logic. Each CLB can implement one or two-bit subtracter slices [XAP13]. An N-bit threshold unit occupies $\lfloor N/2+1 \rfloor$ CLBs.

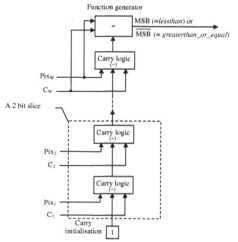

Figure 7.20 A bit parallel Threshold block

7.4.6   2's complement bit parallel 'Equal' operator ('='):

is_tc_par_ISI_op(=, Thresh_value, IWL, OWL, Latency, B)

This operation implements a boolean function which takes a W-bit input and outputs
'1' only if the input bit pattern is equal to a constant value C. A CLB's 4-input LUT
can implement a 4 input '=' operation. One CLB can implement up to a 9 input '='
operation as shown in Figure 7.21.

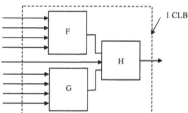

Figure 7.21 A 9 input bit pattern decoding in XC4000

In general, a W-bit '=' operation can be obtained by decoding the input bit pattern into
groups of 9 (one CLB each) and ANDing the partial results.

7.4.7   Online constant division (IS-I): is_online_ISI_op(/, Divisor, IWL, Latency, B)

Division by a constant divisor D can be implemented simply by multiplying by the
reciprocal. The divisor D is first approximated to a fraction $\frac{X}{Y}$, where Y is a power of

two ($Y=2^P$). The division is then reduced to a multiplication by X followed by P right shifts. The online serial-parallel multiplier presented in section 3.3.5 could be used for the multiplication.

Suppose the wordlength of the input data is M and that of X is N. The multiplication by X would then result in $N+M$ digits in full precision. Note that we have to shift this result by P digits to get the division result. Our approach is to limit the output wordlength to the same wordlength as the input i.e. N digits (instead of the full $N+M$ digits). This is equivalent to M right shifts of the full precision result. The remaining shifts (i.e. P-M) will be performed on the bit parallel result, at the end, by just discarding the P-M least significant bits of the result. In order to avoid interference between successive results, the multiplier registers are cleared (asynchronously) at the beginning of each word by 'Is_MSD' signal. The online delay of the resulting division unit is 2.

For instance, consider the *Blur* filter given by a convolution with the following window:

1	1	1	
1	1	1	$\div 9$
1	1	1	

The division by 9 can be approximated by multiplication by $\dfrac{7}{64} = \dfrac{7}{2^6}$. A multiplier by $7=0111_2$ is then needed as shown in Figure 7.22. Since $P = 6$ and $M= 4$, then the 2 (= P-M) least significant bits of the overall operation output should be discarded.

Note that this approximation involves an error, which will propagate in subsequent stages. However, it is possible to control the value of this error by choosing an appropriate approximation.

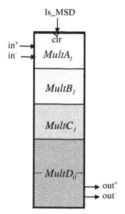

Figure 7.22 An online division by 9 unit implemented by multiplication with its reciprocal ~7/64

7.4.8 Maximum unit based on 2's complement bit serial MSBF (II-I):

is_tc_msbf_III_op(max, IWL, Latency, B)

This unit selects the maximum/minimum of two inputs represented in 2's complement bit serial MSBF. Note that a similar unit based on online arithmetic has already been presented in section 3.3.7. Figure 7.23 shows the transition diagram of a Finite State Machine (FSM) performing the maximum 'O' of two 2's complement operands 'X' and 'Y'. The start state is indicated by a '$^{\clubsuit}$' superscript. The control signal 'Is_MSB' indicates the start of two new operands. The unit operates with a latency of 2. The physical implementation of this machine occupies 4 CLBs.

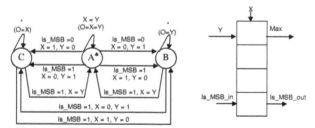

Figure 7.23 State diagram and FPGA floorplan of a 2's complement bit serial MSBF Maximum unit

A minimum unit would be implemented in a similar way knowing that $\text{Min}(X,Y) = \{X,Y\}-\{\text{Max}(X,Y)\}$.

7.5 Compound skeletons- the concept and examples

Compound skeletons result from the process of identifying, from experience, common ways of assembling primitive operations and providing optimised implementations of these. To demonstrate this concept, we will present, in this section, hardware optimisations for two compound hardware skeletons.

7.5.1 Multiple neighbourhood operations on an image

A number of IP operations comprise several concurrent neighbourhood operations which share the same input image, and whose templates have the same size and shape. The outputs of these operations, ultimately, join in a Multi-Image-Image operation. Sobel operation, presented in section 7.2.2 above, is one example of such operations. Prewitt, Kirsch and Roberts operators [Pra91][Ros95] are other examples.

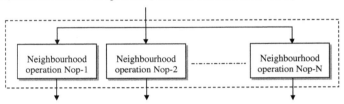

Figure 7.24 Parallel neighbourhood operations sharing the same input image

The hardware implementation of this skeleton offers the possibility for significant optimisations. Let us consider, for simplicity, the case of just two 'parallel' neighbourhood operations. Suppose these two neighbourhood operations are given by the following parameters:

Template A   Template B

A_{PQ}	⋯⋯	A_{P1}		B_{PQ}	⋯⋯	B_{P1}
---	---	---		---	---	---
A_{1Q}	⋯⋯	A_{11}		B_{1Q}	⋯⋯	B_{11}

Neighbourhood_operation(L_1, G_1)   Neighbourhood_operation(L_2, G_2)

where L_i, G_i {i=1,2} are the local and global operations respectively. Since both neighbourhood operations are applied to the same image, only one set of line buffers and buffer units is needed to synchronise the supply of pixels for both operations.

This creates a Complex Processing Element (CPE) instead of two separate PEs as shown in Figure 7.25 assuming a vertical scan direction.

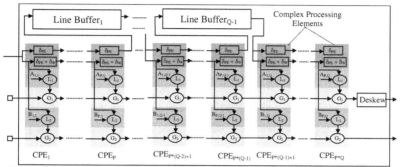

Figure 7.25 Architecture of a generic 2D, compound PxQ neighbourhood operation with two parallel tasks

Figure 7.26 presents a more detailed structure of the complex PE for the case of online arithmetic. Note that the SDNR to 2's complement conversion needs to be done only once and supplied to both PEs corresponding to the two neighbourhood operations. Also, an extra pipeline stage ($\delta_{thru} = 1$) has been added to the second neighbourhood operation to speed up the FPGA implementation. The latter should be performed irrespective of the arithmetic used.

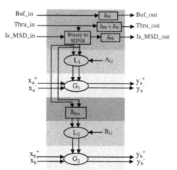

Figure 7.26 Architecture of a complex Processing Element for two parallel neighbourhood operations

The extension of this structure to a general complex PE for 'N' neighbourhood operations is straightforward. All that is needed is to broadcast the two outputs of δ_{thru} to the 'Local' and 'Global' operations of the next parallel neighbourhood operation (via another delay δ_{thru}). Note that, in general, there will be a skew between the output of each neighbourhood operation, which should be compensated. We provide a skeleton implementation of the architecture presented in Figure 7.25 (serial input, serial output), just for parallel convolution operations. This can be constructed by:

- Using online arithmetic:

```
is_online_para_nop(mult, accum, List_of_windows, Buf_size, IWL, Wproc, Latency, B)
```

- Using 2's complement bit serial LSBF:

```
is_tc_lsbf_para_nop(mult, accum, List_of_windows, Buf_size, IWL, Wproc, Latency, B)
```

where **List_of_windows** is a list of window coefficients for each parallel convolution, **IWL** is the input wordlength, **Wproc** is the processing wordlength and **Latency** is the unit's latency.

7.5.2 A second compound skeleton: '*II-I_Op*(Image, Nop(Image))'

In this sub-section, we present a special optimisation for the DAG fragment shown in Figure 7.27.

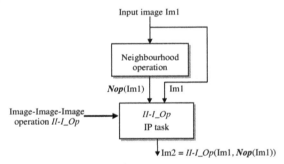

Figure 7.27 The *III_Op*(Image, *Nop*(Image)) skeleton

As mentioned before, the two input operands to the *II-I_Op* operation should be synchronised. Since the result of the neighbourhood operation is characterised by a certain latency $\delta_{neighbourhood}$, the other input to the *II-I_Op* operation (Im1) should be delayed by the same amount (see Figure 7.28).

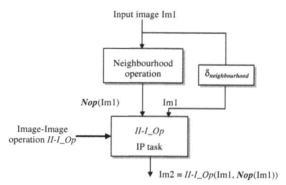

Figure 7.28 Data synchronisation

However, instead of allocating extra hardware to implement the necessary delay for synchronisation ($\delta_{neighbourhood}$), this delayed version of the input image can be picked from *within* the neighbourhood operation hardware. The question is, however, where should 'Im1' be taken from, and what extra internal delay, if any, is necessary? Note first that each Processing Element inputs a pixel value (see signal 'Thru_in' in Figure 7.26) at a particular position within the window neighbourhood. Synchronising the input image 'Im1' with the result of the neighbourhood operation is hence performed by delaying the input signal 'Thru_in' of the PE corresponding to the *target* pixel position by δ_{global} in every remaining PE to the output. An extra delay δ_{extra}, however, should be added. The latter corresponds to the delay in the PE's *input* signal 'Thru_in' reaching the global operation unit. This is illustrated in Figure 7.29 for a 3x3 window case where the target pixel in the centre of the window.

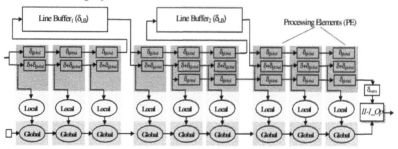

Figure 7.29 Optimised implementation for "*II-I_Op*(Image, *Nop*(Image))" skeleton for 3x3 window with central target pixel position

In the case of online arithmetic (see Figure 7.26 for instance):

$$\delta_{extra} = \delta_{local} + \delta_{sdnr2tc}$$

For binary images, since 2's complement bit parallel is used:

$$\delta_{extra} = 0$$

We provide the implementation of the following skeletons for generating the architecture presented in Figure 7.29:

- For a generic neighbourhood operation defined by **Local, Global** and , **Window** using online arithmetic:

> **is_online_Im_nop_Im(III_Op, Local, Global, Window, Buf_size, IWL, Wproc, Latency, B)**

- For a convolution neighbourhood operation using bit serial 2's complement LSBF:

> **is_tc_lsbf_Im_nop_Im(III_Op, mult, accum, Window, Buf_size, IWL, Wproc, Latency, B)**

7.6 FPGA implementation of practical compound IP operations

In this section, we will present the FPGA implementation of two examples of compound IP operations for which we have no direct skeleton: the first assembles only primitive skeletons (Open&Close), the second will incorporate one compound skeleton (Sobel).

7.6.1 Open and Close operations

A block diagram of both 'Open' and 'Close' operations is given by Figure 7.11. 'Open' and 'Close' involve pipelining two successive neighbourhood operations ('Erode' and 'Dilate'). If online arithmetic is to be used, then 'Erode' and 'Dilate' cannot be placed horizontally on XC4036EX-2 (36x36 CLBs) since each PE width is 3 CLBs. The total width needed for the PE array of one operation ('Erode' and 'Dilate') would have been 27 CLBs. Instead, these two operations are placed vertically as shown in Figure 7.30.

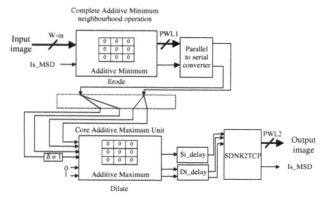

Figure 7.30 Architecture of an 'Open' operation based on online arithmetic

Note that because all the window coefficients for both 'Erode' and 'Open' operations are zeros, there is no need for the local addition operation. The local addition unit is hence removed. Thus, the processing wordlength is equal to the input wordlength (i.e. W-in). This special optimisation has been added to the online IA neighbourhood operation skeleton presented in section 6.2. The following is the HIDE4k code needed to generate an online based 'Open' architecture.

```
is_online_open(W-in, Buf_size, Filename):-
Erode_window =[[0,0,0],[0,0,0],[0,0,0]], Dilate_window =[[0,0,0],[0,0,0],[0,0,0]],
is_IA_online_nop(add, minimum, Erode_window, Buf_size, W-in, PWL1, _, Erode),
is_parallel_2_serial_converter( PWL1, Par2Ser),
Upper_part = horizontal([ Erode, Par2Ser ]),
is_online_core_unit(add, maximum, Dilate_window, Buf_size, PWL1, Core_Dilate_unit),
is_online_core_delay(data, add, maximum, Dilate_window, Data_Delay2),
is_online_processing_wordlength(add, maximum, Dilate_window , PWL1, PWL2),
Extra_data_delay is (PWL2 – Data_Delay2 MOD PWL2) MOD PWL2,
is_dual_delay(Extra_data_delay, Di_delay),
is_online_core_delay(control, add, maximum, Dilate_window, Control_Delay2),
Extra_contol_delay is (PWL2 - Control_Delay2 MOD PWL2) MOD PWL2,
is_single_delay(Extra_contol_delay, Si_delay),
is_sdnr2tcp(PWL2, Sdnr2tcp),
Rp= horizontal([vertical([Di_delay, Si_delay]), Sdnr2tcp)]),
Dilate = horizontal([Core_Dilate_unit, Rp]),
is_single_delay(1, Delay),
Init = vertical([vcc, gnd, Delay]),
Lower_part = horizontal([Init, nc([(1,1),(2,2),(3,3),(thru,4),(thru,5),(thru, 6)]), Dilate]),
Temp1 = alter_ports(east, south, [1,2], Upper_part),
```

```
Temp2= alter_ports(west, north, [1,2,3,4], Lower_part),
Open = vertical([Temp2, nc([ (1,1),(2,1),(3,2),(4,2)]),Temp1]),
is_generated_netlist(Open, Filename).
```

A floorplan of the resulting architecture for a 256x256 input image of 8-bits/pixel, on XC4036EX-2, is presented in Appendix IV. The processing wordlength is 8 bits and the whole circuit occupies 766 CLBs. Timing simulation shows that the circuit can run at a speed of 70MHz which leads to a theoretical frame rate of 133 frames per second.

However, since no addition is used in both 'Erode' and 'Dilate' (window coefficients all equal to zero), bit serial 2's complement MSBF data representation can be used. A serial 2's complement MSBF maximum unit is 1 CLB wide only (see section 7.4.8). 'Erode' and 'Dilate' operations are hence placed horizontally in this case. The corresponding architecture is given by Figure 7.31.

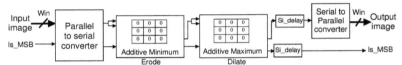

Figure 7.31 Architecture of an 'Open' operation based on 2's complement MSBF data representation

The following special skeleton is provided for building a special architecture for a PxQ Maximum/Minimum neighbourhood operation based on 2's complement MSBF arithmetic (serial input, serial output):

```
is_tc_msbf_core_maxmin_ nop(Max_or_Min, P, Q, Buf_size, W-in, Latency, NOP)
```

The following is the HIDE4k code needed to generate an 'Open' architecture based on bit serial 2's complement MSBF arithmetic:

```
is_tc_msbf_open(W-in, Buf_size, Filename):-
is_parallel_2_serial_converter( W-in, Par2Ser),
is_tc_msbf_core_maxmin_ nop(minimum, 3, 3, Buf_size, W-in, Latency1, Erode),
is_tc_msbf_core_maxmin_ nop(maximum, 3, 3, Buf_size, W-in, Latency2, Dilate),
Extra_delay is (W-in – (Latency1+Latency2) MOD W-in) MOD W-in,
is_single_delay(Extra_delay, Si_delay),
is_ser_2par(W-in, Ser2par), % builds a scaleable serial to parallel converter unit
Rp=vertical([ Si_delay, horizontal([Si_delay, Ser2par])]),
Open =horizontal([Par2Ser , nc([(1,1),(2,2),(2,3)]), Erode, nc([(1,1),(2,2),(2,3)]), Dilate, Rp]),
is_generated_netlist(Open, Filename).
```

A floorplan of the resulting architecture for a 256x256 input image of 8-bits/pixel, on XC4036EX-2, is presented in Appendix IV. The processing wordlength is 8 bits. The circuit occupies 443 CLBs. This is more than 300 CLBs less than the corresponding area occupied by an online arithmetic based implementation. Timing simulation shows that the circuit can run at a speed over 87 MHz which leads to a theoretical frame rate of 165 frames per second. Clearly, such custom solution is more efficient (area and speedwise) than an online arithmetic based solution.

7.6.2 Sobel edge detection operation

This operation involves two neighbourhood operations performed in parallel and has been presented in section 7.2.2. An optimisation for such operations has also been presented in section 7.5.1. As an extra delay ($\delta_{thru} = 1$) has been added to the second neighbourhood operation, an extra delay ($\delta_{extra} = \delta_{thru} = 1$) should be added to the result of the first neighbourhood operation as shown in Figure 7.32. This is performed automatically by the skeleton presented in section 7.5.1.

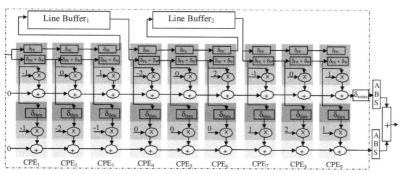

Figure 7.32 Architecture of Sobel operation

In the following, we will present two FPGA implementations of Sobel operation, based on two different arithmetic choices: the first is based on online arithmetic, whereas the second is based on bit serial 2's complement LSBF.

• Online arithmetic based Sobel implementation

In this case, the Sobel circuit is assembled using online arithmetic based components. In particular, we will make use of the online arithmetic based skeleton presented in section 7.5.1.

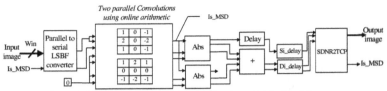

Figure 7.33 Block diagram of an online based Sobel architecture

The following is the HIDE4k code needed to generate an online based 'Sobel' architecture:

```
is_online_sobel(W-in, Buf_size, Filename):-
is_online_para_nop (mult, accum, [ [[1,2,1],[0,0,0],[-1,-2,-1]], [[1,0,-1],[2,0,-2],[1,0,-1]] ],
                    Buf_size, W-in, PWL, Latency, B),
is_parallel_2_lsbf_converter(W-in, Par2Ser), % Parallel to serial with sign extension
Init = vertical([gnd, Par2Ser]),
Lp = horizontal([Init,nc([(1,1),(1,2),(1,3),(1,4),(2,5),(3,6),(3,7)]), B]),
is_online_II_op(abs_2, PWL, Lat_abs, Abs),
Temp = horizontal([ Lp, nc([(1,1),(2,2),(3,4),(4,5),(5,3),(5,6)]), v_seq(2,Abs) ]),
is_online_III_op(+, PWL, Lat_add, Adder),
is_single_delay(Lat_add, Delay),
Temp2 = horizontal([ Temp, nc([ (1,1),(2,2),(4,3),(5,4),(6,5)]), vertical([Adder, Delay])]),
Extra_delay is (PWL-((Latency+Lat_abs+Lat_add) MOD PWL)) MOD PWL,
is_dual_delay(Extra_delay, Di_delay),
is_single_delay(Extra_delay, Si_delay),
Temp3= horizontal([ Temp2, vertical([Di_delay, Si_delay])]),
is_sdnr2tcp(PWL,Sdnr2tcp),
Sobel = horizontal([ Temp3, Sdnr2tcp]),
is_generated_netlist(Sobel, Filename).
```

A floorplan of the resulting architecture for a 256x256 input image of 8-bits/pixel, on XC4036EX-2, is presented in Appendix IV. The processing wordlength is 13 bits (see Equation 3.w1). The circuit occupies 475 CLBs. Timing simulation shows that the circuit can run at a speed of 75MHz which leads to a theoretical frame rate of 88 frames per second.

- **2's complement LSBF based Sobel implementation**

In this case, the Sobel circuit is designed using 2's complement LSBF arithmetic. We will make use of the 2's complement LSBF based skeleton presented in section 7.5.1. Note that in order to perform Absolute operation, the two serial LSBF outputs need first to be converted into bit parallel before a bit parallel absolute unit is used (see section 7.4.2 above). The final addition is also performed in bit parallel. The latter is based on fast dedicated carry logic (see example 5.1).

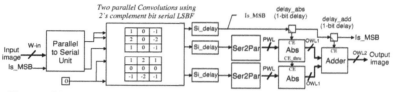

Figure 7.34 Block diagram of a 2's complement bit serial LSBF Sobel architecture

The following is the HIDE4k code needed to generate a bit serial 2's complement LSBF based 'Sobel' architecture is presented.

```
is_tc_lsbf_sobel(W-in, Buf_size, Filename):-
is_tc_lsbf_para_nop(mult, accum, [ [[1,2,1],[0,0,0],[-1,-2,-1]], [[1,0,-1],[2,0,-2],[1,0,-1]] ],
                Buf_size, W-in, PWL, Latency, B),
is_parallel_2_serial_unit(mult, accum, W-in, PWL, _, Par2Ser),
Init = vertical([gnd, Par2Ser]),
Lp = horizontal([Init, nc([(1,1),(1,2),(2,3),(3,4),(3,5)]), B]),
Extra_delay is (PWL-((Latency+1) MOD PWL)) MOD PWL,
is_single_delay(Extra_delay, Si_Delay),
Temp = horizontal([Lp, v_seq(3, Si_Delay)]),
is_ser_2par(PWL, Ser2par),
Temp1=horizontal([Temp, nc([(1,1), (2,2), (3,thru)]), v_seq(2,Ser2par) ]),
is_tc_par_II_op(abs, PWL,OWL1, Lat_abs, Abs),
Temp2 = horizontal([ Temp1, vertical([Abs, Abs, delay_abs]) ]),
is_tc_par_III_op(+, OWL1, OWL2, Lat_add, Adder),
Sobel = horizontal([ Temp2, vertical([Adder, delay_add]) ]),
is_generated_netlist(Sobel, Filename).
```

A floorplan of the resulting architecture for a 256x256 input image of 8-bits/pixel on XC4036EX-2 is presented in Appendix IV. The processing wordlength is 11 bits (see Equation 4.w4). The circuit occupies 340 CLBs. This is more than 100 CLBs less than an online arithmetic based implementation. Timing simulation shows that the circuit can run at a speed of 75MHz which leads to a theoretical frame rate of 104 frames per second. Clearly such custom solution is more efficient (area and speedwise) than an online arithmetic based solution.

7.7 Summary

In this chapter, we have presented a *framework* for generating optimised FPGA architectures, for area and speed, for a wide range of image processing applications that can be modelled by a DAG. This framework is based on the concept of *hardware skeletons*. A hardware skeleton is a parameterised description of a task-specific architecture, to which the user can supply parameters such as values, functions or even other skeletons. A library of hardware skeletons which contains a set of high level descriptions of task-specific architectures is provided. The skeletons built in the previous chapter for IA operations are part of this library. Although our library of compound skeletons is only in its infancy, the two skeletons provided illustrate task-specific optimisations. Different skeletons for the same operation, using different arithmetic representations, are provided, giving the user a range of implementation choices. This supports experimentation with different implementations and choosing the most suitable one for the particular constraints in hand (e.g. speed and area). Two examples (Open and Sobel operations) have been provided to illustrate this latter point. Though this experimentation is performed manually at the moment, it may be possible to do some of it automatically in the future. Ultimately, we would like to reach the point where, given a complete algorithm description in terms of skeletons, an efficient hardware configuration should be generated automatically by our system. This proposed system would give the convenience and rapid development cycle of an application-oriented, high level-programming model, without sacrificing significantly the performance of the solution.

The following tables summarise the skeletons introduced in this chapter:

Image-Image point operations			
Constructor name	**Point_Op**	**Types (Input, Output)**	**Function**
is_online_II_op(**Point_op**, IWL, Latency, B)	**abs**	(Online, Online)	Outputs the absolute value of its input
	neg	(Online, Online)	Outputs the negative of its input
is_tc_par_II_op(**Point_op**, IWL, OWL, Latency, B)	**abs**	(2's C. bit parallel, 2's C. bit parallel)	Outputs the absolute value of its input
	neg	(2's C. bit parallel, 2's C. bit parallel)	Outputs the negative of its input

Image-Scalar-Image point operations			
Constructor name	Point_Op	Types (Input, Output)	Function
is_online_ISI_op(Point_op, Scalar, IWL, Latency, B)	>	(Online, Online)	Outputs '1' if the input is greater than **Scalar** and '0' otherwise
	<	(Online, Online)	Outputs '1' if the input is less than **Scalar** and '0' otherwise
	=	(Online, Online)	Outputs '1' if the input is equal to **Scalar** and '0' otherwise
	+	(Online, Online)	Adds its input to a constant coefficient
	-	(Online, Online)	Subtracts a constant coefficient from its input
	*	(Online, Online)	Multiplies its input with a constant coefficient
	/	(Online, Online)	Divides its input by a constant coefficient
is_tc_par_ISI_op(Point_op, Scalar, IWL, OWL, Latency, B)	>	(2's C. bit parallel, binary)	Outputs '1' if the input is greater than **Scalar** and '0' otherwise
	<	(2's C. bit parallel, binary)	Outputs '1' if the input is less than **Scalar** and '0' otherwise
	=	(2's C. bit parallel, binary)	Outputs '1' if the input is equal to **Scalar** and '0' otherwise
	+	(2's C. bit parallel, 2's C. bit parallel)	Adds its input to a constant coefficient
	-	(2's C. bit parallel, 2's C. bit parallel)	Subtracts a constant coefficient from its input
	*	(2's C. bit parallel, 2's C. bit parallel)	Multiplies its input with a constant coefficient
	/	(2's C. bit parallel, 2's C. bit parallel)	Divides its input by a constant coefficient

Image-Multiple-Scalar-Image operations			
Constructor name	Point_Op	Types (Input, Output)	Function
is_tc_par_IMSI_op(Point_op, [Th1, Th2], IWL, Latency, B)	between	(2's C. bit parallel, Binary)	Outputs '1' whenever its input value is between **Th1** and **Th2**, and '0' otherwise
	outside	(2's C. bit parallel, Binary)	Outputs '0' whenever its input value is between **Th1** and **Th2**, and '1' otherwise

Image-Image-Image point operations			
Constructor name	Point_Op	Types (Input, Output)	Function
is_online_III_op(Point_op, IWL, Latency, B)	+	(Online, Online)	Adds two input operands
	-	(Online, Online)	Subtracts two input operands
	max	(Online, Online)	Selects the maximum of two input operands
	min	(Online, Online)	Selects the minimum of two input operands
is_tc_par_III_op(Point_op, IWL, OWL, Latency, B)	+	(2's C. bit parallel, 2's C. bit parallel)	Adds two input operands
	-	(2's C. bit parallel, 2's C. bit parallel)	Subtracts two input operands
	max	(2's C. bit parallel, 2's C. bit parallel)	Selects the maximum of two input operands
	min	(2's C. bit parallel, 2's C. bit parallel)	Selects the minimum of two input operands
is_tc_lsbf_III_op(Point_op, IWL, OWL, Latency, B)	+	(2's C. bit serial LSBF, 2's C. bit serial LSBF)	Adds two input operands
	-	(2's C. bit serial LSBF, 2's C. bit serial LSBF)	Subtracts two input operands
is_tc_msbf_III_op(Point_op, IWL, OWL, Latency, B)	max	(2's C. bit serial MSBF, 2's C. bit serial MSBF)	Selects the maximum of two input operands
	min	(2's C. bit serial MSBF, 2's C. bit serial MSBF)	Selects the minimum of two input operands

| is_unsigned_msbf_lll_op(Point_op , IWL, OWL, Latency, B) | max | (Unsigned bit serial MSBF, Unsigned bit serial MSBF) | Selects the maximum of two input operands |
| | min | (Unsigned bit serial MSBF, Unsigned bit serial MSBF) | Selects the minimum of two input operands |

Global operations			
Constructor name	**Point_Op**	**Types (Input, Output)**	**Function**
is_tc_par_RS_op(Point_op, IWL, OWL, Latency, B)	accum	(2's C. bit parallel, 2's C. bit parallel)	Accumulates the incoming data
	max	(2's C. bit parallel, 2's C. bit parallel)	Selects the maximum among the incoming data
	min	(2's C. bit parallel, 2's C. bit parallel)	Selects the minimum among the incoming data

Neighbourhood operations			
Constructor name	**Max_or_Min**	**Types (Input, Output)**	**Function**
is_tc_msbf_core_maxmin_ nop(**Max_or_Min, P, Q**, Buf_size, W-in, Latency, NOP)	max	(2's C. bit serial MSBF,	Constructs a PxQ Maximum/Minimum neighbourhood operation
	min	2's C. bit serial MSBF)	

High level (compound) skeletons		
skeleton name	**Types (Input, Output)**	**Function**
is_online_para_nop(mult, accum, List_of_windows, Buf_size, IWL, Wproc, Latency, B)	(2's C. bit serial MSBF, Online)	Performs multiple convolutions in parallel on the same image using online arithmetic
is_tc_lsbf_para_nop(mult, accum, List_of_windows, Buf_size, IWL, OWL, Latency, B)	2's C. bit serial LSBF, 2's C. bit serial LSBF)	Performs multiple convolutions in parallel on the same image using 2's complement, bit serial, LSBF
is_online_lm_nop_lm(lll_Op, Local, Global, Window, Buf_size, IWL, Wproc, Latency, B)	(2's C. bit serial MSBF, Online)	lll-op(Image, Nop(Image))
is_tc_lsbf_lm_nop_lm(lll_Op, mult, accum, Window, Buf_size, IWL, Wproc, Latency, B)	(2's C. bit serial LSBF, 2's C. bit serial LSBF)	lll-op(Image, Nop(Image))

Chapter 8

Novel Image Processing architectures

Chapter 8

Novel image processing architectures

This chapter presents three IP algorithms along with their FPGA implementations. The first is a new formulation of an existing algorithm used for perimeter estimation. This is an application to a more complex compound operation compared with the compound operations presented in the previous chapter. Then, we will present a novel algorithm for median filtering. The latter is an example of a common neighbourhood operation which cannot be expressed in the set of IA operations presented in chapter 3. Finally, we will present an implementation of an algorithm for Connected Component Labelling. This is an example of an algorithm requiring a recursive image processing operation which has not been implemented in the simple IPC instruction set presented in chapter 3. Note that these examples will be presented from an algorithmic point of view rather than the architecture description viewpoint.

8.1 Perimeter estimation

Measurement of perimeters, areas, centroids and other shape related parameters of planar objects is an important task in industrial computerised vision system [Cas96]. In this section, we will illustrate the problem of finding a reasonably accurate measure of the perimeter of an object.

8.1.1 An algorithm for perimeter estimation

Consider a binary image 'Im1' containing only one object. We define the contour of a digitised object as a sequence of boundary pixels of the object (see Figure 8.1c). This contour is often represented by a chain code [Fre74].

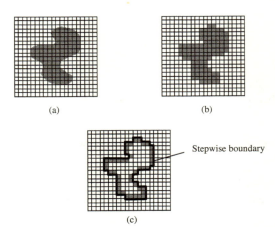

(a)   (b)

Stepwise boundary

(c)

Figure 8.1 (a) Original object shape (b) Object shape after digitisation (discrete form) (c) object contour with its stepwise boundary

Another view of the object contour is the line between the object pixels and the background (the 'crack'). Encoding this line (a sequence of horizontal and vertical pixel edges) yields what is usually called the crack code of the digitised object boundary (identified as the bold line in Figure 8.1c). Clearly the length of the latter contour is greater than the perimeter of the original object, especially for shapes with many corners: hence the problem of finding an efficient and accurate perimeter estimator.

One way of estimating the perimeter of a digitised object [KB89][PR79] is to measure the number of vertical and horizontal cracks, and perform subsequent adjustments (e.g. take the number of corners into consideration).

Another approach is to approximate the real object boundary more accurately, and perform subsequent measurements on this approximated contour [Mon70]. In particular, it is common to represent the contour as a line passing through the centre of boundary pixels – i.e. as a sequence of horizontal, vertical and diagonal links [Cas96]. Area measurements must of course take this into account, as this approach effectively shaves off a little of each boundary pixel of the object. Assuming square pixels, the perimeter is then estimated by:

*Perimeter = No. of horizontal & vertical links + (No. of diagonal links * $\sqrt{2}$)*

In the following, we will present an alternative formulation of this algorithm which is particularly suited to FPGA implementation.

8.1.2 New formulation of the algorithm

Before measuring the object's perimeter, we need first to *find* the perimeter. A simple method for identifying the boundary pixels is to perform an 'Erode' operation on the image. The boundary pixels are those which were eroded, and can be found by subtracting the result from the original image, as shown in Figure 8.2.

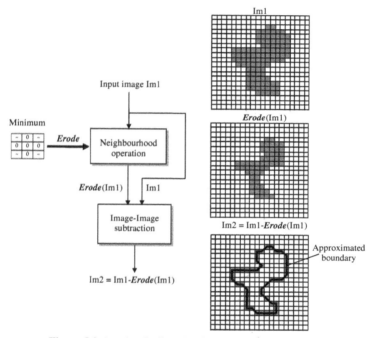

Figure 8.2 An edge finding algorithm for binary images

As mentioned earlier, a simple count of the number of pixel edges does not give an accurate measure of the perimeter (because of corners and diagonal edges). Instead, we will take the contour as a sequence of links between the centres of adjacent boundary pixels (see *Im2* in Figure 8.2). However, rather than focus on the links (each of which straddles two boundary pixels), we will consider the individual contribution of each boundary pixel. This contribution depends on the path which the contour follows *through* the pixel. Assuming a one-pixel wide perimeter, and an aspect ratio of 1.0 (i.e. square pixels), we can classify each edge pixel's contribution to the perimeter into one of the following categories (or any of their rotations) [Cro98]:

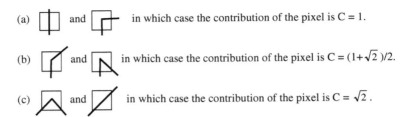

(a) ⬚ and ⬚ in which case the contribution of the pixel is C = 1.

(b) ⬚ and ⬚ in which case the contribution of the pixel is $C = (1+\sqrt{2})/2$.

(c) ⬚ and ⬚ in which case the contribution of the pixel is $C = \sqrt{2}$.

The perimeter is then given by:

$$\begin{aligned} \text{Perimeter} \quad = \quad & \text{No. of (a) pixels} * 1 \\ + \quad & \text{No. of (b) pixels} * (1+\sqrt{2})/2 \\ + \quad & \text{No. of (c) pixels} * \sqrt{2} \qquad \text{(Equation 8.1)} \end{aligned}$$

One way of classifying the contribution of edge pixels (assumed to be '1' against a background of '0's) is to convolve the whole binary image 'Im2' with the following window:

$$T = \text{Im2} <\text{convolve}>$$

10	2	10
2	1	2
10	2	10

The result of this convolution at each pixel position enables the category of the corresponding edge pixel to be deduced:

Result (T[i,j])	category
5 or 15 or 7 or 25 or 27 or 17	(a)
13 or 23	(b)
21 or 33	(c)
anything else	*no contribution*

Table 8.1 Classification of different convolution pixel results

The make up of these result pixels is shown in Figure 8.3.

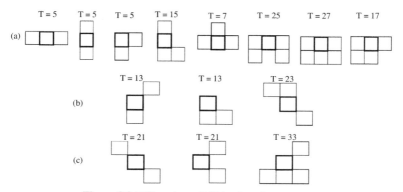

Figure 8.3 Different possibilities for edge segments

The perimeter will then be given by:

$$\text{Perimeter} = \text{count(T=5, 15, 7, 25, 27 or 17)} * 1$$

$$+ \quad \text{count(T=13 or 23)} * (1+\sqrt{2})/2$$

$$+ \quad \text{count(T=21 or 33) Pixels} * \sqrt{2}$$

For hardware implementation purposes, the coefficients will be approximated in binary to eight binary places as follows:

$$1 = 1.00000000_2, (1+ \sqrt{2})/2 \approx 1.00110101_2 \text{ and } \sqrt{2} \approx 1.01101010_2.$$

A block structure of the whole operation is given by Figure 8.4.

8.2.3 FPGA implementation

Since the input image is binary, 'Erode' is performed as shown in section 4.1.4. As the result of a binary 'Erode' operation is itself binary, 'Subtraction' (Im1-Erode(Im1)) operates on binary data and hence reduces to a simple 2-input gate. The operation 'Im1-Erode(Im1)' uses the optimisation presented in section 7.5.2. The convolution operates on binary images and hence is based on the implementation presented in section 4.1.2. The output of this convolution is in bit parallel (7 bits wide). Each 'multiple =' block outputs '1' whenever its input (the convolution result) is equal to one of a particular set of constants (e.g. {13, 23}). This implements a simple boolean function which can be implemented easily using the XC4000 CLB's look up tables as shown in section 7.4.6.

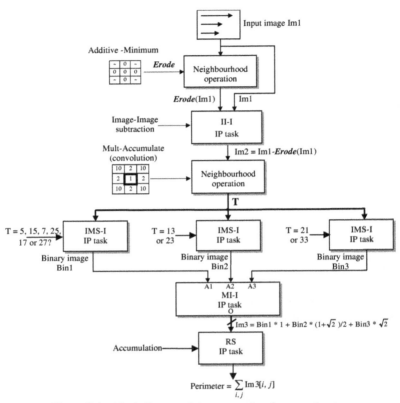

Figure 8.4 A block diagram of the proposed perimeter estimator

The MI-I block outputs the appropriate pixel contribution to the perimeter (i.e. 1, $\sqrt{2}$ or $(1+\sqrt{2})/2$). It receives 3 binary inputs, and outputs a bit parallel result. Again, this can be easily implemented using the XC4000 CLB's look up tables.

Finally, these pixel contributions (in the form of the three possible coefficients 1, $\sqrt{2}$ and $(1+\sqrt{2})/2$) are serially accumulated. The accumulation is in bit parallel and uses fast carry logic.

The perimeter estimator architecture has been described using HIDE4k and targeted the XC4013E-1 FPGA chip (24x24 CLBs). The resulting circuit, for a 512x512 input binary image, occupies 199 CLBs. Timing simulation shows that the circuit can run at a speed of 85MHz which leads to a theoretical frame rate of 324 frames per second.

8.2 Median Filtering

Median filtering has proved an effective way to satisfy the dual requirements of removing impulse noise while preserving rapid signal changes [HYT80][AC89]. In this section, we present a novel bit serial algorithm and architecture for general median filtering. We firstly outline the general structure of a 2D median filter architecture, irrespective of which median finding algorithm is used. Then, we present an FPGA implementation for an existing 'Triple Input Sorter' based algorithm (TIS) [BN97][XCL23]. After that, we present our new bit serial median algorithm (called Bit Voter, or BV) [BC99] which is highly scaleable and easily implemented on small FPGA chips. It is based on a 'Bit Voter' block, and assumes unsigned pixel values in the first instance. Three extensions to the basic BV algorithm are then presented: Weighted Median filtering; Ranked Median filtering; and handling potentially negative (2's complement) pixel values. Finally, comparative timings and area measurements for the FPGA implementation of the two algorithms are given. This will be followed by some conclusions.

8.2.1 Basic architecture outline for a 2D median filter

For the two dimensional (2D) case, a median filter consists of passing an NxM window over an image, and computing the output pixel as the median value of all the pixel values (brightness) within the input window. If NxM is odd, then the median will be the (NxM+1)/2 entry in the list of ordered pixel values. To allow each pixel to be supplied only once to the FPGA, internal line buffers are required. Figure 8.5 shows the outline structure of the 2D median filter for a 3x3 window size (assuming bit serial processing). It is the design of the 'Median Finding Unit', whose inputs are the NxM pixel values and whose output is the median value of these elements, which will differentiate the two following algorithms.

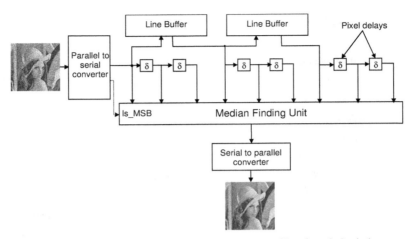

Figure 8.5 Outline structure of a bit serial 2D median filter for a 3x3 window

8.2.2 Existing 'Triple Input Sorter' based Algorithm (TIS)

A block diagram of a median filter design based on a Triple Input Sorter unit [BN97] [XCL23] for a 3x3 window is shown in Figure 8.6. Supposing a horizontal scan direction, the algorithm consists of the following stages:

- Stage 1:   Sorts the elements of each window column.
- Stage 2:   Sorts the elements of each window row.
- Stage 3:   The median is finally obtained by sorting the cross diagonal and picking up the middle value.

This algorithm differs from the 'bubble sort algorithm' [CMP88][Olaf83] in that it does not do a *total* sort of the entire matrix elements. Only three results are guaranteed to be placed in the right place: the maximum, the minimum and the median; this saves a great deal of logic. Note that because the same operation (Triple Input Sort) is applied to the elements of each column, it is possible to use only one column sorter (see Figure 8.6). This saves 2 TIS units.

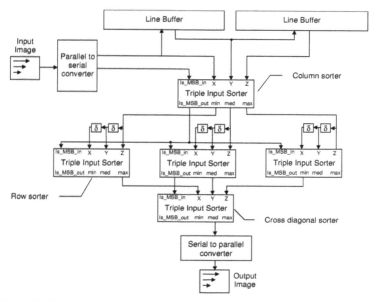

Figure 8.6 Block diagram of a 3x3 Triple Input Sorter based median filter design

The Triple Input Sorter is based on a Dual Input Sorter, as shown in Figure 8.7.

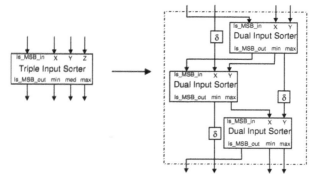

Figure 8.7 Design of the Triple Input Sorter block

The dual input sorter unit is based on the 2-operands maximum/minimum unit presented in section 7.4.8.

A 3x3 bit serial TIS-based median filter has been described using HIDE4k and implemented for a 512x512 image of 8-bits per pixel, on an XC4013E-1 FPGA chip (24x24 CLBs). A serial Triple Input Sorter block occupies 12 CLBs. The Median

Finding Unit occupies 48 CLBs, and the whole circuit takes 369 CLBs. Timing simulation shows that the circuit can run at a speed of 91 MHz. This would enable a theoretical frame rate processing of 43 frames per second. Note finally that the algorithm could also be implemented in a bit parallel [XCL23].

8.2.3 The Novel Algorithm (BV)

We now present the novel BV algorithm [BC99]. We will first describe the general principle of BV, and then discuss its implementation. The description assumes that pixels are unsigned.

Observe that if the candidate values (9 for a 3x3 window) are compared with a pivot value and split into two groups ('<' and '≥'), then the median value must be in the larger group. The smaller group can then be effectively eliminated from the set of possible candidates. If we process all the candidate values together in bit serial, then this partitioning can be achieved by choosing just one pivot bit at each stage.

To implement this approach, the pixels are fed Most Significant Bit First to a 'Voter Block'. This block will examine the candidate bits, and finds which is the larger group by 'voting' – i.e. by finding the most common bit among them. Assuming an odd number of candidates, clearly the median pixel will be among the group that contains more elements than the other. Hence, the output bit at any stage is the most common bit, which has just been found. The other group will be automatically eliminated from the race by latching each of the remaining candidates' bits either to 0 (if it was in a 0's group) or to 1 in the opposite case. This latching method of elimination does not affect subsequent vote results, since all that it does is replace the weak candidates (lower pixel values) by even weaker ones, and strong candidates (higher pixel values) by even stronger ones.

An example trace of the algorithm for finding the median of five values is shown in Figure 8.8. This shows candidate pixels progressively being eliminated, and the eliminated bits being substituted with bit values depending on why they were eliminated.

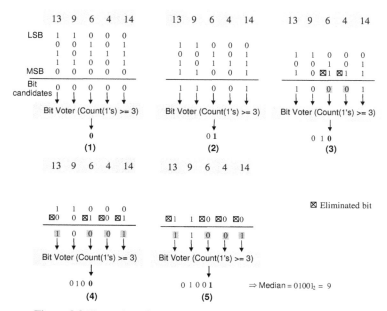

Figure 8.8 Illustration of BV median filtering algorithm for N*M = 5

The design of BV algorithm is given by Figure 8.9.

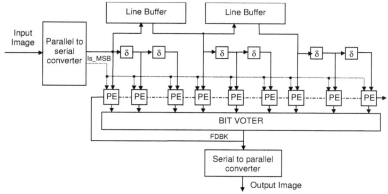

Figure 8.9 Block diagram of the novel algorithm design

The hardware implementation of the novel algorithm consists of two stages:

1. An array of pixel Processing Elements (PE's): Each PE takes the next bit of its input pixel. It will first determine the bit value to be passed to the voting stage: this will be either its input pixel bit value, or the latched 'elimination bit' if the

pixel has been eliminated. When the next result bit is subsequently fed back (from the Bit Voter stage), each PE decides whether or not its future candidate bits are to be eliminated or not. If the input pixel is to be eliminated, the PE's output is latched to the 'elimination bit' value (The last candidate bit). The structure of the Processing Element is given by Figure 8.10.

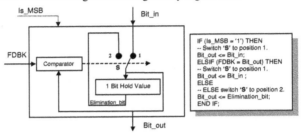

Figure 8.10 BV's Processing Element structure

2. Bit Voter stage (BV): This block receives as its input the entire set of processed candidate bits, and outputs the most common bit among them (1 or 0) as the next bit of the result. This is done simply by counting the number of 1's and comparing the result with a threshold value – which, in the case of a 3x3 window, will be four. Counting the number of 1's in an array can be performed on XC4000 by counting the number of 1's in groups of 4 (using the CLB's 4x1 LUTs) and using a tree of adders to sum the partial count results as shown in Figure 8.11.

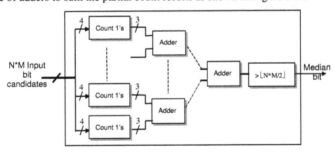

Figure 8.11 Implementation of the Bit Voter unit on XC4000

In the case of 3x3 window, two 4x3 LUTs are needed to count the numbers of 1's in two groups of 4 inputs. The two partial results are then added using a 3 bits adder with the 9th input used as initial carry-in. The final count result is represented in 4 bits and can then be thresholded (> 4, or ≥ 5) using just one 4x1 LUT (see Figure 8.12).

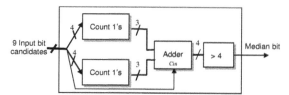

Figure 8.12 Implementation of a 9 input Bit Voter unit on XC4000

Increasing the window size increases the number of PE's accordingly, and implies some additional hardware in the Bit Voter unit. The PE block consumes just one CLB; the Bit Voter block takes 6 CLBs for a 3x3 window size. The scaleability and the compactness of this algorithm make it an ideal candidate for a general-purpose median filter. Note, however, that the feedback signal ('FDBK') must be generated with no skew compared to the BV output ('Bit_out') in order to carry out the comparison operation (see Figure 8.10). Thus, the Bit Voter block must operate with no latency i.e. should be fully combinatorial. As a result, the BV median filter design cannot be speeded up by pipelining.

8.2.4 Extending BV for Weighted Median filtering

In Weighted Median filtering, the user can vary the likelihood of a particular pixel position being selected by giving weights to each window position, as illustrated by the window shown in Figure 8.13 and the corresponding 3x3 neighbourhood from the image being filtered.

1	2	1
2	3	2
1	2	1

a	b	c
d	e	f
g	h	i

Figure 8.13 Window with weights and corresponding 3x3 image neighbourhood

The Weighted Median filter will therefore find the median of 15 numbers:

$$\{ \ a, \ b, \ b, \ c, \ d, \ d, \ e, \ e, \ e, \ f, \ f, \ g, \ h, \ h, \ i \ \}$$

This suggests a simple alteration to our BV architecture above to implement a Weighted Median Filter, in which the input bit pixel candidates are first replicated (by a factor given by the weight in the corresponding window position) before being input to a larger Bit Voter block. The number of inputs to the Bit Voter block will be the sum of the weights in the window. The architecture corresponding to the weighted window in Figure 8.13 is shown in Figure 8.14. Note that the standard median filter is equivalent to the simple case in which all the weights are '1'.

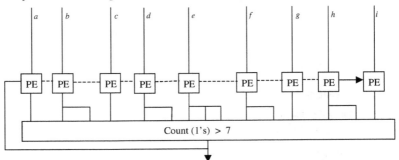

Figure 8.14 Modified Architecture for Weighted Median Filter

Although the architectural extension is straightforward, and requires only a scaleable design for the Bit Voter block, there are performance implications when using weights larger than 1. As the number of candidates to the bit voter block increases, its computational complexity also increases. In general, the computational complexity is $O(\log(N))$, where 'N' is the sum of the weights. Since the BV block cannot be pipelined, the overall performance (speed) will hence decrease.

8.2.5 Extending BV for Ranked Median filtering

The standard median filter conceptually ranks all the values in a neighbourhood, and selects the middle value (e.g. the 5th value for a 3x3 window). A generalisation of this is to select the Rth ranked value (where $R = \lceil N*M/2 \rceil$ finds the standard median, $R = 1$ finds the minimum, and $R = N*M$ finds the maximum). This is called the Ranked Median filter.

A simple modification to our BV architecture is sufficient to implement this more general form of the median filter. For standard median, the BV block counts the number of '1' bits and compares this to $\lfloor N*M/2 \rfloor$. This is just a special case of the threshold value necessary for the Rth ranked value. We generalise the BV block so that it counts the number of '1' bits and compares this count with N*M-R. By supplying any appropriate value of R, a user can obtain any required ranking. This value (R) can be even stored in an on-chip register and modified on the fly. The architecture is outlined in Figure 8.15. Note that there is no performance penalty for generalising to Ranked Median filtering.

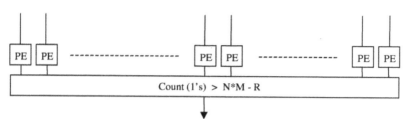

Figure 8.15 Modified architecture for Rank R Median filter

The above extensions to the algorithm can be combined, and used to give a very general median filter which does both Weighted Median and Ranked Median filtering.

8.2.6 Extending BV for signed input values (2's complement format)

The BV algorithm discussed so far assumes unsigned pixel values, and it needs some modification to handle signed numbers represented in 2's complement format. Let us consider the general case of a ranked median of rank R for an NxM window size. Observe that, during the first (MSB) iteration, the group of 1's corresponds to the *smaller* values (negative values) whereas the group of 0's corresponds to the *larger* values (positive values). As a result, the MSB of the result (rank R value) is '1' if the number of 1's in the input candidates is greater than or equal to R (see Figure 8.16a).

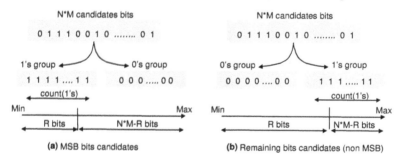

Figure 8.16 Signed bit voting process for an N*M rank R median

The result's MSB is thus found by the following logical relationship:

$$\text{count}(1's) \geq R$$

which can be rewritten as

$$\text{count}(1's) > R\text{-}1 \qquad (1)$$

However, the candidates' bits in _subsequent_ iterations are positively weighted (unlike the MSB) and hence should be treated as in the case of unsigned bit voter i.e. the result bit in subsequent iterations is obtained by the following logical relationship (see Figure 8.16b):

$$\text{count}(1\text{'s}) > N*M\text{-}R \qquad (2)$$

Note that in a simple median filter i.e. $R = (N*M+1)/2$, relations (1) and (2) are the same, and hence there is no difference in bit voting unit between the signed and unsigned case.

    Another difference in the first iteration for signed numbers is setting the value of the elimination bit. As mentioned above, during the MSB, the group of 1's in signed numbers corresponds to the group of smaller values (negative numbers), whereas the group of 0's corresponds to the group of larger values (positive numbers). If the median is among the 0's group, the 1's group should be eliminated, as before. The elimination process should replace this weak group (negative values) by even weaker values in order to preserve the balance in subsequent iterations, as in the unsigned bit voter case. However, since the contribution of subsequent bits to the pixel values is positive, the weakest possible value for the negative group to be replaced with is then _zero_. Hence, the elimination bit for the 1's group is zero. Alternatively, if the median value is among the 1's group in the MSB bits, then the 0's group should be eliminated in subsequent iterations. Since this group represents positive numbers, then its members values should be replaced by the strongest possible positive value in subsequent iterations i.e. 11....1. This means that the elimination bit for the 0's group is _one_. As a result, the elimination process for the first bit (MSB) is different from the one used for subsequent bits. In fact it is the opposite, since the group of 0's is eliminated by pulling each subsequent candidate bit to 1 (as opposed to 0 in subsequent iterations) whereas the group of 1's is eliminated by pulling each subsequent candidate bit to 0 (as opposed to 1 in subsequent iterations). Figure 8.17 illustrates the signed ranked-median algorithm for 5 input pixels and a rank $R = 3$ (standard median).

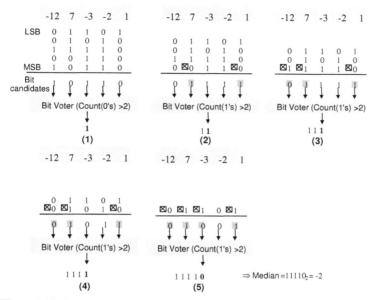

Figure 8.17 Illustration of signed ranked-median filtering algorithm (N*M = 5 and R=3).

Design of a signed Bit Voter median filter

Both relation (1) and (2) need a *count(1's)* operation. The only difference between the two relations is the threshold value. During the MSB, *count(1's)* should be compared to R-1, whereas in subsequent iterations it should be compared to N*M-R. These two comparisons are performed separately. An extra signal 'Is_MSB' (High during the MSB of the input operand) is needed to multiplex the two comparison results to the output. Therefore, the only difference between the unsigned bit voting unit and the signed one is the duplication of the threshold block. (For a 3x3 median filter, the extra logic can actually be packed into the already used CLBs so that the number of CLBs used remains 6 CLBs.)

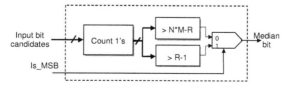

Figure 8.18 Signed bit Voting Unit

Since the elimination bit during the MSB cycle is the opposite of the elimination bit in subsequent iterations, a delayed version of 'Is_MSB' signal is used to invert the elimination bit value of the MSB. This does not consume any extra hardware in the PE, which still consumes just 1 CLB.

8.2.7 Comparison of TIS and BV algorithms

A 3x3 simple median filter based on BV has been described using HIDE4k and implemented for a 512x512 image of 8-bits per pixel, on an XC4013E-1 FPGA chip (24x24 CLBs). The Median Finding Unit occupies 15 CLBs. The whole circuit occupies 320 CLBs. Timing simulation shows that the circuit can run at a speed of 54 MHz. Table 8.2 summarises the performance (area and speed) of both TIS and BV architectures.

	Total Area (CLBs)	Median Finding Unit area (CLBs)	Speed (MHz)	Frame rate (Frames/Sec)
Triple Input Sorter Algorithm (TIS)	369	48	91	43
Bit Voter Algorithm (BV)	320	15	54	25

Table 8.2 Performance of 'Triple Input Sorter' and 'Bit Voter' Median architectures

It can be seen that the Bit Voter design is more compact than the Triple Input Sorter. On the other hand, it operates at a much lower maximum speed. This decrease in the speed, compared to TIS, is due to the feedback loop as explained in the closing remark of section 8.2.3 above. This speed differential may not be so pronounced on other FPGA architectures which have larger asynchronous look-up tables (e.g. Altera's devices). Note that a 54MHz speed will still allow real time median filtering in theory (25 frames per second for a 512x512 image of 8-bit pixels).

The major advantage of the BV design is that it is highly scaleable and it is relatively straightforward to generate an implementation for any window size. It is also easily extensible to Weighted Median and Ranked Median filtering.

8.3 Connected Component Labelling

Connected Component Labelling (CCL) is an important task in intermediate image processing with a large number of applications [Mil88][SP88]. The problem is to assign a unique label to each connected component in the image while ensuring a different label for each distinct object as illustrated in Figure 8.19. By assigning a unique label to each connected region, higher level image processing operations can identify, extract, and process each object separately.

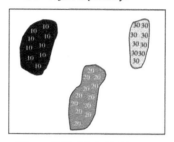

Figure 8.19 A labelled image

Previous hardware implementations of CCL were based on massively parallel approaches as they allocated one PE for each image pixel [AP92][DR81][MLL88][MPK88][OSZ93]. This inevitably requires a great deal of logic, so current solutions are often implemented in VLSI rather than on FPGAs. The FPGA implementation of such parallel approaches [MWJP96] is limited in the size of the image which can be labelled (e.g. 32x32).

In this section, we present an architecture for CCL based on a bit serial, *recursive* algorithm. It is readily scaleable, in that it can label images of any size (within reason), given the appropriate FPGA. We will first describe the algorithm used, and then describe the hardware architecture. Simulation results and conclusions are then given.

8.3.1   The proposed CCL algorithm

Given an arbitrary input image, the CCL algorithm which we use is an iterative one. Initially each object pixel is taken to be a separate object; then, by repeatedly applying a recursive neighbourhood operation, connected pixels are 'merged' by being made to share a common pixel value (the maximum in the neighbourhood). The key to requiring only a small number of iterations is the recursive nature of the neighbourhood operation, in which the result pixel is stored back in the image being labelled: this enables intermediate labels to be propagated across the image in one direction in a single pass.

In more detail, the algorithm, implemented in software by [Bro92], involves the following steps:

- Step 1: Threshold the input image to obtain a binary image. This will make all pixels in the objects equal to 1 and all other pixels equal to 0.

- Step 2: The thresholded binary image is initially labelled by assigning a different label to every non-zero pixel (i.e. initially treating each pixel as a separate object).

- Step 3: Apply a recursive 'non-zero maximum' neighbourhood operation on the image, using the first window in Figure 8.20. During this operation, each result pixel is stored back in the source image as explained in chapter 2. A complete forward pass is followed by an inverse pass, using the second window in Figure 8.20.

- Step 4: Repeat Step 3 until no change in the image occurs.

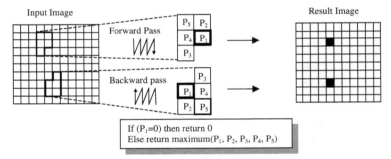

Figure 8.20 CCL neighbourhood operation.

8.3.2 The hardware architecture

The non-zero maximum recursive operation involved in this algorithm can use Donachy's architecture provided in chapter 3 for recursive neighbourhood operations. This architecture is a serial one, where pixels are fed to the FPGA one at a time. Note that since the windows used are 3x2, only one line buffer is required. Note also, that the same FPGA configuration can be used for both forward and backward passes. The latter is achieved by storing the output pixels in the reverse order in which the input pixels have been supplied.

However, even given this architecture, the hardware implementation of this algorithm faces several further challenges:

- If we wish to include the initial thresholding and initial labelling on-the-fly (which we do), then the first pass is special. Subsequent passes should bypass these stages. An unattractive solution would be to reconfigure the whole circuit after the first pass. To avoid that, our implementation provides extra logic for bypassing this stage in subsequent passes without reconfiguring. An extra signal ('Start') is provided to multiplex between the input image data and the initially labelled one.

- As mentioned before, the initial labelling has to assign a different label to every non-zero pixel. For an NxN image size, this could require $2Log_2N$ bits per pixel to represent intermediate label values. In order to reduce the number of bits per pixel, the initial labelling technique we adopt is: firstly to give the first non-zero pixel the highest label, and decrease the label value for subsequent non-zero pixels. Secondly, it gives adjacent non-zero pixels, within the same column (assuming a vertical scan), the same label; this will use fewer label values, thus reducing the required pixel wordlength. The latter could be estimated by knowing of the shape and maximum number of objects. Note that starting this initial labelling technique at the *maximum* label allows us to predetermine the label of one object in advance, which is the maximum pixel value chosen.

- A *conditional* maximum operation is involved. The maximum of five pixel values is divided into four maximum-of-two units, with one special unit implementing the *non-zero maximum condition*.

- In order to eliminate the propagation of the pixel label from the bottom of an image column to the top of another image column and vice versa (see section 3.8.3), a column counter is provided to inhibit this propagation. This column counter block produces two signals: *top* and *bottom*. The first turns high during the top pixel cycle of each column, whereas the second turns high during the bottom pixel cycle of each column.

- Detecting if a pass has resulted in any change needs to be done on the fly. A flag ("Finish") is maintained during processing, and is set to 1 if and when any result pixel differs from its original value. To test for termination of the whole algorithm, this flag must be 0 at the end of a particular pass (either forward or backward).

The organisation of the proposed architecture is given in Figure 8.21. In order to make the design scaleable and compact, we used bit serial arithmetic. For efficient implementation of the 'maximum of two' operators, data is processed Most Significant Bit First (MSBF). Since no addition is involved in this particular algorithm, *unsigned* binary arithmetic is used instead of SDNR. This means that new versions of some arithmetic blocks will need to be developed.

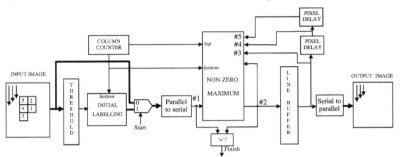

Figure 8.21 Architecture of the Labelling Unit

A forward pass is followed by an inverse one in which the input image (the output image of the previous pass) is scanned in reverse order (actually implemented by storing the output image in reverse order). The process is repeated until no change in the image occurs. The system architecture is illustrated in Figure 8.22.

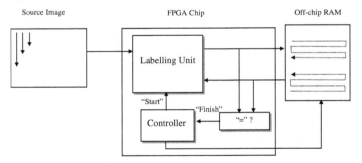

Figure 8.22 System architecture

The controller block generates the proper off-chip RAM address sequence. In addition, it generates the signal 'Start', which initiates the first pass, when it is set to one. It is set to zero in subsequent passes, thus bypassing the Threshold and the Initial Labelling.

Given prior knowledge of the shapes in the source image, an upper limit on the number of required passes can be set in advance, and in some common cases, labelling may need only one forward+backward pass.

8.3.3 FPGA implementation

In this section, we will have a closer look at the FPGA implementation of some new basic building blocks involved in the CCL circuit .

- **Initial labelling unit**

The labelling unit receives a binary pixel as input, and outputs a pixel value (a label) for each non-zero input. It gives the first non-zero pixel the highest label, and decrements the label value for subsequent non-zero pixels. Moreover, it gives adjacent non-zero pixels, within the same column, the same label. Note that this should not happen at the image border (i.e. from the bottom of an image column to the top of the following one). The signal *bottom* (produced by the image column counter) is used to inhibit this propagation (see Figure 8.23). The label decrementation is implemented using dedicated carry logic. The initial label value is assigned to an internal register value through the 'INIT' property for each register's flip-flop. A one bit slice of the labelling unit occupies 3 CLBs (laid out horizontally).

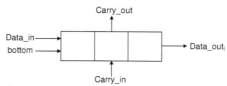

Figure 8.23 A one bit slice initial labelling unit layout

- **Unsigned maximum unit**

This unit selects the maximum of two unsigned inputs presented to its input serially, MSBF. Figure 8.24 shows the transition diagram of the Finite State Machine (FSM) performing the maximum 'O' of two unsigned operands 'X' and 'Y'. The start state is indicated by a '*' superscript. The control signal 'Is_MSB' is used to reset the initial state of the FSM to state 'A' indicating the start of two new operands. The unit operates with a latency of 2. The physical implementation of this machine occupies 4 CLBs.

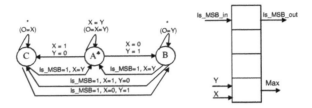

Figure 8.24 State diagram and FPGA floorplan of a 2-operands Maximum unit
Note that a minimum unit is determined in a similar manner.

- **Non-Zero Maximum unit**

This unit differs from an ordinary maximum unit in the sense that it effects a conditional maximum operation. If the incoming image pixel is zero, then the output is zero. Otherwise, the maximum value between this incoming pixel value and four other pixels is output. The unit is based on four 2-operands maximum units (see Figure 8.24 above). Extra logic is needed to detect if the bit serial input pixel is equal to zero or not. Note that both *bottom* and *top* signals (see Figure 8.21) are used to inhibit the propagation of the pixel label from the bottom of an image column to the top of another image column and vice versa.

The whole circuit has been generated from a high level HIDE4k description. It has been implemented on XC4013E-1 FPGA chip (24 by 24 CLBs). For a 256 by 256 image of 8 bits/pixel, the circuit occupies 282 CLBs and fits easily on to this chip.

8.3.4 Simulation results and conclusions

We have simulated the Labelling unit architecture using Xilinx Foundation Simulator for a variety of images. Figure 8.25 presents the simulation results for a simple case of an 8X8 image.

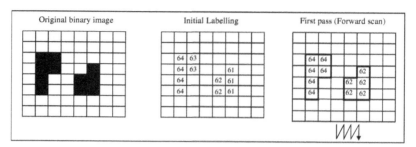

Figure 8.25 Simulation example of Connected Component Labelling

In this particular case, one forward pass is sufficient to label the image. However, that is not true in the general case. Objects of the forms given in Figure 8.26 cannot be labelled in one pass. In this case, two passes – one forward and one backward - are necessary.

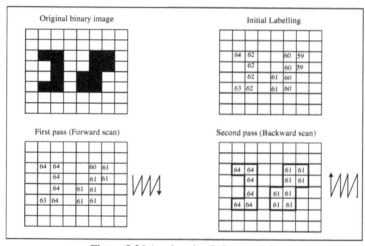

Figure 8.26 Another simulation example

Timing simulations show that the circuit can run at a speed of 77 MHz. For 256x256 images, using 16 bits per pixel, the current architecture delivers 70 passes per second. For the common case where a single forward+backward pass is sufficient, a frame rate of 35 frames per second (fps) can be achieved. In practice, in some circumstances, a smaller wordlength can be used (e.g. 10 bits), which results in proportionately faster operation.

Although the algorithm has been implemented in bit serial, it is possible to implement it using bit parallel in order to speed up the circuit at the expense of more hardware.

The main advantage of this algorithm over previous massively parallel implementations is that its hardware implementation is easily scaleable to full size images. On the other hand, because a single pass is not sufficient to label the whole image in the general case, this algorithm requires off-chip memory to store intermediate images. In addition, it is not possible to predict the number of passes required in the general case. Both these factors mean that the algorithm is not well suited to real time labelling using an FPGA embedded in a camera.

8.4 Conclusions

The following conclusions can be drawn from this chapter:

- The perimeter estimator design has demonstrated the reuse of the parameterised skeletons. Indeed, the whole perimeter design is merely a direct composition of a number of skeletons presented in chapter 7.
- The general-purpose median filter algorithm presented is novel and is hence a contribution to the state of the art of IP algorithms.
- The novel FPGA architecture presented for Connected Component Labelling (CCL) extends the maximum size which can be labelled on FPGAs. A labelling unit for a 256x256 image can easily fit on XC4013E (24x24 CLBs). Note that we had to come back to the hardware level to implement a specific architecture for this algorithm. This is due to:
- The use of unsigned arithmetic: this requires the design of unsigned binary based components. These were not available in the library but have been added.
- CCL is based on a recursive neighbourhood operation. Further, the latter is based on a *conditional* operation (non-zero-maximum). No skeleton has been designed for this type of operation.
- The CCL operation uses an on-the-fly detection of a condition (no change in the image occurred as a result of the application the non-zero maximum operation) to

determine the end of the operation. Again, no skeleton has been designed for this sort of operations.

This is an instance where an *ad hoc* solution had to be derived since no skeleton was provided for it in the library. Note that no matter how mature the hardware skeleton library is, it is likely that there will always be an instance where a particular operation cannot be modelled in terms of the existing skeletons. If these instances are not very common, it might be more appropriate to design ad hoc solutions for these, rather than adding specific skeletons into the library. The latter would condense the hardware skeleton library and hence confuse the user.

Chapter 9

Bit Parallel Implementation of the IPC

Chapter 9

Bit Parallel Implementation of the IPC

The basic functions required for nearly any signal processing operation include addition/subtraction, shifts and delays. These can then be used to construct more complicated structures such as multipliers and comparators. The existence of dedicated fast carry logic in the XC4000 makes parallel addition very efficient and hence makes a bit parallel implementation of the IPC an attractive solution.

In this chapter, we will present a bit parallel implementation of the basic Image Algebra (IA) operations set presented in chapter 3, and its extension for compound IP operations. We will first present the hardware implementation of the bit parallel basic building blocks. Then, we present the full architectures of IA neighbourhood operations along with their high level HIDE4k descriptions. To assist in building compound operations, three reusable high level skeletons will then be presented. Implementation results (timing and area) will then be given and discussed. Finally, conclusions will be drawn.

9.1 Bit parallel implementation of IA neighbourhood operations

In this section, we will present the FPGA implementation of the IA neighbourhood operations presented in chapter 3 (already implemented in bit serial) using 2's complement bit *parallel* arithmetic. A generic model of neighbourhood operations is given in Figure 3.3. Generally, a bit parallel architecture consumes more logic resources than a serial one. The area consumed by a bit parallel implementation grows with the pixel wordlength unlike a bit serial based implementation. It is then necessary to optimise the implementation for area even though this may lead to a more irregular structure.

Note that a W-bit parallel delay unit consumes 'W' times as much hardware as a bit serial delay unit (assuming 2's complement). One way of optimising the area of the bit parallel implementation would be to minimise the number of delay units. That is why we have decided to remove the global delay within each PE (see δ_{PE} in Figure 3.3). This in turn enables us to perform the global operation in a more parallel fashion, using a tree structure instead of the linear, chain structure used in the bit serial implementation. This actually dismantles the PE structure and exposes the pixel delay δ as shown in Figure 9.1. The latter shows a generic PxQ bit parallel neighbourhood operation, with a local operation **L** and a global operation **G** (assuming a horizontal scan direction).

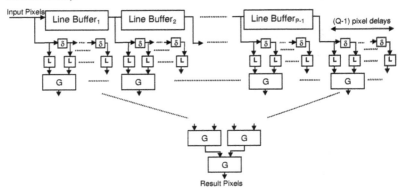

Figure 9.1 A conceptual generic PxQ bit parallel neighbourhood operation structure

9.1.1 Bit parallel basic building blocks

The following bit parallel blocks are needed for the implementation of all five IA operations:

- Bit parallel *local addition*
- Bit parallel *local multiplication*
- Bit parallel *global accumulation*
- Bit parallel *maximum/minimum unit*
- Pixel delays
- Line delays

9.1.1.1 Bit parallel local addition

In this operation, an input pixel is added to a constant coefficient. This is implemented using dedicated carry logic as explained in example 1 of chapter 5. Note that one operand represents the constant coefficient. A **W-in**-bit local addition unit with a constant coefficient **Coeff** is constructed by:

> is_tc_par_local_adder(Coeff, W-in, W-out, B)

9.1.1.2 Bit parallel local multiplication

Multiplication involves two basic operations: the generation of the partial products and their accumulation. To speed up the multiplication process, we should try to minimise the number of the partial products. Note that the partial products corresponding to '0' bits in the multiplier coefficient do not have to be included in the sum (see Figure 9.2).

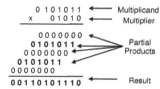

Figure 9.2 Multiplication process example

Secondly, in the case where the coefficient contains a string of consecutive 1's (e.g. 15=01111), the multiplication can be implemented using only two partial products (e.g. 15 = 16-1). This is equivalent to recoding the coefficient in Signed Digit notation (e.g. $15=16-1=1000\bar{1}$). Thus the multiplication is reduced to a simple subtraction (with input shift) as shown in Figure 9.3.

```
        0101011                        0101011
   x      01111                  x       01000ī
        0101011                  111111010101
       0101011                      0000000
      0101011                      0000000
     0101011                       0000000
    0000000                       0101011
    01010000101                   0000000
                                  01010000101
```

Figure 9.3 Multiplier coefficient recoding

Note that in practice, many window coefficients are suited to this optimisation and thus the use of this method for multiplication yields to a considerable reduction in hardware complexity.

The question that we have to answer now is: what is the minimal number of partial products required for a given multiplier? This is equivalent to the problem of finding the smallest number of non-zero digits in a Signed Digit representation of the multiplier. It has been shown that a sequence $z_{n-1}z_{n-2}....z_0$ is a minimal representation of an SD number if $z_i.z_{i-1}=0$ for $1 \leq i \leq n-1$, given that the most significant bits can satisfy $z_{n-1}.z_{n-2} \neq 1$. The algorithm for obtaining the minimal representation of a number is called *canonical recoding* [Hwa79][Kor93][KP99]. It has been also shown that using Canonic Signed Digit (CSD) representation for multiplication requires, on average, and for long wordlengths, 33% fewer adders than binary [Gar65]. We provide the following HIDE4k constructor for finding the CSD representation of an integer:

> **is_csd_representation(Integer_num, CSD_representation)**

where **CSD_representation** is a list containing the resulting CSD representation, as ± powers of 2 (e.g. [-1, 16] for **Integer_num** = 15).

In general, if R is the number of 1's and −1's in the minimal SD representation of a multiplier coefficient C, the multiplication is then performed by the accumulation of R values. Each value is in fact equal to the multiplicand value (M) multiplied by a certain power of two (N_k) as shown in the following equation:

$$C \times M = \left(\sum_{k=1}^{R} \text{sgn}_k \, 2^{P_k} \right) \times M = \sum_{k=1}^{R} \left(\text{sgn}_k \, 2^{P_k} \times M \right) \quad \text{where } \text{sgn}_k = 1 \text{ or } -1$$

$$= \sum_{k=1}^{R} \left(N_k \times M \right)$$

Multiplication by a power of two is simply a shift operation and does not consume any hardware. The multiplication then reduces to a reduction operator which can be performed by a tree structure as shown in Figure 9.4.

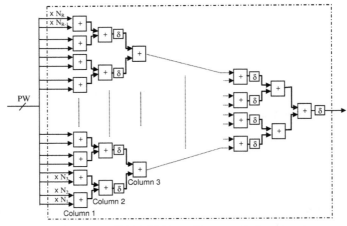

Figure 9.4 Bit parallel Multiplier architecture: Reduction operator

In order to speed up the circuit, a pipeline stage is added after each two columns of the tree (see Figure 9.4). Note that it is still possible to speed up the circuit even further by inserting a pipeline stage at each tree column at the expense of extra hardware.

We provide a utility for generating a generic reduction operator based on a tree structure. The corresponding skeleton is given by:

is_tc_par_reduction_op(Op_2, Input_List, Delay_pos, Max_width, Output_wordlength, Latency, B)

where:

Op_2 defines the 2-input operation in each node of the tree. In our multiplication case, to get a global accumulation, **Op_2 = add_sub**.

Input_List is a list of 2-tuples of the following form:

$$[(PW_1, N_1), (PW_2, N_2),\dots, (PW_i, N_i), \dots]$$

in which each tuple contains a particular input wordlength PW_i and its corresponding power of two coefficient N_i.

Delay_pos is a constant which determines the position of the delay elements and can have 4 possible values:

- '0' in which case no delays are used.
- '1' in which case the delay elements are inserted after each odd numbered column of the tree.
- '2' in which case the delay elements are inserted after each even numbered column of the tree (as in Figure 9.4).
- '3' in which case the delay elements are inserted after each column of the tree.

Max_width is the maximum output wordlength. This is needed to restrict the pixel width from growing unnecessarily.

Output_wordlength is the resulting output pixel wordlength and **Latency** is the latency of the resulting unit **B**.

In a multiplication case, the tree nodes (particularly in the first column) perform a *weighted* addition/subtraction since each input should be first multiplied by a power of two value (perhaps negative).

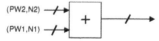

Figure 9.5 Basic component: A weighted adder/subtracter

The following HIDE4k constructor is provided for generating a weighted adder/subtracter unit:

> **is_tc_par_reduce2(add_sub, PW1,N1,PW2,N2, Max_width, Output_wordlength, B)**

The tree structure presented in Figure 9.4 is constructed from this weighted adder/subtracter constructor.

Using the above reduction operator and the canonical recoding utilities, a multiplication unit can be easily generated. The corresponding skeleton is:

> **is_tc_par_mult(Coeff, W-in, Max_width, Output_wordlength, Latency, B)**

where **Coeff** is the multiplier's constant coefficient, **W-in** is the input wordlength, **Max_width** is the maximum output wordlength.

9.1.1.3 Bit parallel global accumulation

Again, this unit is based on dedicated fast carry logic (see example 1 in chapter 5). It is generated by the above weighted adder/subtracter skeleton.

9.1.1.4 Bit parallel global maximum/minimum selectors

The maximum/minimum of two numbers A and B is performed by carrying out the subtraction A-B in bit parallel (using dedicated fast carry logic), and examining the sign of the result, i.e. the most significant bit (MSB) of the subtraction result as explained in section 4.1.3 (see Figure 9.6).

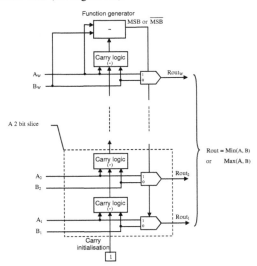

Figure 9.6 Bit parallel Maximum/Minimum unit

We provide a weighted maximum/minimum unit similar to the weighted addition/subtraction unit presented above (see Figure 9.7).

Figure 9.7 A weighted maximum/minimum

This is generated by the following skeleton:

> **is_tc_par_reduce2(Max_or_Min, PW1,N1,PW2,N2, Max_width, Output_wordlength, Latency, B)**

where **Max_or_Min** is either **max** or **min**. For maximum/minimum, **Max_width** does not need to be defined.

A full maximum/minimum reduction operator can then be constructed using the same skeleton as the one used for an adder/subtracter (+/-) reduction operation, i.e. by invoking:

> **is_tc_par_reduction_op(Max_or_Min, Input_List, Delay_pos, Max_width, Output_wordlength, Latency, B)**

9.1.1.5 Pixel buffers

A bit parallel pixel buffer is generated by the following skeleton:

> **is_tc_par_delay_unit(Wordlength, Delay, B)**

where **Wordlength** is the input pixel wordlength and **Delay** is the desired delay amount.

9.1.1.6 Line buffers

Bit parallel line buffers are implemented using the CLB's 16x1 synchronous RAMs with an address counter as explained in section 3.3.1. A line buffer of W-bit pixels is implemented by 'W' 1-bit line buffers operating in parallel.

Note that in bit serial, the line buffers should hold the input image pixels in 'W-proc' bits (W-proc: Processing wordlength) instead of just 'W-in' (W-in: Input Pixel wordlength). In bit parallel though, data will be buffered in 'W-in' bits as there are no bit-level synchronisation issues. This results in considerable area savings.

A set of **P-1** line buffers of size **Buffer_size** is generated by the following skeleton (see Figure 9.8):

> **is_tc_par_line_buffers(P, Buffer_size, Input_wordlength, B)**

Note that the input pixel is also passed through to the output.

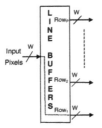

Figure 9.8 Line buffers

9.2 HIDE4k description of IA neighbourhood operations

As was the case in the previous chapters, we will first start by describing a convolution operation. The other IA operations will follow a similar template. For each IA operation, we will derive a suitable instance of the constructor predicate:

is_tc_par_nop(neighbourhood(Local_Op, Global_Op, Window, Buffer_size),
Input_wordlength, Output_wordlength, Latency, B)

Note first that since the architectures are implemented in bit parallel (and are less regular than a bit serial equivalent) and because the implementation makes extensive use of dedicated carry logic which runs in the vertical direction only (on XC4000), HIDE's simple placement heuristic is not appropriate. Although the intermediate HIDE4k description will still be in terms of horizontal and vertical composition, we will not generate actual placement information for bit parallel implementations. We will leave this task to Xilinx PAR tools and switch off our automatic placement:

is_automatic_placement(false)

9.2.1 A PxQ convolution operation

Consider a convolution operation with a generic PxQ window represented by a list of lists as follows:

$$[[C_{P,Q}, ..., C_{P,1}], [C_{P-1,Q}, ..., C_{P-1,1}], ...,[C_{1,Q}, ..., C_{1,1}]]$$

Unused window positions are represented by '~'.

Suppose the image is scanned horizontally. The line buffers (see section 9.1.1.6 above) generate a column of pixels within the window neighbourhood. The remaining Q-1 pixel columns are obtained by simple pixel delays (see 'Pix_delay' unit in Figure

9.10). Based on the bit parallel pixel buffer unit presented in section 9.1.1.5, and given a high level description of the IP operation to be performed, the whole 'Pix-delay' unit is generated by the following HIDE4k constructor:

is_tc_par_pix_delay(Input_wordlength, Op_description, Pix_delay)

In the case of IA neighbourhood operations:

Op_description = neighbourhood(Local_Op, Global_Op, Window, Buffer_size)   (9.1)

Once all the PxQ pixels of a particular neighbourhood are available, the local operation (multiplication) needs first to be performed, followed by the global operation (accumulation). In this particular case, we can do a useful optimisation by noting that the local multiplication (which essentially is an *accumulate* of partial results) and the global *accumulation* can be combined in a single large accumulator. This will result in the saving of delay elements, which would have been necessary if each local multiplication has been performed separately. Figure 9.9 illustrates this for the two coefficients 21 and 1. In effect, we are just balancing the complete accumulation tree.

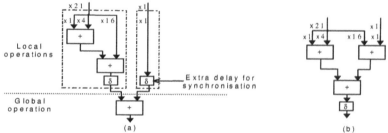

Figure 9.9 Convolution process: (a) Local multiplications performed separately (b) Merging the local multiplications with the global accumulation

For a coefficient $C_{i,j}$, each incoming pixel within the neighbourhood is replicated $R_{i,j}$ times, where $R_{i,j}$ is the number of 1's and -1's in the minimal CSD representation of $C_{i,j}$. In general, the whole multiplication process within the window neighbourhood will result in $Pn = \sum_{i,j} R_{i,j}$ pixels ($1 \leq i \leq P$, $1 \leq j \leq Q$), where each replicated pixel has a particular power of two weight $(N_{i,j})_k$, $1 \leq k \leq R_{i,j}$, such as:

$$C_{i,j} = \sum_{k=1}^{R_{i,j}} sgn_{i,j} \, 2^{(P_{i,j})_k} = \sum_{k=1}^{R_{i,j}} (N_{i,j})_k \quad \text{where } sgn_{i,j} = 1 \text{ or } -1$$

The multiplication operation results effectively in the replication of each set of pixel ports in the outer ports of **Pix-delay** unit i.e. creates a *network connection* instead of a physical block. This process is performed by the following constructor:

> **is_tc_par_local_op(mult, accum, Window, New_Coeff_List, Latency, B)**

where:

Window is the list of lists containing the window coefficients.

New_Coeff_List is a list containing each output pixel wordlength $PW_{i,j}$ along with its corresponding power of two coefficient $(N_{i,j})_k$:

$$[..,(PW_{i,j}, (N_{i,j})_1), (PW_{i,j}, (N_{i,j})_2),.., (PW_{i,j},(N_{i,j})_{R_{i,j}}),..], i = 1,2,..,P \text{ and } j=Q,Q\text{-}1,..,1$$

$$(9.2)$$

The global operation (accumulation) can then be seen as a tree of two-operand additions/subtractions. Each addition/subtraction operand has an associated power of two weight (particularly in the first column of the tree).

The maximum possible pixel wordlength (i.e. the minimum necessary processing wordlength) depends on the nature of the neighbourhood operation (convolution in this case) and on the window coefficients. In general, this can be deduced from a high level description of the IP operation to be performed, using the following rule:

> **is_maximum_pixel_width(Input_wordlength, Op_description, Max_width)**

The convolution processing unit can then be described as follows:

```
is_tc_par_proc_unit(neighbourhood(mult, accum, Window, Buffer_size),
                    Input_wordlength, Output_ wordlength, Latency_in, Latency_out, B):-
is_tc_par_ local_op(mult, accum, Window, New_Coeff_List, Latency_Loc, Local),
is_maximum_pixel_width(Input_wordlength, neighbourhood(mult, accum, Window,
                    Buffer_size), Max_width),
is_tc_par_reduction_op(add_sub, New_Coeff_List, 2, Max_width, Output_ wordlength,
                    Latency_Glo, Global),
B =horizontal([Local, Global]),
Latency_out is Latency_in+Latency_Loc + Latency_Glo.
```

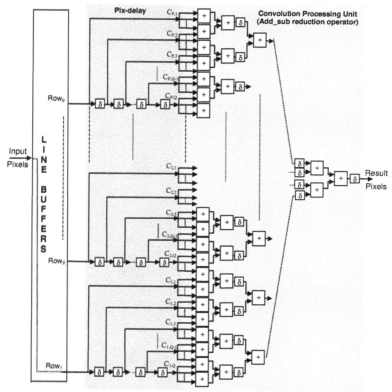

Figure 9.10 Architecture of a PxQ bit parallel convolution

9.2.2 A PxQ Multiplicative Maximum/Minimum operation

The structure of this unit is presented in Figure 9.11. The local operation (multiplication) is performed as explained in section 9.1.1.2. An *add_sub* reduction operator is used for each local multiplication. Based on this reduction operator, the whole local operation unit can be generated by invoking:

---
is_tc_par_local_op(mult, Max_or_Min, Window, New_Coeff_List, Latency, B)
---

where **Max_or_Min** is **max** or **min**.

The global operation uses a maximum/minimum reduction operator similar to an *add_sub* one as explained in section 9.1.1.4 above. The core Multiplicative Maximum-Minimum processing unit can then be described as follows:

is_tc_par_proc_unit(neighbourhood(mult, Max_or_Min, Window, Buffer_size),

                Input_wordlength, Output_ wordlength, Latency_in, Latency_out, B):-

is_tc_par_local_op(mult, Max_or_Min, Window, New_Coeff_List, Latency_Loc, Local),

is_maximum_pixel_width(Input_wordlength, neighbourhood(mult, Max_or_Min,

                Window, Buffer_size), Max_width),

is_tc_par_reduction_op(Max_or_Min, New_Coeff_List, 1, Max_width,

                Output_ wordlength, Latency_Glo, Global),

B = horizontal([Local, Global]),

Latency_out is Latency_in+Latency_Loc + Latency_Glo.

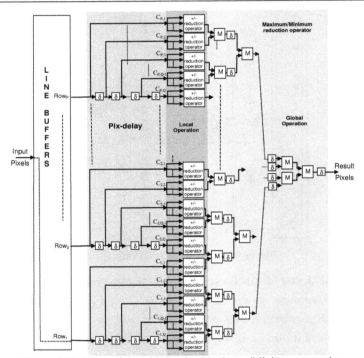

Figure 9.11 Bit parallel Multiplicative Maximum/Minimum operation

9.2.3   A PxQ Additive Maximum/Minimum operation

In this case, the local operation is a simple addition whereas the global one is a maximum/minimum operation as in the previous case. The design of this unit, follows immediately, from the two previous cases and is shown in Figure 9.12.

    The whole local addition operation can be easily derived from the constant adder constructor (see section 9.1.1.1). It is generated by:

> **is_tc_par_ local_addition(add, Max_or_Min, Window, New_Coeff_List, Latency, B)**

where:

New_Coeff_List is a new list containing each output pixel wordlength $PW_{i,j}$ along with its corresponding power of two coefficient $(N_{i,j})_k$ as given in (**9.2**). Note that $(N_{i,j})_k = 0$ in this neighbourhood operation type.

The core Additive Maximum-Minimum processing unit can be described as follows:

> **is_tc_par_proc_unit(neighbourhood(add, Max_or_Min, Window, Buffer_size),**
> **Input_wordlength, Output_ wordlength, Latency_in, Latency_out, B):-**
> **is_ tc_par_ local_op(add, Max_or_Min, Window, New_Coeff_List, Latency_Loc, Local),**
> **is_maximum_pixel_width(Input_wordlength, neighbourhood(add, Max_or_Min, Window,**
> **Buffer_size), Max_width),**
> **is_tc_par_reduction_op(Max_or_Min, New_Coeff_List, 1, Max_width,**
> **Output_ wordlength, Latency_Glo, Global),**
> **B=horizontal([Local, Global]),**
> **Latency_out is Latency_in+Latency_Loc + Latency_Glo.**

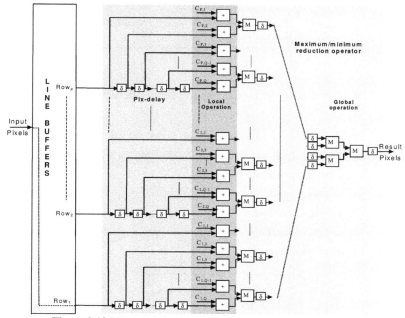

Figure 9.12 Bit parallel Additive Maximum/Minimum operation

9.2.4 Overall description of a generic PxQ IA neighbourhood operation

We can see from the previous sections that a core neighbourhood description (B) can be constructed by the following generic skeleton:

---
is_tc_par_proc_unit(neighbourhood(Local_Op, Global_Op, Window, Buffer_size),

            Input_wordlength, Output_ wordlength, Latency_in, Latency_out, B)

Based on the line buffer constructor and the pixel delay one, and given a high level description of the IP operation to be performed, the following generates the necessary line and pixel buffers:

---
is_tc_par_line_and_pixel_buffers(Input_wordlength, Op_description, B)

The full neighbourhood operation can then be easily built as follows:

---
is_tc_par_nop(neighbourhood(Local_Op, Global_Op, Window, Buffer_size),

         Input_wordlength, Output_ wordlength, Latency, B):-

is_tc_par_line_pixel_buffers(Input_wordlength, neighbourhood(Local_Op, Global_Op,

                 Window, Buffer_size), Buffers),

is_tc_par_proc_unit(neighbourhood(Local_Op, Global_Op, Window, Buffer_size),

         Input_wordlength, Output_ wordlength, 0, Latency, Proc_Unit),

B =horizontal([Buffers, Proc_Unit]).

9.3 Extending the model to compound operations

In this section, we will show how to extend the previous simple instruction set to certain compound operations. In the following, we will present three skeletons for three frequently used sets of IP operations.

9.3.1 Pipeline skeleton

In this type of operation, a neighbourhood operation is followed by zero or more point operations (see Figure 9.13).

Figure 9.13 Instruction Pipelining skeleton

A point operation can be with parameter(s), i.e. Image-Scalar-Image (e.g. Division, Multiplication) or Image-Multi-Scalar-Image operations (e.g. multi-threshold), or without parameters i.e. Image-Image point operations (e.g. Absolute). The pipeline operations for these two cases are described respectively as:

> **point_op(Previous_pipeline_stage, Parameters)**
>
> **point_op(Previous_pipeline_stage)**   (9.3)

where

point_op: is a point operation identifier (e.g. **'div'** or **'/'** for division, **'mult'** or **'*'** for multiplication and **'abs'** for Absolute).

Previous_pipeline_stage: is the high level description of the pipeline structure up to **point_op**.

For instance a convolution with the following template (*Blur*):

1	1	1
1	1	1
1	1	1

$\div 9$

is described as:

> **div(neighbourhood_operation(mult, accum, [[1,1,1],[1,1,1],[1,1,1]], Buf_size), 9)**

Note that the prefix **'div'** can, for readability, be written in infix form as **'/'**, as follows:

> **neighbourhood_operation(mult, accum, [[1,1,1],[1,1,1],[1,1,1]], Buf_size)/ 9**

Similarly, an absolute Laplace filter would be described as follows:

> **abs(neighbourhood_operation(mult, accum, [[~,-1,~],[-1,4,-1],[~,-1,~]], Buf_size))**

As presented in chapter 7, we provide the following skeletons for I-I, IS-I and IMS-I operations respectively:

> **is_tc_par_II_op(Point_op, IWL, OWL, Latency, B)**
>
> **is_tc_par_ISI_op(Point_op, Param, IWL, OWL, Latency, B)**
>
> **is_tc_par_IMSI_op(Point_op, List_of_param, IWL, OWL, Latency, B)**

The processing unit of any pipeline structure of the sort presented in Figure 9.13 can then be constructed as follows:

```
% For point operations without parameters
is_tc_par_proc_unit(Point_op(Previous_pipeline_stage), IWL, OWL, Lat_in, Lat_out, B):-
is_tc_par_proc_unit(Previous_pipeline_stage, IWL, OWL_temp, Lat_in,
                    Lat_temp, B_temp),
is_tc_par_II_op(Point_op, OWL_temp, OWL, Point_op_lat, Point_op_desc),
B = horizontal([B_temp, Point_op_desc]),
Lat_out is Lat_temp+Point_op_lat.

% For point operations with parameters: IMSI operations case (ISI case is similar)
is_tc_par_proc_unit(Point_op(Previous_pipeline_stage, List_of_param), IWL, OWL,
                    Lat_in, Lat_out, B):-
```

```
is_tc_par_proc_unit(Previous_pipeline_stage, IWL, OWL_temp, Lat_in, Lat_temp,
                B_temp),
is_tc_par_IMSI_op(Point_op, List_of_param, OWL_temp, OWL, Point_op_lat,
                Point_op_desc),
B = horizontal([B_temp, Point_op_desc]),
Lat_out is Lat_temp+Point_op_lat.
```

Note that a multiplication point operation is implemented by the *add_sub* reduction operator presented in section 9.1.1.2 above. Note also that a bit parallel implementation of an absolute unit has already been presented in section 7.4.2.

The following will present the FPGA implementation of a bit parallel, constant division point operation.

Parallel constant division (IS-I, point_op = div)

Consider a constant division by D. If the divisor D is approximated to a fraction $\frac{X}{Y}$, where Y is a power of two, then the division is reduced to a multiplication followed by a right shift. The multiplication is performed as explained in section 9.1.1.2 above. For instance, consider the case of the *Blur* operation. The division by 9 could be approximated to a multiplication by $\frac{7}{64} = \frac{7}{2^6}$, which implies a multiplication by 7 followed by 6 right shifts. Using the *canonical recoding* algorithm, the multiplication by $7 = 2^3 - 1$ is performed using only one subtraction block. Therefore, a division by 9 consumes only one subtraction unit. In general, divisors are optimised offline and stored in a look-up table. The following IS-I skeleton generates a division unit:

```
is_tc_par_ISI_op(div, Divisor, Input_wordlength, Output_wordlength, Div_latency, B)
```

9.3.2   Parallel neighbourhood operations skeleton

In this type of operations, 'N' neighbourhood operations having the same window size (followed by zero or more point operations) are performed in parallel before they join in a Multi-Image-Image operation.

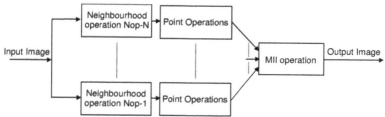

Figure 9.14 parallel IP operations on the same input image

Each parallel operation can be generated using the previous skeleton. The MI-I operation can be decomposed into a tree of Image-Image-Image (II-I) operations as shown in Figure 9.15. The supported II-I operations are addition (+), subtraction (-), maximum (max) and minimum (min). Note that a MI-I operation can use a mixture of II-I operation types.

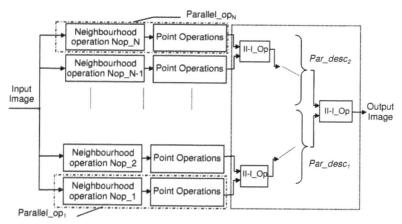

Figure 9.15 Parallel operations supported structure

The high level description (**Par_desc**) of this operation would be defined using iii_op (for II-I_op in Figure 9.15) as follows:

$$\text{Par\_desc} = \text{Iii\_op}(\text{Par\_desc}_1, \text{Par\_desc}_2) \qquad (9.4)$$

Par_desc$_1$ and **Par_desc$_2$** are defined either recursively as compound operations of the form (9.4) itself, or as ('terminal') pipeline skeletons (**Parallel_op$_i$**) of the form (9.3), i.e.

$$\text{Parallel\_op}_i = \text{point\_op}_{i,1}(....\text{point\_op}_{i,k}(\text{neighbourhood\_operation}(\text{Local}_i, \text{Global}_i,$$
$$\text{Window}_i, \text{Buf\_size}_i), \text{par}_{ik}),..., \text{par}_{i,1})$$

For instance, a Sobel operation will be described by:

$$\text{abs}(\text{neighbourhood}(\text{mult},\text{accum},[[1,2,1],[0,0,0],[-1,-2,-1]], \text{Buf\_size}))$$

$$+$$
$$\text{abs(neighbourhood(mult,accum,[[1,0,-1],[2,0,-2],[1,0,-1]], Buf\_size))}$$

Note that when two parallel operations join in an II-I operation, they need to be synchronised. Extra delay should be added to the least latent operation. The following constructor is provided for that purpose:

```
is_synchronised(Blk1, Lat1, Blk2, Lat2, New_Blk1, New_Blk2, New_Lat)
```

Blk1, Blk2 are the two parallel operations units to be synchronised. **Lat1, Lat2** is their respective output latency.

New_Blk1, New_Blk2 are the new synchronised blocks, and **New_Lat** is their corresponding latency (= **max(Lat1, Lat2)**).

Given a high level description such as in (**9.4**), the following implements the corresponding FPGA processing unit:

```
is_tc_par_proc_unit(III_op(Par_desc1, Par_desc2), IWL,OWL, Lat_in, Lat_out, B):-
is_tc_par_proc_unit(Par_desc1, IWL, OWL_1, Lat_in, Lat_1, B_1),
is_tc_par_proc_unit(Par_desc2, IWL, OWL_2, Lat_in, Lat_2, B_2),
is_synchronised(B_1, Lat_1, B_2, Lat_2, New_B1, New_B2, New_Lat),
is_tc_par_III_op(III_op, OWL_1, OWL_2, OWL, III_op_Lat, III_op_unit),
B = horizontal([ vertical([New_B1, New_B2]), III_op_unit]),
Lat_out is New_Lat+III_op_Lat.
```

The whole architecture is then constructed by adding the necessary line and pixel buffers as shown in section 9.2.4 above.

9.3.3 Pipelining neighbourhood operations

In this type of operations, compound operations of the form (9.3) or (9.4) are cascaded in a pipeline as shown in Figure 9.16. Each pipeline stage contains *one* neighbourhood operation (simple or parallel).

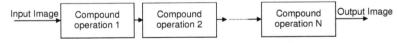

Figure 9.16 neighbourhood operation pipeline

This structure is described by:

Op_description = pipeline(List_of_compound_operation_descriptions) (9.5)

For instance, an open operation applied on 256x256 images of 8-bits/pixel would be described by:

Open = pipeline([neighbourhood(add, min, [[0,0,0],[0,0,0],[0,0,0]], 256)),

neighbourhood(add, max, [[0,0,0],[0,0,0],[0,0,0]], 256))])

Skeletons were provided above for generating the architecture of each compound operation within the list. Note the need for a wordlength converter between two compound operations if the resulting pixel wordlength of one operation is different from the required input pixel wordlength of the following operation. For that purpose, we provide the following I-I point operation skeleton:

> **is_tc_par_II_op(tc_wl_converter, IWL, OWL, Latency, B)**

This converts an IWL-bit input into an OWL-bit result. It could be either a limiter if IWL >OWL or a sign extension in the opposite case.

Figure 9.17 Format converter

The whole architecture (including pixel and line buffers) corresponding to (9.5) is generated by the following skeleton:

```
is_tc_par_nop(pipeline(List_of_operation), IWL, OWL, Latency, B):-
is_tc_par_nop_x(List_of_operation, , IWL ,OWL, 0, Latency, List_Op),
B = horizontal(List_Op).

is_tc_par_nop_x([ ],IWL, IWL, Latency, Latency, [ ]).
is_tc_par_nop_x([H|T], IWL, OWL, Latency_in, Latency_out, [B_1|Tail]):-
is_tc_par_proc_unit(H, IWL, OWL1, Latency_in, Lat1, B_1_temp),
is_tc_par_line_pixel_buffers(IWL, H, Buffers_H),
B_1 = horizontal([Buffers_H, B_1_temp]),
is_tc_par_nop_x(T, OWL1, OWL, Lat1, Latency_out, Tail_temp),
is_tc_par_line_pixel_buffers(OWL1, T, Buffers_Tail),
Tail = horizontal([Buffers_Tail, Tail_temp]).
```

If point operations need to be performed before any neighbourhood operation, then this can be done by considering these point operations as a compound operation applied on an identity neighbourhood operation represented by **ident** (treated as a special case). For instance, if a threshold operation needs to be performed before an Erode operation, then the corresponding operation high level description would be:

> **pipeline([threshold(ident), neighbourhood(add, min, [[0,0,0],[0,0,0],[0,0,0]], 256)])**

A significant achievement of our system is that the skeletons (9.3), (9.4) and (9.5) can be nested to any depth and interchangeably (FPGA area permitting). This has been a big problem in software skeletons [Ham00].

9.4 Implementation results

FPGA configurations have been generated from the above HIDE4k descriptions for the five IA operators, in addition to Sobel and Open compound operations. The generated EDIF netlists do not contain placement information. This task is left to Xilinx PAR tools.

The resulting area and simulated performance of all operators are summarised in the following tables. These figures are compared with the corresponding figures of the bit serial based architectures. The architectures were generated for 256x256 images of 8 bits per pixel and targeted XC4036EX-2. The FPGA floorplans of some of these architectures are presented in Appendix V.

- **Convolution (Laplace)**

is_tc_par_nop(neighbourhood(mult, accum,[[~,-1,~],[-1,4,-1],[~,-1,~]], 256), 8, OWL, Latency, B)

Arithmetic	Speed (MHz)	Pixel throughput (MPixel/sec)	Total Area(CLBs)	Total Area – Line Buffer Area (CLBs)
2's complement Bit parallel	47	47	228	68
2's complement Bit serial LSBF (see section 6.5)	75	6.25	283	79

- **Multiplicative Maximum/Minimum**

is_tc_par_nop(neighbourhood(mult, max, [[1,2,1],[2,4,2],[1,2,1]], 256), 8, OWL, Latency, B)

Arithmetic	Speed (MHz)	Pixel throughput (MPixel/sec)	Total Area(CLBs)	Total Area – Line Buffer Area (CLBs)
2's complement Bit parallel	29	29	292	132
Online Arithmetic (see section 6.4)	75	6.25	442	238

- **Additive Maximum/Minimum**

is_tc_par_nop(neighbourhood(add, max, [[1,1,1],[1,1,1],[1,1,1]], 256), 8, OWL, Latency, B)

Arithmetic	Speed (MHz)	Pixel throughput (MPixel/sec)	Total Area(CLBs)	Total Area – Line Buffer Area (CLBs)
2's complement Bit parallel	30	30	330	170
Online Arithmetic (see section 6.4)	75	7.5	458	286

- **Open**

```
is_tc_par_nop(pipeline([ neighbourhood(add, min, [[0,0,0],[0,0,0],[0,0,0]], 256)),
                 neighbourhood(add, max, [[0,0,0],[0,0,0],[0,0,0]], 256))]),
           8, OWL, Latency, B)
```

Arithmetic	Speed (MHz)	Pixel throughput (MPixel/sec)	Total Area(CLBs)	Total Area – Line Buffer Area (CLBs)
2's complement Bit parallel	30	30	528	208
2's complement bit serial MSBF (see section 7.6.1)	87	10.8	443	123

- **Sobel**

```
is_tc_par_nop(abs(neighbourhood(mult, accum, [[1,2,1],[0,0,0],[-1,-2,-1]], 256))
         + abs(neighbourhood(mult, accum, [[1,0,-1],[2,0,-2],[1,0,-1]], 256)),
           8, OWL, Latency, B)
```

Arithmetic	Speed (MHz)	Pixel throughput (MPixel/sec)	Total Area(CLBs)	Total Area – Line Buffer Area (CLBs)
2's complement Bit parallel	44.6	44.6	322	162
2's complement bit serial LSBF (see section 7.6.2)	75	6.8	340	136

We can see from these figures that all bit parallel architectures operate at a slower clock speed than their corresponding serial architectures. However, the pixel throughput is substantially higher for the bit parallel implementations.

Concerning the area, the bit parallel architectures compete very well with the bit serial ones. In fact, the bit parallel ones consume less area in some cases (most noticeably, compared to the online based architectures). This is partly due to the line buffer area saving (see section 9.1.1.6 above). It is also due to the sparsity of the above windows (e.g. Laplace filter) and the fact that no multiplications are needed for all the above examples, as all the coefficients are powers of two. These two cases occur frequently in IP filters. Note, however, that the area consumed by the bit parallel architectures grows linearly with the input pixel wordlength, which is not the case for the bit serial architectures where the area consumed is independent of the pixel wordlength. In addition, the speed of the bit parallel architectures is expected to decrease with the wordlength as more routing resources would be needed (routing congestion). This makes the performance of bit parallel architectures less predictable than bit serial ones. Another disadvantage of the bit parallel architectures is that they are massively based on the dedicated fast carry logic which runs only in the vertical direction. This makes the placement alternatives fewer and may result in placement congestion in much bigger architectures.

9.5 Conclusions

In this chapter, we have presented a bit parallel implementation of the proposed IP Coprocessor. Since parallel architectures are generally irregular, a simple placement based on horizontal and vertical constructors is not appropriate. Instead, although the description still appears in term of horizontal and vertical predicates, the placement task is left to the Xilinx PAR tools. The implementation makes extensive use of dedicated fast carry logic available on the XC4000. The use of CSD representation reduces the number of partial products in a multiplication and is very useful in the case of Image Algebra operations where integer coefficients are used. Further, these are often powers of two, which make the multiplication operation redundant. This makes the bit parallel implementation very competitive area-wise compared with the bit serial one. In fact, it can lead to even less area consumption in certain cases though the consumed area grows with the pixel wordlength.

Although bit parallel architectures result in slower clock speeds, the pixel throughput is substantially higher than the corresponding bit serial ones. The time-hardware product (Pixel clock period x Area) is hence definitely smaller (i.e. better) for a bit parallel implementation on XC4000 FPGAs at least for our particular application. This is not the same conclusion found in fine grain FPGAs or VLSI [DR85][And93][Øye96] where a bit serial implementation often leads to a better time-hardware product. The reason for this is the existence of the dedicated fast carry logic on the XC4000 FPGAs. This logic is separate from the CLBs' LUTs and uses dedicated fast routing tracks. It is available for the digital designer with no extra cost.

Another advantage of using bit parallel arithmetic resides in its simple control scheme compared to bit serial. Indeed, bit parallel architectures do not need both a pixel clock and a bit clock as all the pixel bits are processed simultaneously.

Although the CSD technique employed here reduces significantly the number of adders/subtracters needed in a multiplication, it is not the optimal solution. Better results can be obtained by applying Dempster-MacLeod algorithm (DM) [DMac94]. The latter optimises the number of adders needed in a multiplication by factoring the constant coefficient (if possible) as illustrated in Figure 9.18 for a multiplication by 45.

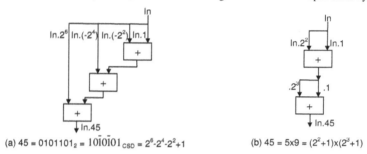

(a) $45 = 0101101_2 = 10\overline{1}0\overline{1}01_{CSD} = 2^6-2^4-2^2+1$ (b) $45 = 5 \times 9 = (2^2+1) \times (2^3+1)$

Figure 9.18 Constant multiplication using (a) CSD (b) DM

Note, however, that the coefficients used in IP windows are generally small and hence may not benefit greatly from this optimisation.

Another way of optimising the number of adders/subtracters needed in an IA neighbourhood operation is to exploit the fact that a particular coefficient value might figure more than once in a window. In such cases, a global operation could be applied first to the common elements, and then the local operation (multiplication in particular) would need to be performed just once on the result. This is illustrated for the case of a convolution in Figure 9.19 (with just two identical coefficients for illustration).

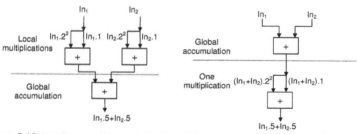

Figure 9.19 Another possible optimisation of the number of adders (convolution case)

In general, the problem of optimising the hardware needed for a bit parallel IA neighbourhood operation should also take into consideration the number of delays necessary for meeting the required timing constraints and for synchronisation as well (in addition to the minimisation of the number of adders/subtracters) [Har91][SB95][SS94]. Our actual system does not claim to be optimal. The application of the above optimisations into our system, is a possible area of future work.

This chapter has also presented three present three high level skeletons for three frequently used sets of IP operations. An important feature of these skeletons is that they can be nested to any depth and interchangeably (FPGA area permitting).

The following tables summarise the skeletons introduced in this chapter (all based on 2's complement bit parallel arithmetic):

Skeleton name	Op	Function
is_tc_par_reduce2(Op, PW1, N1, PW2, N2, Max_width, Output_wordlength, B)	**add_sub**	performs a 2-operand *weighted* addition/subtraction
	max	performs a 2-operand *weighted* maximum operation
	min	performs a 2-operand *weighted* minimum operation
is_tc_par_reduction_op(Op, Input_List, Delay_pos, Max_width, Output_wordlength, Latency, B)	**add_sub**	reduces a set of N inputs (provided in 'Input_List') into one result using a tree of 2-operands II-I operations (**Op**)
	max	
	min	

Skeleton name	Function
is_tc_par_delay_unit(Wordlength, Delay, B)	Constructs a bit parallel pixel buffer
is_tc_par_line_buffers(P, Buffer_size, Input_wordlength, B)	Constructs a set of 'P-1' line buffers of size 'Buffer_size'
is_tc_par_II_op(tc_wl_converter, IWL, OWL, Latency, B)	Constructs a wordlength converter (IWL → OWL)

Skeleton name	Par_desc	Function
is_tc_par_nop(Par_desc, Input_wordlength, Output_wordlength, Latency, B)	**See (9.3)**	Constructs a pipeline skeleton composed of a neighbourhood operation followed by zero or more point operations

	See (9.4)	Constructs a skeleton composed of 'N' neighbourhood operations having the same window size (followed by zero or more point operations) performed in parallel on the same image. The results, then, join in a Multi-Image-Image operation
	See (9.5)	This skeleton pipelines compound operations of the form (9.3) or (9.4)

Chapter 10

Realisation of the IPC on an FPGA Video board

Chapter 10

Realisation of the IPC on an FPGA Video Board

In this chapter, we will present a real hardware implementation of the IPC working on a commercial FPGA based video processing board. First, we will explain our choice of FPGA board and give details of the chosen hardware platform (the Visicom's Vigra Vision board). An implementation of the IPC on this board using the skeleton-like approach is then presented. This is limited to a video processing IPC rather than a full coprocessor model. The final working system will then be illustrated by some practical examples.

It will be seen that going from the designs of the previous chapters to a fully working system with real video input is fraught with many low level difficulties. This chapter will address a number of these difficulties. Although these problems are not central to the main focus of this book, they are an important part of any system intended for video processing, and they have influenced the final design of the image processing architectures.

10.1 Choice of the FPGA Board

Two possible FPGA boards were available as hardware platforms for this project:
1. Microtech's Aristotle board [Mir99] with whom we had an already established contact.
2. Visicom's Vigra Vision PCI video board [Vig98]. The latter have expressed interest in our work and were prepared to donate the necessary hardware and support.

These two boards were briefly presented in chapter 1. The selection of the Vigra Vision board was influenced by the following factors:
- Integrated real time video capture and display.
- Software/Hardware components for image capture and storage made available.
- Support from the manufacturers.

We now examine the structure of Visicom's Vigra Vision board in more detail.

10.2 The Vigra Vision PCI Video Board

The Vigra Vision PCI video board from Visicom is a single slot PCI card which combines video acquisition, FPGA based real-time processing, and display. A function block diagram for the Vigra Vision video board is given by Figure 10.1.

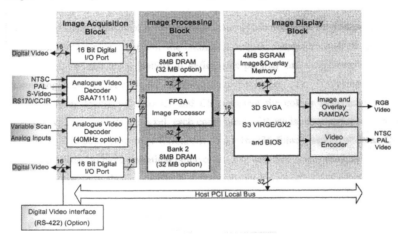

Figure 10.1 Functional block diagram of Vigra Vision PCI video board

The Vigra Vision structure can be subdivided into three main anatomical blocks: the image acquisition block, the image processing block and the image display block. The following will describe these main parts in more detail.

10.2.1 The Image Acquisition Block

Images are captured by the Philips SAA7111A chip [Phi98a]. The latter combines a two-channel analogue pre-processing circuit including source selection, anti-aliasing filter and an Analogue to Digital Converter (ADC), an automatic clamp and gain control, a clock generation circuit (CGC), a digital multi-standard decoder (PAL, NTSC, SECAM), a brightness/contrast/saturation control circuit and a colour space matrix.

The Philips SAA7111A accepts four analogue video inputs. These could be four composite video streams, two S-video streams or one S-video and two composite video streams. Internal analogue source selectors multiplex one of these four inputs. The rate at which the digitised video stream is clocked into the FPGA depends on the output format chosen. The Philips SAA7111A supports a wide range of video output formats. An on-chip control register is provided to select the type of video output. Currently, Vigra Vision uses the CCIR-656 8-bits video format, where video data is clocked to the FPGA at 27 MHz.

CCIR-656 standard

CCIR-656 is the successor of CCIR-601 standard which specifies the image format acquisition sematic, and parts of the coding for digital standard television signals (PAL, NTSC and SECAM) [Int99]. It defines the parallel and serial interfaces for transmitting 4:2:2 YCbCr digital video between equipment. The Y represents the luminance (grey level), whereas Cr and Cb represent the colour information (see Appendix VI). For 16-bits per pixel, each component of these is represented on 8 bits (unsigned). Y is defined to have a nominal range 16-235 (black-white) whereas Cb and Cr are defined to have a nominal range of 16-240 with 128 corresponding to zero. Figure 10.2 represents the data layout in video memory for a 4:2:2 YCbCr 8-bits pixel format.

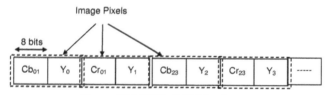

Figure 10.2 CCIR-656 Video format

Each pixel is assigned a unique value for Y, but eh Cb, Cr information is shared by a pair of adjacent pixels. For instance, Pixel$_0$ is represented by Y$_0$, Cb$_{01}$, Cr$_{01}$; Pixel$_1$ is represented by Y$_1$, Cb$_{01}$, Cr$_{01}$ and Pixel$_2$ is represented by Y$_2$, Cb$_{23}$, Cr$_{23}$ etc.

Pixels are supplied sequentially row by row (pixel by pixel) in an interlaced mode i.e. odd rows first (odd field), then even rows (even field) as shown in Figure 10.3 Each video line is sampled at 27MHz, generating 720 active pixel samples (720 active samples of Y per line and 360 active samples each of Cb and Cr per line). In CCIR-656 standard, active video resolutions are 720x486 for NTSC video systems or 720x576 for PAL/SECAM video systems.

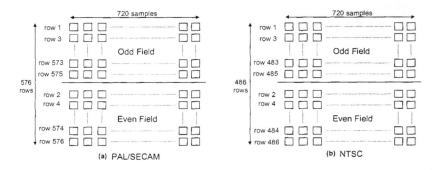

Figure 10.3 PAL/SECAM and NTSC video systems

In addition to the YCbCr video data, the Philips SAA71111A outputs video timing signals on separate pins [Phi98a]. These include:

- LLC (Line Locked Clock): A clock running at 27MHz which is the line video sampling rate.

- VS (Vertical Synchronisation signal): This signal indicates the vertical synchronisation with respect to the 4:2:2 YCbCr output video signal.

- HREF (Horizontal Reference signal): this signal is used to indicate data on the output bus. The positive slope marks the beginning of a new active line. The HIGH period of HREF is 720 Y samples long.

- FIELD: This signal is the odd/even field identification, where a HIGH level identifies an odd field and a LOW identifies an even one.

10.2.2 The Image processing block

The image processing block consists of a Xilinx XC4013E-3 FPGA (24x24 CLBs) and two 8 MB banks of EDO DRAM. The FPGA processes the digitised video data it receives from the video acquisition block, and can use the two memory banks for the storage of intermediate image data. The FPGA has access to a master clock MCLK generated by a PLL controlled by the onboard S3 chip.

10.2.3 The Image display block

The Image display block consists of the S3 Virge/GX2 video accelerator [S3] and 4MB of synchronous graphic memory (SGRAM). The data can be moved directly from the

SGRAM to the host main memory either through host reads or through the S3 DMA controller. The S3 Virge/GX2 has an integrated RAMDAC which converts the digitally encoded images into RGB analogue signals that can be displayed by the monitor. Note that the S3 chip has also access to a video encoder for output to NTSC or PAL compliant video devices.

10.2.4 Bus interface

The Vigra Vision board interfaces with the host via a PCI bus. In addition, the Vigra Vision uses two additional bus systems namely the I^{2}C bus, and a local peripheral bus. The I^{2}C bus [Phi98b] is a 2-wire multi-master bus implemented on the Vigra Vision board for communication between the peripheral IC's, mainly the SAA7111A ADC and the S3 video accelerator. The I^{2}C protocol is based on a serial, 8-bit oriented, bi-directional data transfer. The LPB bus [S3] is used to interface the S3 video accelerator to the Xilinx FPGA. This bus has three modes of operation including video-8 (4:2:2 YcBCr -8 bits-), video-16 (4:2:2 YCbCr -16 bits-), and bi-directional. Note that the bi-directional mode can be used by the host system to access the onboard DRAM through the PCI bus.

In our configuration, analogue video (RS170, CCIR, PAL or NTSC) is captured via the SAAA7111 ADC, passes to the FPGA which processes the incoming video in real time using the DRAMs as intermediate storage. The processed video is then passed, through the S3 chip, to the video memory (4MB SGRAM) from where it can be visualised on the PC's monitor. The processed data can also be downloaded to the host memory using routines supplied by Visicom.

10.3 Arithmetic choice: Bit Serial vs Bit Parallel

A discussion of the advantages and disadvantages of both bit serial and bit parallel arithmetic has been presented in chapter 9 (see sections 9.4 and 9.5). We have seen that our bit parallel implementation leads to a better time-hardware product. It can even beat our bit serial implementation area-wise in some cases. However, in the context or processing real time video, the Vigra Vision board influences the choice of the arithmetic. If bit serial arithmetic is to be used, there is a need to generate a bit clock from the pixel clock. The bit clock frequency is 'N' times the pixel's clock (for an 'N'-bit pixel). For practical real time video processing, the luminance pixel sampling rate is 13.5 MHz. This implies a bit clock frequency of 108 MHz for 8-bit length pixel processing, and 216 MHz for 16-bit length pixel processing. The XC4013-3 cannot operate at these frequencies (These frequencies are feasible with the latest Xilinx Virtex chips [Vir99]). This excludes the use of bit serial arithmetic on this particular FPGA chip. As a result, we have chosen parallel arithmetic rather than bit serial, for video processing.

Note that a trade-off in the form of digit serial arithmetic would still be possible. However, this implies the use of an external PLL for the digit clock frequency generation, and extra care for data synchronisation. A bit parallel implementation, as presented in chapter 9, can be efficiently implemented using dedicated fast carry logic. However, the use of our bit parallel arithmetic implies that the automatic placement is left to Xilinx PAR tools. This sacrifices one of the objectives set in chapter 3 (automatic place and route). Nonetheless, the choice of a bit parallel implementation is necessary under the constraints in hand (real time video on this particular board).

10.4 Implementation of the FPGA based IPC

As far as this project is concerned, we process only the luminance (grey level) information. Since the pixel's luminance and chrominance information are interleaved in YCbCr 4:2:2 8-bit video, the grey level information needs first to be separated from the composite video. This can be performed easily by enabling the grey level processing unit only during the luminance period of the composite video (see 'Luma' signal in Figure 10.4). However, since the displayable data should be in YCbCr 4:2:2 8-bit format [Vig98], the chrominance cannot just be ignored. It is delayed by the same amount as the luminance latency before being mixed again with the processed luminance data to form an interleaved YCbCr 4:2:2 8-bit video at the output. As in the luminance, the chrominance is separated from the composite video by the enable signal 'Chroma' (see Figure 10.4). both 'Chroma' and 'Luma' signals are generated from the horizontal reference (HREF) and the pixel clock (LLC) signals.

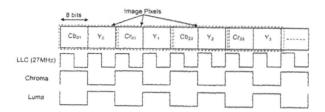

Figure 10.4 'Luma' and 'Chroma' control signals

Note that since the input images are supplied in interlaced mode, the image rows immediately to the top and the bottom of the actually transmitted row belong to the previously transmitted field (see Figure 10.5).

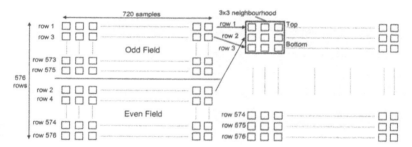

Figure 10.5 Original image reconstruction from an interlaced video-in

Hence, in order to implement a line buffer, we need to store each incoming field ready to be used during the next field. This means that a whole image needs to be stored in memory. Note that since we process only the grey level information, we need to store only the latter information. This means that 576x720 grey level samples need to be stored in memory for PAL video. This is equivalent to the memory capacity of 100K CLBs. Clearly, this is not feasible on-chip. Instead, the line buffers design will use the external DRAM interface is needed to store the incoming video into DRAM and read the remaining (P-1) rows from DRAM as shown in Figure 10.6 where an overall view of the FPGA configuration is given.

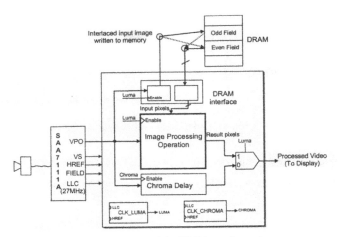

Figure 10.6 Overall view of the FPGA configuration

An interface to the DRAM allowing the buffering of two image rows (see 'top' and 'bottom' rows in Figure 10.5) was provided by Visicom. This allows performing any 3xQ-neighbourhood operation. The following describes this interface in some details.

10.4.1 DRAM interface for line buffering- A 3xQ neighbourhood operation

In the case of a 3xQ neighbourhood operation, two neighbourhood pixels belonging to the previous field are needed (see 'top' and 'bottom' in Figure 10.5). Each incoming pixel (grey level only) is written into DRAM for use during the next field. The corresponding *top* and *bottom* pixels necessary in a 3xQ neighbourhood are read from the previous field stored into DRAM. Hence, for each byte received two bytes read and one byte write from and to DRAM are needed. The average bandwidth that must be maintained by the DRAM should hence be three times the input rate, i.e. ~40MB/s (= 3 x13.5MB/s). Note that the other (Q-1) columns needed for particular 3xQ neighbourhood can be obtained by (Q-1)*3 pixel delays within the FPGA.

Each 8 MB DRAM is organised into a 1024x2048 double word memory. One bank of memory is used to implement the line buffering. Three 16x32-bits Input/Output FIFOs are implemented on FPGAs to interface to the DRAM. Two 16x32-bits input FIFOs are used to store the *top* and the *bottom* rows pixels read from the DRAM. One 16x32-bits output FIFO is used to store incoming video data before it is written to the DRAM. The FIFO's are accessed (read and write) by the FPGA internal circuitry at a rate of 13.5 MB/s. They, however, communicate with the DRAM at a higher rate (~40MB/s) using another clock 'K2' running at 40MHz. The latter is generated from the input clock MCLK which runs at 80MHz. Figure 10.7, shows a simplified state machine which controls the DRAM bank.

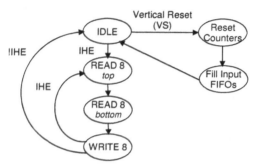

Figure 10.7 State machine of the DRAM controller

In general, refresh cycles are performed while IDLE. At the beginning of each field (VS signal), the DRAM address generators are reset and the input FIFOs are filled. When an input FIFO is half empty (IHE signal), eight double words are read into each one of the two input FIFOs, and eight double words are written from the output FIFO to the DRAM.

In general, line buffers are designed offline for windows with different number of rows. Given a high level description of the operation to be carried out on the video input in addition to the input pixel wordlength, the following invokes the proper line buffer (FIFO interface to the external DRAM):

```
is_video_line_buffers(Input_wordlength, High_Level_Dsc, Line_Buffers)
```

For the time being, only a DRAM interface implementing two line buffers of 8-bit pixels is available for use.

10.4.2 Putting it all together: a generic IA neighbourhood operation

As hinted above, we only process the grey level information. The corresponding processing unit is enabled by 'Luma' signal. The Chroma information is just delayed by the same amount as the latency of the grey level processing unit (δ_{Luma}). 'HREF', 'VS', and 'FIELD' synchronisation signals will be delayed by 2* δ_{Luma} (see Figure 10.8).

Note that since our bit parallel designs (presented in chapter 9) process 2's complement data, the incoming unsigned video data should be converted into 2's complement by adding an extra bit MSB = 0 to the pixels before they are input to the grey level processing unit (see blocks 'S' in Figure 10.8). One block of these is constructed by the following constructor:

```
is_tc_par_unsigned_2_tc(Input_wordlength, Output_wordlength, S)
```

Based on this constructor and given a high level description of the operation to be carried out, in addition to the input pixel wordlength, the following generates the whole array of block 'S':

```
is_array_of_unsigned_2_tc(High-Level_Desc, Input_wordlength, Output_wordlength, S)
```

HIDE4k descriptions of 2's complement bit parallel architectures have already been presented in chapter 9. Indeed, the core processing unit of a bit parallel neighbourhood operation is constructed by:

```
is_tc_par_proc_unit(High_level_desc, Input_wordlength, Putput_wordlength,
                    Latency_in, Latency_out, B)
```

where **High_level_desc** is the high level description of the desired IP operation. This has either one of the forms given by (**9.3**) or (**9.4**) i.e.

- For the pipeline skeleton (see section 9.3.1):

$$\text{High\_level\_desc} = \text{point\_op(Previous\_pipeline\_stage, Parameters)}$$

Or $$\text{High\_level\_desc} = \text{point\_op(Previous\_pipeline\_stage)} \qquad (10.1)$$

- For parallel neighbourhood operations (see section 9.3.2):

$$\text{Par\_desc} = \text{iii\_op(Par\_desc}_1\text{, Par\_desc}_2\text{)} \qquad (10.2)$$

Par_ desc$_1$ and **Par_ desc$_2$** are defined either recursively as compound operations of the form (10.2) itself, of pipeline skeletons of the form (10.1).

At the output, the pixels should be presented to the S3 chip 8 bits wide (unsigned), a 'limiter' unit is used to limit the output pixels' values to an unsigned byte. If the processed pixel value is greater than 255, it will be limited to 255, and if it is less than 0 (negative), it is then set to 0. Given the input pixel word length, the following constructor generates the limiter unit:

```
is_limiter(Input_wordlength, Latency, B)
```

It has been mentioned earlier (see section 10.4.1 above) that the DRAM is accessed at 40MHz rate. This clock (see signal K2 in Figure 10.8) is generated from the master clock MCLK by division over 2. We provide the following utility for generating a clock division unit by an integer N (N$\leq$ 16) [XAP09]:

```
is_clock_divider(N, B)
```

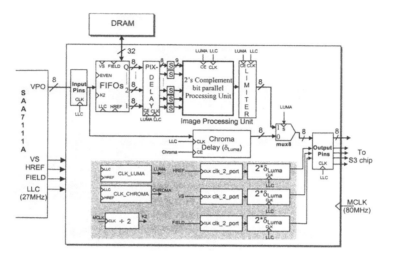

Figure 10.8 FPGA configuration block structure

Timing constraints should be added in order to guarantee the proper functioning of the circuit at video rate. In particular, the image processing unit should be able to process data at 13.5 MHz. The bit parallel architectures developed in chapter 9 are perfectly capable of sustaining this rate (see section 9.4). The timing constraints are input to the PAR tools in a user constraint file.

10.5 HIDE4k description of video processing operations

Nearly all the skeletons necessary for the construction of the full FPGA architectures corresponding to the operations described by (10.1) and (10.2), on the VigraVision board, have been presented above.

Control signals 'LLC', 'VS', 'HREF' and 'FIELD' are considered as global signals to the circuit. 'Luma' and 'Chroma' are global signals and are generated from 'LLC' and 'HREF' signals. Note that 'VS', 'HREF' and 'FIELD' are global control signals, but they need to be delayed: this means they have to be converted into ordinary port signals. For this purpose we provide a dummy block 'clk_2_port' which transfers a clock input signal into an outer port (on the east side).

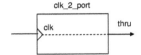

Figure 10.9 Clock to port dummy block

Given a high level description (**High_Level_Desc**) of the operation to be carried out on the video input, the following HIDE4k code generates the whole Image Processing Unit (see Figure 10.8):

```
is_tc_par_image_proc_unit(High_Level_Desc, Input_wordlength, Lat_in, Lat_out, B):-
is_video_line_buffers(Input_wordlength, High_Level_Desc, Line_Buffers),
is_tc_par_pix_delay(Input_wordlength, High_Level_Desc, Pix_delay),
is_array_of_unsigned_2_tc(High_level_desc , Input_wordlength, OWL, Array_of_S),
Lp=horizontal([Line_Buffers, Pix-delay, Array_of_S]),
is_tc_par_proc_unit(High_Level_Desc, OWL, Output_width, Lat_in, Lat2, TC_Par_unit),
is_limiter(Output_width, Limiter_Lat, Limiter),
Lat_out is Lat2+ Limiter_Lat,
B = horizontal([Lp, TC_Par_unit, Limiter ]).
```

Normally, a user will supply '0' for the initial input latency **Lat_in**. The whole circuit description is then given by:

```
is_VigraVision_config(High_Level_Desc, FPGA_config_desc):-
Input_wordlength is 8,
% Grey Level Processing
is_tc_par_image_proc_unit(High_Level_Desc, Input_wordlength, 0, Latency, Im_temp),
Im_proc_unit = rename_signals([(clk,llc),(ce,luma)], Im_temp),
% Chroma Processing part
is_tc_par_delay_unit(Input_wordlength, Latency, Delay_Byte),
Chroma_delay = rename_signals([(clk,llc),(ce,chroma)], Delay_Byte),
% Image Processing Unit + Chroma Delay
Tmp = vertical([Chroma_delay, Im_proc_unit]),
Mux8 = rename_signals([ (s,luma)], mux8),
Im_proc_Chroma_parts = horizontal([input_Pins, nc([p_seq(i, 1,1,8, [(i,i), (i,i+8)] )], Tmp,
Mux8]),
% Synchro.
is_single_delay(2*Latency, Delay_sync),
Synchro_delay_temp = rename_signals([(clk,llc)], v_seq(3,Delay_sync)),
Clk_2_port1 = rename_signals([(clk,field)], clk_2_port),
```

```
Clk_2_port2 = rename_signals([[(clk,vs)], clk_2_port),
Clk_2_port3 = rename_signals([[(clk,href)], clk_2_port),
Clk_2_port = vertical([Clk_2_port1, Clk_2_port2, Clk_2_port3]),
Synch_delay = horizontal([Clk_2_port , Synchro_delay_temp ]),
is_clock_divider(2, Clock_div),
K2_clock = rename_signals([[(clk,mclk)], Clock_div),
% Putting it all together
Temp1_all = vertical([Synch_delay, Im_proc_Chroma_parts]),
Temp2_all = horizontal([ Temp1_all, output_pins],
is_cfg_driven(High_Level_Desc, Temp2_all, Temp3_all), % see section 10.5.2 below
Temp4_all = drive_signals( [(_,clk_luma,[luma],_,_), (_,clk_chroma,[chroma],_,_),
                            (bufg, K2_clock,[k2],_,_)], Temp3_all),
FPGA_config_desc = drive_signals( [(_,href_clk,[href],_,_), (_,vs_clk,[vs],_,_),
         (_,field_clk,[field],_,_), (_,llc_clk,[llc],_,_), (_,mclk_clk,[mclk],_,_)], Temp4_all)
```

Thus, if the user wants to generate a complete configuration, including all the detailed components discussed above, he or she merely has to call this predicate with the required high level description (which must confirm to the format in 10.1 and 10.2).

10.5.1 Two pipelined neighbourhood operations

This section will present a third skeleton to extend the ones given by (10.1) and (10.2). This consists in pipelining two *neighbourhood* operations. The neighbourhood operations could be compound (i.e. based on (10.1) or (10.2)).

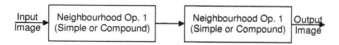

Figure 10.10 Two pipelined neighbourhood operations

In this case, one neighbourhood operation will use one DRAM for line buffering, while the other will use the other DRAM on the VigraVision board as shown in Figure 10.11.

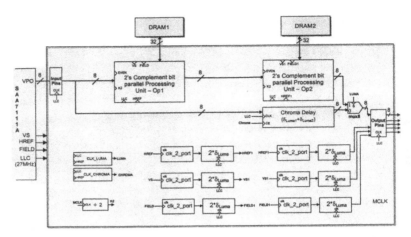

Figure 10.11 FPGA block configuration for two pipelined neighbourhood operations

Given a high level description of the form:

Pipeline(Op1_desc, Op2_desc)   **(10.3)**

where **Op1_desc, Op2_desc** are high level descriptions of type (10.1) and (10.2), he
following code generates the corresponding FPGA configuration.

```
is_VigraVision_config(pipeline(Op1, Op2), FPGA_config_desc):-
Input_wordlength is 8,
% FIRST OP. Processing
is_tc_par_image_proc_unit(Op1, Input_wordlength, 0, Latency1, Im1_temp),
Im_proc_unit1 = rename_signals([[(clk,llc),(ce,luma)], Im1_temp),
is_tc_par_delay_unit(Input_wordlength , 0, Delay_Byte1),
Temp1 = vertical([Chroma_delay1, Im_proc_unit1]),
First_Op = horizontal([input_Pins, nc([p_seq(i, 1,1,8, [(i,i), (i,i+8)] ]), Temp1]),
% Synchro 1.
is_single_delay(2*Latency1, Delay_sync1),
Synchro_delay_temp1 = rename_signals([[(clk,llc)], Delay_sync1),
Clk_2_port1 = rename_signals([[(clk,href)], clk_2_port),
Href1_clk = horizontal([Clk_2_port1 , Synchro_delay_temp1]),
Clk_2_port2 = rename_signals([[(clk,vs)], clk_2_port),
Vs1_clk = horizontal([Clk_2_port2 , Synchro_delay_temp1]),
Clk_2_port3 = rename_signals([[(clk,field)], clk_2_port),
Field1_clk = horizontal([Clk_2_port3 , Synchro_delay_temp1]),
is_clock_divider(2, Clock_div),
K2_clock = rename_signals([[(clk,mclk)], Clock_div),
% Second Operation
is_tc_par_image_proc_unit(Op2, Input_wordlength, 0, Latency2, Im2_temp),
```

```
Im_proc_unit2 = rename_signals([[(clk,llc),(ce,luma)], Im2_temp),
is_tc_par_delay_unit(Input_wordlength , Latency1+Latency2, Delay_Byte2),
Chroma_delay2 = rename_signals([[(clk,llc),(ce,chroma)], Delay_Byte2),
Temp2 = vertical([Chroma_delay2, Im_proc_unit2])
Mux8 = rename_signals([ (s,luma)], mux8),
Second_Op = horizontal([Temp2, Mux8]),
% Synchro 2
is_single_delay(2*Latency2, Delay_sync2),
Synchro_delay_temp2 = rename_signals([[(clk,llc)], v_seq(3,Delay_sync2)),
Clk_2_port1_2 = rename_signals([[(clk,field)], clk_2_port),
Clk_2_port2_2 = rename_signals([[(clk,vs)], clk_2_port),
Clk_2_port3_2 = rename_signals([[(clk,href)], clk_2_port),
Clk_2_port = vertical([Clk_2_port1_2, Clk_2_port2_2, Clk_2_port3_2]),
Synch_delay2 = horizontal([Clk_2_port , Synchro_delay_temp2 ]),
% Putting it all together
Temp1_all = vertical([Synch_delay2, Second_Op]),
Temp2_all = horizontal([ Temp1_all, output_pins]),
Temp3_all = drive_signals( [(_,Href1_clk,[href],_,_), (_,Vs1_clk,[vs],_,_),
                        (_,Field1_clk,[field],_,_)], Temp2_all),
% First +Second Op
Op_1_2 = horizontal([First_Op, Temp3_all]),
is_cfg_driven(pipeline(Op1, Op2), Op_1_2, Temp4_all), % see section 10.5.2 below
Temp5_all = drive_signals( [(_,clk_luma,[luma],_,_),(_,clk_chroma,[chroma],_,_),
                        (bufg,K2_clock,[k2],_,_)], Temp4_all),
FPGA_config_desc = drive_signals( [(_, href_clk, [href],_,_), (_, vs_clk, [vs],_,_),
        (_, field_clk, [field],_,_), (_, llc_clk ,[llc],_,_), (_, mclk_clk ,[mclk],_,_)], Temp5_all).
```

As in 9.3.3, if a number of point operations (**point_op$_1$, point_op$_2$,...., point_op$_N$**) need to be performed before any neighbourhood operation, then this can be done by considering these point operations as a compound operation applied on an identify neighbourhood operation represented by indent (treated as a special case):

pipeline(point_op$_1$(point_op$_2$,...., point_op$_N$(ident, parN)), Op$_1$_desc)

or **pipeline(point_op$_1$(point_op$_2$,...., point_op$_N$(ident, parN)), Op$_1$_desc), Op2_desc)**

This requires minor modifications in the above presented, code listing and has been implemented.

10.5.2 Dynamically reconfigurable designs

At times, it is desirable to change certain parameters in an FPGA configuration without having to reconfigure the whole chip. A threshold operation is an example, where the threshold value may need to be adjusted dynamically by the user. In this case, the threshold value is held in a specific on-chip register. The register should be mapped into the I²C address space from where it can be accessed (note that the FPGA itself needs to be mapped onto the I²C address space first). To implement this approach, in general, reconfigurable data is held in internal registers each with a specific and unique sub-address. An interface to the I²C bus is provided (based on one provided by Visicom) to decode the FPGA address and the internal registers sub-addresses. This interface (see block *iic_interface* in Figure 10.12) enables a particular on-chip register whenever it is addressed, hence initiating the data transfer. Different enable signals are provided for different internal registers (three sub-addresses are provided in Figure 10.12: '0xC0', 0xC1' and 0xC2'). This number can be easily increased by decoding other sub-addresses. A particular on-chip register is mapped onto the I2C address space simply by driving one of these enable signals to its clock enable signal. The data is then serially loaded into the register whenever it is enabled.

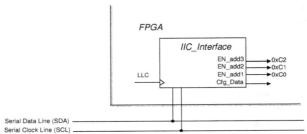

Figure 10.12 *iic_interface* block

We provide two operations, which can be dynamically reconfigured:

1- **cfg_thresh(Previous_Op, Reg_address):** This is an IS-I operation in which the data is compared to a threshold value (*thresh_value*) which can dynamically reconfigured.

Figure 10.13 Dynamically reconfigurable Threshold block

The user can dynamically specify one of the following four operations to be carried out:

- **Bypass:** In this mode, the unit limits the output data to 8 bits (unsigned) but does not apply any threshold operation.

- **Greaterthan:** in which the output of this unit will be 255 if the input data is greater than the threshold value and 0 otherwise.

- **Lessthan:** in which the output of this unit will be 255 if the input data is less than the threshold value and 0 otherwise.

- **Equal:** in which the output of this unit will be 255 if the input data equals the threshold value and 0 otherwise.

These modes are dynamically adjustable by the user.

2- **cfg_multi_thresh(Previous_Op, Reg_address): IMS-I**

In this operation, a two-level threshold is applied to the image. Two internal 8-bit registers are used to store the two threshold values. These two registers are considered as a 16 bit address so only one address is needed. In addition to specifying the two threshold values (*thresh_low* and *thresh_high*), the user can also dynamically specify one of the following four operations to be carried out:

- **Bypass:** In this mode, the unit limits the output data to 8 bits (unsigned) but does not apply any threshold operation.

- **Between:** in which the output of this unit will be 255 if the input data is between *thresh_low* and **thresh_high** (inclusive) and 0 otherwise.

- **Outside:** in which the output of this unit will be 0 if the input data is between *thresh_low* and *thresh_high* and 255 otherwise.

In fact, this operation supersedes the previous one since:

$$greaterthan(X) = between(X + 1, 255)$$
$$lessthan(X) = between(0, X-1)$$
$$equal(X) = between(X, X)$$

The *iic_interface* block is considered as a clock generator. Each output enable signal should drive the corresponding configuration enable signal of a particular internal reconfigurable register. Since the sub-addresses are supplied as parameters, the driven signals can be known given the high level description of the operation to be carried out. Given this high level description in addition to the HIDE4k description of the block to be driven, the following constructor generates the resulting driven block (B):

is_cfg_driven(High_Level_Desc, Block_to_be_Driven, B)

This explains the use of this constructor in the previous code listings.

10.6 Overall system for application development

From the previous sections, we can see that the ser can generate the HIDE4k description of full FPGA architectures by invoking the following constructor:

> **is_VigraVision_config(High_Level_Desc, FPGA_config_desc)**

Where **High_Level_Desc** can have one of the three forms defined in (10.1), (10.2) or (10.3). This high level description of the IP algorithm in hand can even be input graphically as a DAG [McE00].

The EDIF description of this architecture can then be generated by:

> **is_generated_netlist(FPGA_config_desc, Filename)**

This is performed automatically by the HIDE4k system. The circuit is not fully placed, as we are not performing automatic placement. Only the basic components are pre-placed.

Once the EDIF description is generated, it is then fed to the Xilinx PAR tools to generate the FPGA configurable bitstream. This may take a long time (~1hr on a Pentium 233 running Windows 95 with 32M or RAM) since the placement task is left to the general-purpose placement tools. The automatically placed bit serial architectures presented in chapter 6, however, needed few minutes to go through the PAR tools.

At the application level, the user interfaces tot eh VigraVision board through a C-callable library (VigraVision ToolBox- VTB DLL). The ToolBox includes hardware initialisation and register control functions, image acquisition functions and image processing functions [Vig98]. For instance, the application developer downloads a particular FPGA configuration by invoking the following function:

> **u_loadXilinx**(Xilinx_Chip_ID, Configuration_filename)

He or she can then copy the processed image from the video buffer to the host processor, for further analysis, by:

> **u_readRect**(LPRECT *lpImgRect*, LPVOID *imgData*)

Where *lpImgRect* specifies the rectangle in the frame buffer where data is to be read from, and *imgData* is a pointer to the image transferred to the host memory.

The Tool Box is supported in Microsoft Visual C/C++ 5.0. Its functions can be accessed by application software which has been linked with the VTB import library and accessed via Windows as a DLL library. The resulting IPC (see Figure 10.14) is based on a library of bitstream configurations ready to use (download to the FPGA) from a high level language (VC++ in our case). This library is extensible over time using our

HIDE4d system. Thanks to our skeleton oriented approach, this task is relatively easy to perform and requires little FPGA hardware knowledge (if any). This has been illustrated in this chapter by three skeletons. Other skeletons can be designed using a similar approach and added to the library.

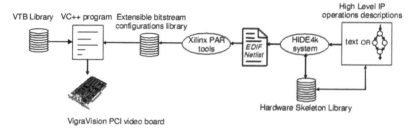

Figure 10.14 Overall view of the VigraVision based IPC

10.6.1 A Demonstration Program

We present in this section a Visual C++ based demo programme built on the top of an existing Visicom Demo program [Vig98]. The latter is a user friendly, menu driven program, running under Windows, which demonstrates the main functions of the VigraVision board. In particular, this program inputs, processes and displays a live video stream. The user can select the operation to be performed on the input video from a simple menu. Using the system we developed in this chapter, the set of operations has been extended very conveniently to give operations including: Sobel, Prewitt, Laplace, Blur, Sharpen, grey level Erosion, grey level Dilation and Open&Close IP operations. The following gives the high level description from which the FPGA configurations of these IP operations have been generated automatically (Note that all these operations have a multi-level threshold option; the threshold register address is '0xC2'):

- Sobel

```
High_Level_Desc = cfg_multi_thresh(
            abs(neighbourhood(mult,accum,[[1,2,1],[0,0,0],[-1,-2,-1]]))
            +
            abs(neighbourhood(mult,accum,[[1,0,-1],[2,0,-2],[1,0,-1]])), '0xC2')
```

- Prewitt

```
High_Level_Desc = cfg_multi_thresh(
            abs(neighbourhood(mult,accum,[[1,1,1],[0,0,0],[-1,-1,-1]]))
            +
            abs(neighbourhood(mult,accum,[[1,0,-1],[1,0,-1],[1,0,-1]])), '0xC2')
```

- Laplace

High_Level_Desc = cfg_multi_thresh(
            neighbourhood(mult,accum,[[~,-1,~],[-1,4,-1],[~,-1,~]]), '0xC2')

- Blur

High_Level_Desc = cfg_multi_thresh(
            neighbourhood(mult,accum,[[1,1,1],[1,1,1],[1,1,1]])/9, '0xC2')

- Sharpen

High_Level_Desc = cfg_multi_thresh(
            neighbourhood(mult,accum,[[-1,-1,-1],[-1,12,-1],[-1,-1,-1]])/4, '0xC2')

- Erode

High_Level_Desc = cfg_multi_thresh(
            neighbourhood(add,min,[[~,0,~],[0,0,0],[~,0,~]]), '0xC2')

- Dilate

High_Level_Desc = cfg_multi_thresh(
            neighbourhood(add,max,[[~,0,~],[0,0,0],[~,0,~]]), '0xC2')

- Open

High_Level_Desc = pipeline(
        neighbourhood(add,min,[[~,0,~],[0,0,0],[~,0,~]]),
        cfg_multi_thresh(neighbourhood(add,max,[[~,0,~],[0,0,0],[~,0,~]]), '0xC2'))

- Close

High_Level_Desc = pipeline(
        neighbourhood(add,max,[[~,0,~],[0,0,0],[~,0,~]]),
        cfg_multi_thresh(neighbourhood(add,min,[[~,0,~],[0,0,0],[~,0,~]]), '0xC2'))

In addition to these skeleton instances, a special design for median filtering based on TIS algorithm using 2's complement bit parallel (see section 8.2) has been described in HIDE4k. The corresponding configuration is simply generated from the following high level description:

High_Level_Desc = tc_par_TIS_median

The following figures present the demo GUI that the user uses to apply an operation on the video stream.

Figure 10.15 VTB Demo GUI

Figure 10.16 Image Processing Menu Item

Figure 10.17 Applying Sobel filter

Figure 10.18 Dynamic reconfiguration using the Multi-threshold dialog box

Figure 10.19 Sobel filter followed by a Multi-threshold

10.7 Conclusions

In this chapter, we have presented an implementation of the Image ProcessingCoprocessor on Visicom's VigraVision video PCI board. The choice of this hardware platform was motivated by the features of the latter (video capture and display circuitry all included in one PCI board) and the willingness of Visicom's staff to offer the necessary hardware and software support.

The implementation of the IPC was successful and a working system allowing video processing at real time was designed. The high level skeletons presented in chapter 9 were used successfully. This allows for very rapid generation of FPGA architectures from very high level descriptions and opens the way to enabling image processing application developers to exploit the high performance capability of a direct hardware solution, while programming in an application-oriented model.

The process of realising the IPC in a real video processing board prompted certain design decisions as well as a number of changes to the designs developed previously:

- Bit parallel instead of bit serial: The implementation of the IPC was based on 2's complement bit parallel arithmetic as a bit serial implementation would have required very high bit clock frequencies.

- Use of off-chip memory for line buffering: As a result of processing interlaced video, a whole image should be stored to be able to implement a line buffer. This requires a huge amount of memory storage which cannot be provided on-chip. Instead, external RAM has been used to implement the line buffers.

- There are many control signals needed in video processing designs. This required a number of low level management for multiple clocks. HIDE4k has proved powerful enough to handle these details.

However, a number of limitations have emerged during this exercise:

- The memory interface necessary for line buffering depends on the particular IP operation in hand (size of template in particular). As this interface is based on fairly complex state machines, the corresponding logic is not readily scaleable. The solution we propose is to design an interface for the maximum template size possible and rely on the vendor's placement and routing tools to trim away an unused logic if a smaller template size is used.

- An important factor in judging the ease of use of our skeleton oriented approach is the choice of the skeletons themselves. This should be driven by the reusability of a particular hardware pattern. We do not claim that our particular skeleton choices are the best. Other choices might give more powerful high level descriptions, and have still to be investigated further.

- A number of nasty low level details often need to be addressed (see the dynamically reconfigurable designs in section 10.5.2 and the closing remark in section 10.5.1 for example). These often need the implementation of special case predicates. However, we have proved that these details can be hidden from user's point of view.

Chapter 11

Conclusion

Chapter 11

Conclusion

In this chapter, we first review the main achievements and novel contributions of this work. Although the various stages of the work were reviewed or evaluated in the appropriate chapter, we will give a number of evaluation comments on the project as a whole in section 11.2. From these, a number of suggestions for future work are outlined.

11.1 Achievements and novel contributions

The main achievements and novel contributions of the research presented in this book are:

- We have ported and extended the HIDE6k hardware description environment for the Xilinx XC4000 series (HIDE4k system). This means that HIDE4k has inherited the main strength of HIDE6k system. These can be summarised in the following points:
    - HIDE4k allows for very concise descriptions of FPGA architectures. The parameterised block composition allows for very concise descriptions of parameterised and scaleable circuits which often occur in digital signal processing. Also, the automatic port matching, in particular, saves the user from specifying explicitly the interconnections between adjacent blocks, unlike in VHDL.
    - The direct generation of EDIF netlist speeds up the design cycle as no extra synthesiser tools are necessary. This also reduces the total cost.
    - The use of Prolog has proven very beneficial. The notion of *unbound variables* was extremely useful for describing entities with uncommitted factors (e.g. Block size, placement). The automatic pattern matching feature has been useful in expressing conditions in a smart way.

- HIDE4k includes several practical enhancements of the previous HIDE6k system, including:
    - Increased facilities for block interconnection
    - A more flexible control management scheme
    - A more flexible placement scheme. HIDE4k gives the user the possibility to undo the automatic placement if need be. This can be even done partially for certain components of the circuit.
    - HIDE4k generates FPGA configurations in VHDL format as well as EDIF

- We have developed an efficient library of architectures on Xilinx 4000. This library is much more extensive than the XC6000 based one. For instance, the architectures developed in this book provide a range of alternative arithmetic implementations: radix-2 online arithmetic, 2's complement bit serial LSBF and MSBF, unsigned binary arithmetic, 2's complement bit parallel and some components for the special case of binary images (1 bit per pixel).

- We have developed three novel IP architectures in this book: perimeter estimation, median filtering and connected component labelling. This is a contribution to the state of the art of IP architectures.

- This book has put forward the new concept of *hardware skeletons* as a way of satisfying the dual requirement of generating efficient FPGA architectures while retaining the convenience and rapid development cycle of an application-oriented, high level programming model. This approach promises to save the FPGA user from having to go through the classical, slow and error-prone process of FPGA design. The same concept exists in the software domain (in a more mature form), though our approach emerged independently.

- The generator from application-oriented skeletons to the intermediate HIDE4k notation has included many optimisations:
- The generated architectures are not tied to a fixed processing wordlength. Rather, based on the input pixel wordlength and the details of the operation to be

performed (e.g. window coefficients), the minimum necessary processing wordlength is used.

- The generator takes advantage of the details of each particular operation (e.g. particular coefficient values) to generate a solution specifically optimised for the IP operation in hand (e.g. CSD based bit parallel multiplier architecture).

- Optimised hardware solutions, for area and speed, are generated for a number of common hardware patterns (e.g. neighbourhood operations on the same input image).

• A major achievement of the research presented in this book is that our system has ultimately been tested on real hardware. The exercise threw up a number of low level problems particularly to do with video i/o and interfacing to off-chip RAM. Despite these problems, our skeleton-based approach was successfully implemented on the VigraVision video board for a useful subset of IP algorithms. This enabled the generation of efficient FPGA architectures (running at video rate) from algorithm-oriented high level descriptions.

11.2 Evaluation comments

Bearing in mind the original objectives of the research presented in this book (presented in section 2.4) and taking into account the above achievements, the following, sometimes critical, points can be made:

• We have shown in this book that it is possible to exploit the high performance capability of a direct hardware solution, while programming in an application-oriented model. If the desired system/algorithm is expressible in terms of skeletons available in the library, then the architecture developer does not require any detailed hardware knowledge. Otherwise, the library needs to be extended. In that case, the HIDE4k system is a useful tool for the rapid building of new, parameterised (and hence reusable) library components (skeletons).

• It had originally been hoped to provide on the fly generation of FPGA configurations. However, it became apparent that this was not achievable within the timescale of this project. One reason is that the details of the bitstream configuration file of the XC4000 are not public domain, so PAR tools had to be used. The possibility of using JBits [Jbits99] to address this problem should be investigated, although with increasing complex and irregular architectures, on the fly generation of placed and routed configurations will become increasingly non trivial.

- At the start of this project, we assumed the desirability of generating full placement information. However, with the increasing complexity and irregularity of the architectures, and with steady improvement in PAR tools, the argument for generating full placement information is getting weaker.

- In the process of using HIDE4k for generating fully placed architectures, it was observed that when the architectures become less regular, HIDE4k descriptions can become cumbersome. This is due to the fact that horizontal and vertical block composition is mainly suitable for array-like architectures. The assumption that blocks are rectangular and non-overlapping is a major restriction. Also, the facilities for port interconnection can become rather complicated. These were designed for regular architectures, and their limitations begin to appear for irregular circuits.

- The concept of *hardware skeletons* which has been proposed in this book has been put forward in an informal way. Nonetheless, the general concept has been demonstrated, and as a method for bridging the gap between application-oriented design and optimised hardware solutions, the concept has exciting possibilities.

- The concept of hardware skeletons could certainly be extended beyond the domain of Image Processing to other areas of signal processing (e.g. speech processing).

The following points are the result of evaluating the work against the original objectives as stated in section 2.5 (see page 61):

- We have met our first objective in designing an environment which allows an IP application developer to program FPGAs at an algorithmic level (Tulip-like).

- Our environment acts as an optimising silicon compiler in the sense that it performs a number of optimisations customised to the IP operation in hand (e.g. takes into account the window coefficients values and the input pixel wordlength). This satisfies another objective put forward in section 2.5.

- We have met our objective in generating FPGA configurations using different arithmetic types and data representations.

- We have extended the IP operations library to new operations not provided by Donachy (e.g. Median filtering, Connected Component Labelling). This satisfies another objective put forward in section 2.5.

- Finally, we have also met our final objective in implementing our software environment on a commercial FPGA board.

However, the produced environment is not complete and suffers from the following limitations:

- Our objective "The environment would ideally *hide the FPGA hardware details completely* from the user's point of view" was not completely satisfied, as some awareness of the hardware limitations is still necessary. For instance, area limitation will reveal itself in a restriction on the maximum size of window which can be used.

- The range of IP operations supported is not complete. For instance, a general framework for recursive operations was not implemented.

- Though our environment performs a number of optimisations, it is not optimal. There is still room for further optimisations (see section 9.5 for instance).

- The range of arithmetic types (bit serial LSBF, MSBF and bit parallel) is not complete. For instance, digit serial versions of our architectures were not implemented.

- The FPGA based coprocessor that has been implemented on the VigraVision™ board was only for video processing. An FPGA based image coprocessor was not implemented on this board.

11.3 Future work

This research presented in this book has opened the way for a number of possible future directions:

- One of the successes of this work was the implementation of the IPC in *bit parallel*. However, although our bit serial architectures were not implemented on our video processing system (mainly due to the high clock speed needed), bit serial arithmetic should not be ruled out in future work. After all, bit serial architectures have a consistent performance (fixed speed and area) regardless of the input wordlength. The fact that interconnections are local makes bit serial architectures highly regular and hence it is possible to generate them on the fly from a high level description. With the latest FPGA chips offering speeds over 200MHz, a bit serial implementation of the IPC should be able to achieve real time video performance, and should still be considered in the future.

- The work presented in this book has presented both bit serial and bit parallel architectures. It would be interesting to extend the library to digit serial architectures, to give the user greater flexibility in the trade off between speed and area.

- As far as HIDE4k system is concerned, it is desirable to extend it in order to handle non-rectangular blocks and allow for overlapping. It is also desirable to extend its expressive power to handle less regular architectures (not just array-like architectures). The use of hardware skeletons at the lower, block level is a suggested starting point for this. An explicit support for the management of buses (as opposed to simple ports) is also desirable to describe bit parallel architectures.

- The HIDE system has been implemented now on Xilinx 6000 and 4000 series. It would be useful to target another architecture (say Altera devices) and investigate the problem of portability across different architectures. This issue was not addressed in this book. An obvious next step would be to transfer the environment to the Virtex family. This should take advantage of the features of Virtex architecture (e.g. use of Block SelectRAM for line buffering instead of the distributed synchronous RAMs, use of DLLs for clock frequency division and multiplication and for clock deskew etc.).

- We recommend further investigation of the concept of *hardware skeletons*. For instance, the following issues need further study and experimentation:
- A formalisation of the definition of hardware skeletons.
- For a particular application area (e.g. image processing), what range of skeletons should be provided in the library?
- For a particular FPGA card (e.g. with multiple RAM banks), what 'support' skeletons should be provided (e.g. interface to RAM banks)?
- When developing an application, there could be several arrangements of skeletons for the same operation. How is the best arrangement chosen?

- The library should be extended to include a much wider range of IP tasks, such as DCT and wavelet transforms. The possibility of generating these using a similar approach to the one presented in this work should be investigated. These architectures are necessary components in the field of image compression, which is an area of increasing interest.

- The current library is not complete; for instance histogramming and other vector operations need to be added. Also, not all operations have the full range of arithmetic versions available. These gaps should be filled.

- There is room for further optimisation of existing architectures. For instance, the bit parallel multiplication can be optimised further by using the Dempster-McLeod algorithm and taking advantage of an eventual symmetry in the coefficients used (see section 9.5).

- A recent opportunity has been put to us to develop tools for Visicom's new Virtex-E based V8 VISIon COMputer™ [Vig00]. One attractive development is the design of a *graphical programming environment* allowing the automatic generation of FPGA architectures from graphical, data flow type programs.

We also suggest that the use of our skeleton oriented approach could be usefully investigated for application areas other than FPGA based Image Processing:

- Because of improving power of FPGA technology, there is an increasing overlap between VLSI and FPGA design issues. Thus the skeleton approach may have some applicability for VLSI design.

- One of the reasons behind the success of our skeleton-oriented approach is the existence of an algebra for image processing. Other application domains where there is an established algebra such as numerical processing can also benefit from the skeleton approach.

   The use of skeletons for network processing might also give enormous benefits. Indeed, because skeletons are inherently parameterised and scaleable, they might be an efficient way to adopt new protocols and emerging standards quickly and easily. Note that, thanks to their increased performance and memory capability, FPGAs are now capable of addressing network processing applications.

- Skeletons could be used for rapid prototyping of a System-On-a-Chip. Indeed, a whole System-On-a-Chip could be modelled as a high level skeleton into which are plugged lower level skeletons (e.g. processors) as parameters.

References

[AAA94]   Akiyama T, Aono H, Aoki K, et al, 'MPEG2 video codec using Image compression DSP', *IEEE Transactions on Consumer Electronics*, Vol 40, No 3, pp 466-472, 1994.

[ABD92]   Arnold J M, Buell D A and Davis E G, 'Splash-2', Proceedings of the 4th Annual ACM Symposium on Parallel Algorithms and Architectures, ACM Press, pp 316-324, Jun. 1992.

[AC89]   Astolla J T, and Campbell T G, 'On computation of the running median', *IEEE Trans. Acoustic Speech and Signal Processing*, ASSP-37, pp.572-574, Apr. 1989.

[AL96]   Aubury M and Luk W, 'Binomial filters', *Journal of VLSI signal processing*, Vol. 12, No. 1, pp 35-50, Jan 1996.

[Alg91]   Algotronix Ltd., *The CAL 1024 datasheet*, Nov. 1991.
            http://www.algotronix.com

[Alo99]   Alotaibi K, 'A High Level Hardware Description Environment for FPGA-Based Image Processing Applications', PhD Thesis, Department of Computer Science, The Queen's University of Belfast, 1999.

[Alt99]   Altera Ltd., 'MAX 7000 Programmable Logic Device Family Data Sheet', ver. 6.01, July 1999.
            http://www.altera.com/document/ds/m7000.pdf

[Alt00a]   Altera Ltd, 'FLEX 10K Embedded Programmable Logic Family Data Sheet', ver. 4.02, May 2000.
            http://www.altera.com/document/ds/dsf10k.pdf

[Alt00b]   Altera Ltd, 'APEX 20K Programmable Logic Device Family Data Sheet', ver. 2.06, March 2000.
            http://www.altera.com/document/ds/apex.pdf

[And93]   Andraka, R., 'FIR filter fits in an FPGA: A bit serial Approach', 3rd PLD Conference, March 1993.
            http://www.andraka.com/files/fir.pdf

[Atm99]   Atmel Corporation, 'AT40K FPGA Interactive Architecture Guide', April 1999.
            ftp://www.atmel.com/pub/atmel/at40k.hlp

[Avi61]   Avizienis A, 'Signed-digit number representations for fast parallel arithmetic', *IRE Transactions on electronic computers*, vol. 10, pp 389-400, 1961.

[BBDS93]   Bailey D H, Barszcz E, Dagum L, and Simon H D, 'NAS Parallel Benchmark Results', *The IEEE Parallel and Distributed Technology Journal*, pp 43-51, Feb 1993.

[BC99]   Benkrid K and Crookes D, 'Design and FPGA implementation of a novel general purpose median filter', Proc. IMVIP'99, Dublin, pp.280-287, September 1999.

[BCB99]   Benkrid K, Crookes D, Bouridane A, Corr P and Alotaibi K, 'A high level software environment for FPGA based image processing', Proc. IPA'99, IEE Seventh International Conference on Image Processing and its Applications, Manchester, pp.112-116, July 1999.

[BCC92]   Birkner J, Chan A, Chua H T, et al, 'A very high speed field programmable gate array using metal-to-metal anti-fuse programmable elements', *Microelectronics Journal*, v 23, n 7, pp. 561-568, Nov 1992.

[BN97]   Bates G L, Nooshabadi S, 'FPGA implementation of a median filter', IEEE Region 10 Annual International Conference, Proceedings/TENCON, Vol.2, pp.437-440, 1997.

[BR93]   Brown S, and Rose J, 'Architecture of FPGAs and CPLDs: A Tutorial', *IEEE Design and Test of Computers*, Vol. 13, No. 2, pp. 42-57, 1996.

[Bro92]   Brown T J, 'Language Development For Transputer Based Image Processing', PhD Thesis, Department of Computer Science, The Queen's University of Belfast, 1992.

[Cas96]   Castleman K R, 'Digital Image Processing', Prentice Hall, 1996.

[Cav84]   Cavanagh J, 'Digital Computer Arithmetic, Design and Implementation', McGraw-Hill, Inc, pp. 137-234, 1984.

[CM94]   Clocksin W F and Mellish C S, 'Programming in Prolog', 4th edition, Springer-Verlag, 1994.

[CMMc90]   Crookes D, Morrow PJ and McParland P J, 'IAL: a parallel image processing programming language', IEE proceedings, Part I, Vol. 137, No. 3, pp 176-182, June 1990.

[CMP88]   Christopher L A, Mayweather W T and Perlman S S, 'VLSI median filter for impulse noise elimination in composite or component TV signals', *IEEE Trans. On consumer Electronics*, Vol 34, No. 1, pp. 263-267, 1988.

[CNH93]   Chan S C, Ngai H O and Ho K L, 'A programmable image processing system using FPGAs', *International Journal of Electronics*, Vol. 75, No. 4, pp. 725-730, 1993.

[Col89]   Cole M, 'Algorithmic Skeletons: structured management of parallel computation', MIT Press, 1989.

[Con96]   Conner D, 'Reconfigurable logic-Hardware speed with software flexibility', *EDN magazine*, Vol. 41, No. 7, pp. 53, 1996.

[COPS99]   Cucchiara R, Onfiani P, Prati A, Scarabottolo N, 'Segmentation of Moving Objects at Frame Rate: A dedicated Hardware Solution', Proc. IPA'99, IEE Seventh International Conference on Image Processing and its Applications, Manchester, pp.138-142, July 1999.

[CP90]   Choudhary A N, Patel J H, 'Parallel Architectures and Parallel Algorithms for Integrated Vision Systems', Kluwer Academic Publishers, 1990.

[Cra84]   Crawford J D, 'EDIF: A Mechanism for the Exchange of Design Information', *IEEE Design and Test of Computers*, Vol. 2, No. 1, pp. 63-69, 1984.

[Cro88]   Crookes D, 'Introduction to Programming in Prolog', 1st edition, Prentice Hall International (UK) Ltd, 1988.

[Cro98]   Crookes D, 'Digital Image Processing', Course Notes, School of Computer Science, The Queen's University of Belfast, 1998.

[CS94]   Crookes D, Steele J A, 'The Tulip Machine: Another Blooming Abstract Machine for Image Processing', Proc. Workshop on Mapping Signal and Image Processing Algorithms onto Parallel Processors, London 4-5 July 1994.

[CSR99]   Chow P, Seo S, Rose J, et al., 'The Design of an SRAM-Based Field-Programmable Gate Array: Part I: Architecture', *IEEE Transactions on VLSI*, Vol. 7 No. 2, June 1999, pp. 191-197.

[DGT93]   Darlington J, Ghanem G, and To H W, 'Structured Parallel Programming', In Programming Models for Massively Parallel Programming Computers, IEEE Computer Society Press, pp. 160-169, Sept 1993.

[DMac94]   Demspter A G and MacLeod M D, 'Constant integer multiplication using minimum adders', IEE Proceedings Circuits Devices Systems, vol. 141, No. 5, pp.407-413, Oct. 1994.

[Don96]   Donachy P, 'Design and Implementation of A High Level Image Processing Machine Using Reconfigurable Hardware', PhD Thesis, Department of Computer Science, The Queen's University of Belfast, 1996.

[DR81]   Dyer C R and Rosenfeld A, 'Parallel image processing by memory augmented cellular automata', *IEEE Transactions on Pattern Analysis and Machine Intelligence*, pp. 29-41, Jan. 1981.

[DR85]   Denyer P and Renshaw D, 'VLSI Signal Processing: A Bit-Serial

Approach', Addison-Wesley, 1985.

[DW81]   Driscoll T and Walker C, 'Evolution of Image-Processing algorithms from software to hardware', Proceedings of the society of photo-optical instrumentation engineers, Vol. 271, pp. 43-50, 1981.

[EL87]   Ercegovac M and Lang T, 'On-the-fly conversion of redundant into conventional representation', *IEEE trans. Computer*, Vol. C-36, No. 7, pp. 895-897, July 1987.

[EL90]   Ercegovac M and Lang T, 'Fast multiplication without carry-propagate addition', *IEEE trans. Computer*, Vol. 39, No. 11, pp. 1385-1390, 1990.

[ERC84]   Ercegovac M D, 'On-line arithmetic: an overview', SPIE Vol. 495, Real time signal processing VII, pp. 86-93, 1984.

[ESL99]   The Embedded Solutions Limited, 'Handel C information sheets', 1999.
http://www.embeddedsol.com

[ET77]   Ercegovac M D and Trivedi K S, 'On-line algorithms for division and multiplication', *IEEE Trans. on Computer*, Vol. C-26, No.7, pp. 681-687, July 1977.

[Fnd98]   Xilinx Ltd., Foundation Series, Software Documentation, 1998.
http://toolbox.xilinx.com/docsan/

[Fre74]   Freeman H, 'Computer processing of line drawing images', *Computer Surveys*, Vol. 6, pp. 57-97, 1974.

[Gar65]   Garner H L, 'Number systems and arithmetic', *advanced Computers*, 1965, 6, pp. 131-194.

[GHB93]   Greene J, Hamdy E, and Beal S, 'Antifuse field programmable gate arrays', *Proceedings of the IEEE*, Vol. 81, No. 7, pp. 1024-1056, 1993.

[Gig94]   Gigaops Ltd., The G-800 System, 2374 Eunice St. Berkeley, CA 94708

[GL96a]   Gehring S, Ludwig S, 'The Trianus system and its application to custom computing'. Proceedings of the 6th international workshop on Field-Programmable Logic and Applications. Springer Verlag, 1996.

[GLW94]   Gehring S, Ludwig S, Wirth N, 'A Laboratory for a digital course using FPGAs'. Proceedings of the 4th international workshop on Field-Programmable Logic and Applications, Springer Verlag, 1994.

[Gok90]   Gokhale M, et al, 'Splash: A reconfigurable linear logic array', Proceedings of the international conference on Parallel Processing, pp. 526-532, Aug 1990.

[Har91]   Hartley R, 'Optimization of canonic signed digit multipliers for filter design', in Proceedings of the IEEE International Symposium on Circuits and Systems, Singapore, pp. 1992-1995, June 1991.

[Ham00]   Hamdan M, 'A combinational framework for parallel programming using algorithmic skeletons', PhD, Dept of Computing and Electrical Engineering, Heriot-Watt University, January 2000
            ftp://ftp.cee.hw.ac.uk/pub/funcprog/mh.phd.ps.Z

[Hoa93]   Hoang D T, 'Searching Genetic Databases on Splash-2', Proceedings of the IEEE workshop on FPGAs as Custom Computing Machines, pp.185-191, IEEE computer Society Press, pp. 172-177, April 1993.

[Hwa79]   Hwang K, 'Computer Arithmetic Principles, Architecture, and Design', Wiley, 1979.

[HYT80]   Huang T S, Yang G J and Tang C Y, 'A fast two-dimensional median filtering algorithm', *IEEE Trans. Acoustic Speech and Signal Processing*, ASSP-28, pp. 415-421, Aug. 1980.

[IEEE87]   IEEE std 1076-1987, IEEE standard VHDL reference manual, 1987.

[Int99]   Intersil Corporation, 'BT.656 Video Interface for ICs', Application Note, 1999.
            http://www.intersil.com/data/AN/AN9/AN9728/an9728.pdf

[JBits99]   Xilinx Ltd., JBits tool, 1999.
            http://www.xilinx.com/xilinxonline/jbits.htm

[JS90]   Jones G, Sheeran M, 'Circuit design in Ruby', in Jorgen Staunstrup (ed.), Formal methods for VLSI design, North-Holland, pp. 13-70, 1990.

[JS91]   Jones G, Sheeran M, 'Collecting butterflies', Feburary 1991, (ISBN 0-902928-69-4).

[JS94]   Jones G, Sheeran M, 'Designing arithmetic circuits by refinement in Ruby', Science of Computer Programming, Elsevier Science Publishers B.V, Amsterdam, pp. 107-135, April 1994.

[KB89]   Koplowitz J and Bruckstein A M, 'Design of Perimeter Estimators for Digitized Planar Shapes', *IEEE transactions on Pattern Analysis and Machine Intelligence*. Vol. PAMI(11), pp. 611-622, 1989.

[KD97]   Kean T, Duncan A, 'A 800 Mpixel/sec Reconfigurable Image Correlator on XC6216', Field Programmable Logic and Applications proceedings, pp. 382-391, 1997.

[Kea89]   Kean T A, 'Configurable Logic: A Dynamically Programmable Cellular Architecture and its VLSI Implementation', PhD Thesis CST-26-89, University of Edinburgh, 1989.

[KKSH90]   Kamp W, Kunemund H, Soldner and Hofer H, 'Programmable 2D linear filter for video applications', *IEEE journal of Solid State Circuits*, pp. 735-740, 1990.

[KL96]   Krikelis A and Lea R M, 'A modular massively-parallel computing approach to image processing', Proceedings of the IEEE, Vol. 84, No. 7, pp. 988-1004, 1996.

[Kor93]   Koren I, 'Computer arithmetic algorithms', Prentice-Hall, Inc, pp. 99-126, 1993.

[KP99]   Keshab K Parhi, 'VLSI Digital Signal Processing Systems: Design and Implementation', John Wiley & Sons, 1999

[LGSZ96]   Luk W, Guo S, Shirazi N, and Zhuang N, 'A framework for developing parameterised FPGA libraries', in Proceedings of Field-Programmable Logic, Smart Applications, New Paradigms and Compilers, R. W. Arnold and M. Glesner (editors) LNCS 1142, Springer, pp. 24-33, 1996.

[LH95]   Lee C K, Hamdi M, 'Parallel Image-Processing applications on a network of workstations', *Parallel Computing*, Vol. 21, No. 1, pp. 137-160, 1995.

[LMcW98]   Luk W, Mc Keever S and Weinhardt M, 'A tutorial introduction to Pebble 3.0', Technical report, Imperial College, England, 1998.

[McE00]   McElwaine M, 'A graphical Editor for a Hardware Image Coprocessor', Final year project report, The Queen's University of Belfast, April 2000.

[McLoe94]   McLoed J, 'Reconfigurable computer changes architecture', *Electronics*, pp. 25, Apr. 1994.

[Mil88]   Milgram D L, 'Region extraction using convergent evidence', Computer Graphics and Image Processing, Vol. 5, No. 2, pp. 561-572, 1988.

[Mir99]   Mirotech Microsystems Inc., *Aristotle board*, 1999.
              http://www.mirotech.com/product/aristotle.html

[MMcC99]   Masud S, McCanny J V, 'Rapid VLSI design of biorthogonal wavelet transform cores', IEEE Workshop on Signal Processing Systems, SiPS: Design and Implementation, pp. 291-300, 1999.

[MMF98]   Mencer O, Morf M, Flynn M, 'PAM-blox: High Performance FPGA Design for Adaptive Computing', Proceedings of IEEE Workshop on FPGAs as Custom Computing Machines, April 1998.

[MMS91]   Muroga H, Murata Y, Saeki T, et al, 'A large scale FPGA with 10K core cells with CMOS 0.8 µm 3-layered metal process', Custom Integrated Circuits Conference, CICC, pp. 641-644, May 1991.

[MLL88]   Maresca M, and Li H, Lavin M, 'Connected component labeling on Polymorphic-Torus architecture', IEEE International Conference on Computer Vision and Pattern Recognition, Ann Arbor, pp. 951-956, 1988.

[MLM84]   McIlroy C D, Linggard R and Monteith W, 'Hardware for real-time image processing', IEE Proceedings, computer and digital techniques, Vol. 131, No. 6, pp 223-229, 1984.

[Mon70]   Montanari U, 'A note on minimal length polygonal approximation to a digitized contour', Communications ACM, Vol. 13, pp. 41-46, 1970.

[Moo92]   Moorby P, 'History of Verilog', IEEE Design & Test of Computers, Vol.9, No.3, pp.62-63, 1992.

[MPK88]   Miller R, and Prasanna-Kumar V K, 'Meshes with reconfigurable buses', Proceedings of the 5th MIT Conference on Advanced Research in VLSI, pp. 163-178, March 1988

[MRM94]   Moran J, Rios I and Meneses J, 'Signed Digit Arithmetic on FPGAs', *More FPGAs*, pp. 250, 1994.

[MSW95]   Michaelson G J, Scaife N R, and Wallace A M, 'Prototyping parallel algorithms in Standard ML', Proceedings of British Vision Conference, Birmingham, Sep. 1995.
              ftp://ftp.cee.hw.ac.uk/pub/funcprog/msw.bmvc95.ps.Z

[Mul91]   Muller J M, 'On-line computations : a survey and some new results', IFIP Workshop on Algorithms and Parallel VLSI Architectures, Bonas, France, June 1991

[MWJP96]   Mozef E, Weber S, Jaber J and Prieur G, 'Parallel architecture dedicated to image component labeling in O(nLog n): FPGA implementation', Proc. SPIE, Vol. 2784, pp.120-125, 1996.

[Nav92]   Navabi Z, 'A High Level Language for design and modeling of hardware', Journal of System Software, pp. 5-18, 1992.

[Olaf83]   Olafzar K, 'Design and implementation of a single chip 1-D median filter', *IEEE Trans. Acoustic Speech and Signal Processing*, ASSP-31, pp. 1164-1168, Oct. 1983.

[Omo94]   Omondi A, 'Computer arithmetic systems : algorithms, architecture and implementation', New York; London : Prentice-Hall, 1994.

[OSZ93]   Olariu S, Schwing J L and Zhang J, 'Fast component labelling and convex hull computation on reconfigurable meshes', *Image and Vision Computing Journal*, Vol. 11, No. 7, pp.447-455, 1993.

[Øye96]   Øye J E, 'A High Speed Cell Library in CMOS for Bit-Serial Implementation of DSP Algorithms', Ph.D. thesis, Norwegian University of Science and Technology, Trondheim, Norway, 1996.

[PA96]   Peterson J B and Athanas P M, 'High speed 2-D convolution with a Custom Computing Machine', *Journal of VLSI signal processing*, Vol. 12, No. 1, pp 7-20, Jan 1996.

[PAM96]   Digital Equipment Corporation, 'The PCI Pamette FPGA board', 1996.
http://www.research.digital.com/SRC/pamette/

[PCC99]   Paar C, Chetwynd B, Connor T, Deng S Y, Marchant S, 'Algorithm-agile cryptographic co-processor based on FPGAs', Proceedings of SPIE - The International Society for Optical Engineering, Vol. 3844, pp. 11-16, 1999.

[Phi98a]   Philips Electronics, 'SAA7111A: The Enhanced Video Input Processor (EVIP)', Product datasheets, 1998.
http://www.semiconductors.com/acrobat/datasheets/SAA7111A_4.pdf

[Phi98b]   Philips Electronics, 'I^{2}C bus specification', 1998.
http://www.semiconductors.com/acrobat/various/I2C_BUS_SPECIFICATION_3.
pdf

[PK94]   Phatak D and Koren I, 'Hybrid signed-digit number systems: A unified framework for redundant number representations with bounded carry propagation chains', *IEEE transactions on computer*, Vol. 43, No. 8, pp. 880-891, Aug 1994.

[Ple88]   Plessey, 'PDSP16488 Single Chip Convolver with integral line delay', Technical report, Plessey Semiconductors Ltd., Cheney Manor, Swindon, Wiltshire SN2 2QW, UK, 1988.

[PR79]   Profitt D and Rosen D, 'Metrication errors and coding efficiency of chain coding schemes for the representation of lines and edges', Computer Graphics Image Processing, Vol. 10, pp. 318-332, 1979.

[Pra91]   Pratt W K, 'Digital Image Processing', 2nd edition, Wiley, 1991.

[RFLC90]   Rose J, Francis R J, Lewis D and Chow P, 'Architecture of Programmable Gate Arrays: The Effect of Logic Block Functionality on Area Efficiency', *IEEE Journal of Solid State Circuits*, pp. 1217 – 1225, Oct. 1990.

[RGV93]   Rose J, El Gamal A, Sangiovanni-Vincentilli A, 'Architecture of Field Programmable Gate Arrays', Proceedings of the IEEE, Vol. 81, No 7, pp 1013-1029, 1993.

[RH97]   Rencher M, Hutching B, 'Automated Target Recognition on Splash II', Proceedings of the IEEE workshop on FPGAs as Custom Computing Machines, April 1997.

[Ros95]   Ross J, 'The Image Processing Handbook', CRC Press, 1995.

[RSR93]   Rajan K, Sangunni K S and Ramakrishna J, 'Dual-DSP systems for signal and image-processing', *Microprocessing & Microsystems*, Vol. 17, No 9, pp. 556-560, 1993.

[RTR99]   Reza A M, Turney R D, 'FPGA implementation of 2D wavelet transform', Proceedings of the Asilomar Conference on Signals, Systems and Computers, Vol. 1, pp. 584-588, 1999.

[RWD90]   Ritter G X, Wilson J N and Davidson J L, 'Image Algebra: an overview', Computer Vision, Graphics and Image Processing, No 49, pp 297–331, 1990.

[S3]   S3 Incorporated, 'Virge GX2 video accelerator'. http://www.s3.com/products.htm

[SB95]   Soderstrand M A and Balasubramanian N, 'An optimal automated implementation of FIR filters on field programmable gate arrays', in Proceedings ICSPAT-95, Boston, MA, Oct. 1995.

[SD99]   Scott Smith and David Black, 'Pushing the Limits with Behavioral Compiler', Synopsys Inc, 1999. http://www.synopsys.com/products/beh_syn/bc_compaq_wp.pdf

[Sho94]   Shoup R G, 'Parameterised Convolution Filtering in an FPGA', *More FPGAs*, W. Moore and W. Luk (editors) Abington EE&CS books, pp. 274, 1994.

[SIA]   The Semiconductor Industry Association publications. http://www.semichips.org/

[Sin95]   Singh S, 'Architectural Descriptions for FPGA circuits', Proceedings of the IEEE workshop on FPGAs for Custom Computing Machines, IEEE computer Society Press, Apr. 1995.

[SP88]   Sanz L C and Petkovic D, 'Machine vision algorithms for automated inspection of thin-film disk heads', *IEEE Transactions on Pattern*

Analysis and Machine Intelligence, Vol. 10, No. 6, pp. 830-848, 1988.

[SS94]   De la Serna A and Soderstrand M, 'Tradeoff between FPGA resource utilization and roundoff error in optimized CSD FIR digital filters', IEEE Asilomar Conference, Vol. 1, pp. 187-191, 1994.

[SS98]   Satnam S, Slous R, 'Accelerating Adobe Photoshop with Reconfigurable Logic', FCCM'98, Proceedings of the IEEE symposium on Field Programmable Custom Machines, CA, April 1998.

[Ste94]   Steele J A, 'An abstract machine approach to environments for image interpretation on transputers', Ph.D. Thesis, The Queen's University of Belfast, 1994.

[Syn99]   Synopsys Inc., FPGA Express tool, 1999.
            http://www.synopsys.com/products/fpga/fpga_express.html

[Teu93]   Teuber, J, 'Digital Image Processing', International series in Acoustics, Speech and Signal processing, Prentice Hall, 1993.

[TI]   Texas Instruments Incorporated, Digital Signal Processors products.
            http://www.ti.com/sc/docs/products/dsp/index.htm

[Vcc99]   Virtual Computer Company, ' The H.O.T. Works', 1999.
            http://www.vcc.com

[Vig00]   Visicom Laboratories, Real Time Image Processing and Video Products.
            http://www.visicom.com/products/products.shtml

[Vig98]   Visicom Laboratories, 'The VigraVision PCI video board: user's manual', 1998.
            www.visicom.com

[Wir95]   Wirth N, 'Digital Circuit Design, An introductory textbook', Springer, 1995.

[WMcC92]   Woods R F and McCanny J V, 'Design of a high performance IIR digital filter chip', IEE Proceedings, Vol. 139, No. 3, pp. 195-202, May 1992.

[WTH98]   Woods R, Trainor D, Heron J-P, 'Real Time Image Processing Using the Xilinx XC6200', IEEE Design and Test of Computers, pp. 30-38, 1998.

[WWD98]   Wong K, Wark M, Dawson E, 'Single-chip FPGA implementation of the Data Encryption Standard (DES) algorithm', Proceedings of the IEEE Global Telecommunications Conference, Vol. 2, pp. 827-832, 1998.

[XAP13]   Xilinx Ltd., 'Using the Dedicated Carry Logic in XC4000E', Xilinx
            Application Notes, XAPP 013, July 1996.
            http://www.xilinx.com/xapp/xapp013.pdf

[XAP09]   Xilinx Application Notes, 'Harmonic Frequency Synthesizer and
            FSK Modulator', XAPP009.
            http://www.xilinx.com/xapp/xapp009.pdf

[XAP52]   Xilinx Application Notes, 'Efficient Shift Registers, LFSR
            Counters, and Long Pseudo-Random Sequence Generators', XAPP
            052, July 1996.
            http://www.xilinx.com/xapp/xapp052.pdf

[XCL23]   Xilinx Ltd., 'Implementing Median Filters in XC4000E FPGAs',
            XCELL journal 23, April 1996.
            http://www.xilinx.com/xcell/xl23/xl23_16.pdf

[XCL42]   Xilinx Ltd., 'Advanced Carry Logic Techniques', XCELL journal
            42, July 1996.
            http://www.xilinx.com/xcell/xl21/xl21-42.pdf

[Xil96]   Xilinx Ltd., 'The X6200 Family preliminary datasheet', 1996.

[Xil99a]   Xilinx Ltd., 'Virtex 2.5 V Field Programmable Gate Arrays –
            Product Specification', 1999.
            http://www.xilinx.com/products/virtex

[Xil99b]   Xilinx Ltd., 'Xilinx XC9500, In-System Programmable CPLD
            Family Datasheet', Vol. 5.0 1999.
            http://www.xilinx.com/partinfo/9500.pdf

[Xil99c]   Xilinx Ltd, 'XC4000E and XC4000X Series Field Programmable
            Gate Arrays –Product Specification', 1999.
            http://www.xilinx.com/partinfo/4000.pdf

[YA94]   Yalamanchili S, Aggarwal J, 'Parallel Processing methodologies for
            Image Processing and Computer Vision', *Advances in electronics
            and electron physics*, Vol. 87, pp. 259-300, 1994.

[ZB99]   Zahir Jaffer and Bryan Piotto, 'Experiences Using Behavioral
            Synthesis on an ATM Traffic & Queue Management ASIC',
            Synopsys Inc, 1999.
            http://www.synopsys.com/products/beh_syn/bc_nortel_wp.pdf

Appendix I

Configuration data structure of an 8 bit adder

Configuration data structure of an 8 bit adder

```
Adder_8 = vertical([init_0, v_seq(4, add_2), add_carry_out ])
```

```
CDS_adder =
cds_node([1,0,0,1,6,
          [cds_node(1,init_0,0,0),
           cds_node(2,[1,4,0,1,1,4,add_2,
            child_locs([copy_locs(1,0,0),copy_locs(2,0,1),copy_locs(3,0,2),copy_locs(4,0,3)]),
            controls(external_signals_view([]),internal_signals_view([])),
            link_list([ link( [port(1,cout,cout,out,0,0), port(2,cin,cin,in,0,1)] ),
                        link( [port(2,cout,cout,out,0,1), port(3,cin,cin,in,0,2)] ),
                        link( [port(3,cout,cout,out,0,2), port(4,cin,cin,in,0,3) ]) ]),
            port_list([ [port(4,cout,1,out,0,3)],[(1,cin,2,in,0,0)],
                        [port(1,s0,3,out,0,0), port(1,s1,4,out,0,0), port(2,s0,5,out,0,1),
                         port(2,s1,6,out,0,1), port(3,s0,7,out,0,2), port(3,s1,8,out,0,2),
                         port(4,s0,9,out,0,3), port(4,s1,10,out,0,3)],
                        [port(1,a0,11,in,0,0), port(1,b0,12,in,0,0), port(1,a1,13,in,0,0),
                         port(1,b1,14,in,0,0), port(2,a0,15,in,0,1), port(2,b0,16,in,0,1),
                         port(2,a1,17,in,0,1), port(2,b1,18,in,0,1), port(3,a0,19,in,0,2),
                         port(3,b0,20,in,0,2), port(3,a1,21,in,0,2), port(3,b1,22,in,0,2),
                         port(4,a0,23,in,0,3), port(4,b0,24,in,0,3), port(4,a1,25,in,0,3),
                         port(4,b1,26,in,0,3)],
                        [],[],[],[]]),
             auto_placement]),
           csd_node(3,add_carry_out,0,5)],
           controls(external_signals_view([]),internal_signals_view([])),
           link_list([ link( [port(1,cout,cout,out,0,0), port(2,cin,cin,in,0,1)] ),
                       link( [port(2,cout,1,out,0,4), port(3,cin,cin,in,0,5) ]) ]),
           port_list([ [], [],
                        [port(2,3,1,out,0,1), port(2,4,2,out,0,1), port(2,5,3,out,0,2),
                         port(2,6,4,out,0,2), port(2,7,5,out,0,3), port(2,8,6,out,0,3),
                         port(2,9,7,out,0,4), port(2,10,8,out,0,4), port(3,cyn,9,out,0,5)],
                        [port(2,11,10,in,0,1), port(2,12,11,in,0,1), port(2,13,12,in,0,1),
                         port(2,14,13,in,0,1), port(2,15,14,in,0,2), port(2,16,15,in,0,2),
                         port(2,17,16,in,0,2), port(2,18,17,in,0,2), port(2,19,18,in,0,3),
                         port(2,20,19,in,0,3), port(2,21,20,in,0,3), port(2,22,21,in,0,3),
                         port(2,23,22,in,0,4), port(2,24,23,in,0,4), port(2,25,24,in,0,4),
                         port(2,26,25,in,0,4)],
                        [],[],[],[]]),
           auto_placement])
```

Appendix II

**FPGA Floorplans of the basic IA
operations using bit serial arithmetic
from both EDIF and VHDL descriptions**

Floorplan of a Laplace filter using online arithmetic

The following is the physical XC4036EX-2 FPGA configurations for a Laplace filter based on online arithmetic for 256x256 input image of 8 bits/pixel. These were generated from (a) an EDIF description (b) a VHDL description which were generated by:

is_online_IA_nop(mult, accum, [[~,-1,~],[-1,4,-1],[~,-1,~]], 256, 8, OWL, Latency, B)

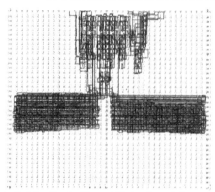

(a) From EDIF (Note that the line buffers width has been taken equal to the whole chip width).

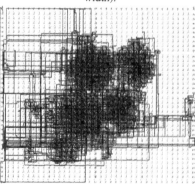

(b) From VHDL.

Floorplan of a Multiplicative-Maximum neighbourhood operation using online arithmetic

The following is the physical XC4036EX-2 FPGA configuration for a Multiplicative Maximum neighbourhood operation, based on online arithmetic for 256x256 input image of 8 bits/pixel. These were generated from (a) an EDIF description (b) a VHDL description, which were generated by:

is_online_IA_nop(mult, maximum, [[1,2,1],[2,4,2],[1,2,1]], 256, 8, OWL, Latency, B)

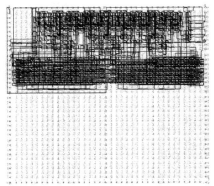

(a) From EDIF (Note that the line buffers width has been taken equal to the whole chip width).

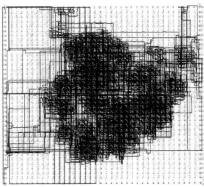

(b) From VHDL.

Appendix

FPGA Floorplans of special case architectures

Floorplan of a Laplace filter using 2's complement bit serial LSBF arithmetic

The following is the physical XC4036EX-2 FPGA configuration for a Laplace filter based on 2's complement bit serial LSBF arithmetic for 256x256 input image of 8 bits/pixel. This was generated from an EDIF description which was generated by:

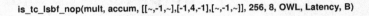

is_tc_lsbf_nop(mult, accum, [[~,-1,~],[-1,4,-1],[~,-1,~]], 256, 8, OWL, Latency, B)

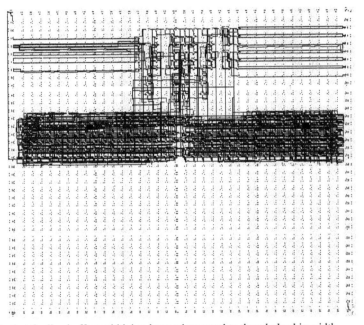

Note that the line buffers width has been taken equal to the whole chip width.

Floorplan of a convolution neighbourhood operation applied on binary images

The following is the physical XC4036EX-2 FPGA configuration for a convolution neighbourhood operation applied on a 512x512 input binary image. This was generated from an EDIF description which was generated by:

is_binary_IA_nop(mult, accum, [[10,2,10],[2,1,2],[10,2,10]], 256, 8, OWL, Latency, B)

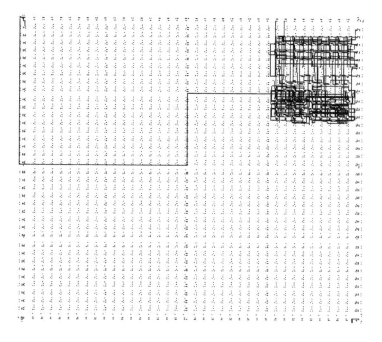

Appendix IV

FPGA Floorplans of compound IP operations using bit serial arithmetic

Floorplan of an Open operation using online arithmetic

The following is the physical XC4036EX-2 FPGA configuration for an 'Open' operation based on online arithmetic for 256x256 input image of 8 bits/pixel. This was generated from an EDIF description which was generated by (see section 7.6.1):

is_online_open(8, 256, Filename)

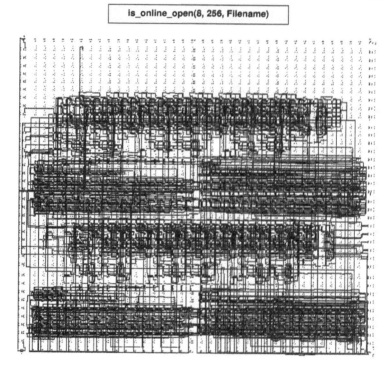

Note that the line buffers width has been taken equal to the whole chip width.

Floorplan of an Open operation using 2's complement bit serial MSBF

The following is the physical XC4036EX-2 FPGA configuration for an 'Open' operation based on 2's complement bit serial MSBF for 256x256 input image of 8 bits/pixel. This was generated from an EDIF description which was generated by (see section 7.6.1):

is_tc_msbf_open(8, 256, Filename)

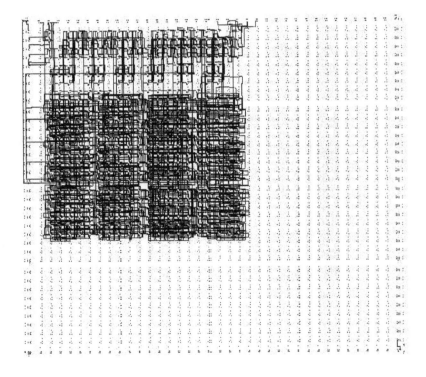

Floorplan of a Sobel operation using online arithmetic

The following is the physical XC4036EX-2 FPGA configuration for a 'Sobel' operation based on online arithmetic for 256x256 input image of 8 bits/pixel. This was generated from an EDIF description which was generated by (see section 7.6.2):

> **is_online_sobel(8, 256, Filename)**

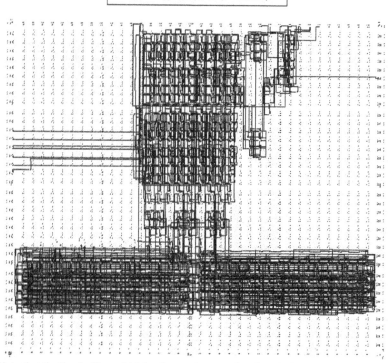

Note that the line buffers width has been taken equal to the whole chip width.

Floorplan of a Sobel operation using 2's complement bit serial LSBF

The following is the physical XC4036EX-2 FPGA configuration for a 'Sobel' operation based on 2's complement bit serial LSBF for 256x256 input image of 8 bits/pixel. This was generated from an EDIF description which was generated by (see section 7.6.2):

is_tc_lsbf_sobel(8, 256, Filename)

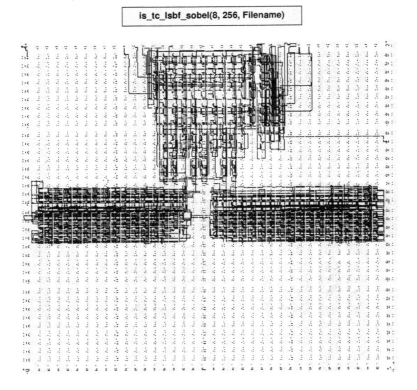

Note that the line buffers width has been taken equal to the whole chip width.

Appendix $\boxed{\text{V}}$

FPGA Floorplans of simple and compound IP architectures using bit parallel arithmetic

Floorplan of a Laplace filter using 2's complement bit parallel arithmetic

The following is the physical XC4036EX-2 FPGA configuration for a Laplace filter based on 2's complement bit parallel arithmetic for 256x256 input image of 8 bits/pixel. This was generated from an EDIF description which was generated by:

is_tc_par_nop(neighbourhood(mult, accum, [[~,-1,~],[-1,4,-1],[~,-1,~]], 256), 8, OWL, Latency, B)

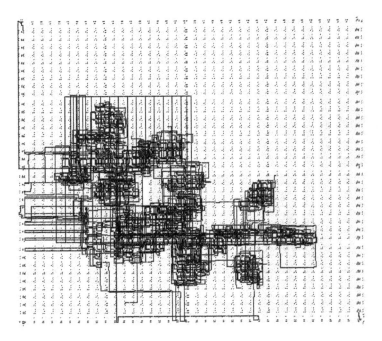

Floorplan of a Multiplicative-Maximum neighbourhood operation using 2's complement bit parallel arithmetic

The following is the physical XC4036EX-2 FPGA configuration for a Multiplicative Maximum neighbourhood operation, based on 2's complement bit parallel arithmetic for 256x256 input image of 8 bits/pixel. This was generated from an EDIF description which was generated by:

is_tc_par_nop(neighbourhood(mult, max, [[1,2,1],[2,4,2],[1,2,1]], 256), 8, OWL, Latency, B)

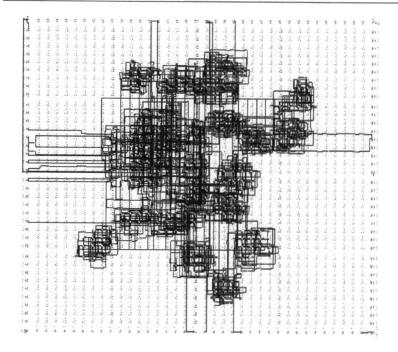

Floorplan of a Sobel operation using 2's complement bit parallel arithmetic

The following is the physical XC4036EX-2 FPGA configuration for a 'Sobel' operation based on 2's complement bit parallel arithmetic for 256x256 input image of 8 bits/pixel. This was generated from an EDIF description which was generated by:

```
is_tc_par_nop(abs(neighbourhood(mult, accum, [[1,2,1],[0,0,0],[-1,-2,-1]], 256))
            + abs(neighbourhood(mult, accum, [[1,0,-1],[2,0,-2],[1,0,-1]], 256)),
            8, OWL, Latency, B)
```

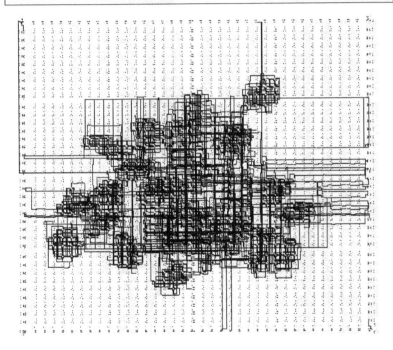

Floorplan of an Open operation using 2's complement bit parallel arithmetic

The following is the physical XC4036EX-2 FPGA configuration for an 'Open' operation based on 2's complement bit parallel arithmetic for 256x256 input image of 8 bits/pixel. This was generated from an EDIF description which was generated by:

```
is_tc_par_nop(pipeline([ neighbourhood(add, min, [[0,0,0],[0,0,0],[0,0,0]], 8, 256)),
                         neighbourhood(add, max, [[0,0,0],[0,0,0],[0,0,0]], 8, 256)) ]),
             8, OWL, Latency, B)
```

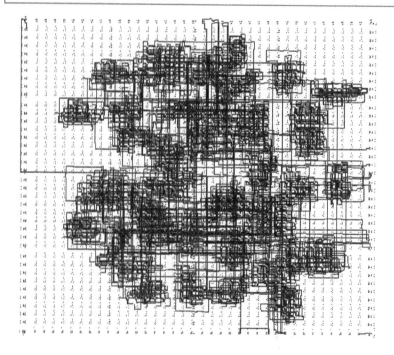

Appendix VI

YC$_b$C$_r$ ↔ RGB conversion

YC$_b$C$_r$ ↔ RGB conversion

If RGB (Red-Green-Blue) components are 8 bits each and have a range of 0-255 as it is commonly found in PCs, then the following equations are used to convert between 24-bit RGB data and YCbCr:

- Y = 0.257 R + 0.504 G + 0.098 B +16

  Cb = -0.148 R – 0.291 G +0.439 B +128

  Cr = 0.439 R – 0.368 G – 0.071 B +128

- R = max(0, min(255, 1.164 (Y-16) + 1.596 (Cr-128)))

  G = max(0, min(255, 1.164 (Y-16) – 0.813 (Cr-128) – 0.392 (Cb-128)))

  B = max(0, min(255, 1.164 (Y-16) + 2.017 (Cr-128)))